ASSESSING THE COMMON CORE

ASSESSING THE COMMON CORE

WHAT'S GONE WRONG— AND HOW TO GET BACK ON TRACK

ROBERT C. CALFEE and KATHLEEN M. WILSON

Foreword by Milton Chen

THE GUILFORD PRESS
New York   London

Library of Congress Cataloging-in-Publication Data

Names: Calfee, Robert C. | Wilson, Kathleen M. | Chen, Milton.
Title: Assessing the common core : what's gone wrong and how to get back on
   track / Robert C. Calfee, Kathleen M. Wilson, Milton Chen.
Description: New York ; London : Guilford Press, a Division of Guilford
   Publications, Inc., [2016] | Includes bibliographical references and index.
Identifiers: LCCN 2015022777 | ISBN 9781462524327 (pbk. : alk. paper) |
   ISBN 9781462524334 (hardcover : alk. paper)
Subjects: LCSH: Common Core State Standards (Education) |
   Education—Standards—United States—States. | Educational change—United
   States.
Classification: LCC LB3060.83 .C357 2016 | DDC 379.1/580973—dc23
LC record available at *http://lccn.loc.gov/2015022777*

To educators who create engaging learning environments
in which all children thrive

In memoriam:
Bob Calfee—
cherished mentor, colleague, and friend to many

About the Authors

Robert C. Calfee, PhD, until his death in 2014, was Professor Emeritus of Education at Stanford Graduate School of Education. He was also a former dean of the Graduate School of Education at the University of California, Riverside. A cognitive psychologist, Dr. Calfee conducted research on the effect of schooling on the intellectual potential of individuals and groups, the assessment of beginning literacy skills, and the broader reach of the school as a literate environment.

Kathleen M. Wilson, PhD, is Associate Professor Emerita of Teaching, Learning, and Teacher Education at the University of Nebraska–Lincoln. As a founding director of the university's Schmoker Reading Center, she studies teacher professional development in formative assessment and instruction of children experiencing difficulty with literacy acquisition. Most recently, Dr. Wilson has been exploring teachers' integration of digital technologies into literacy instruction.

Foreword

I am honored to write the Foreword for a critical book that comes at a critical time, not only for its cogent and valuable interpretation of the Common Core State Standards (CCSS) but also to help honor two scholars who have embraced educational innovation throughout their careers, always with a focus on how children learn best.

In fact, my path to this page has taken a circuitous route, over several decades. In February 2015, I had the opportunity to give a lecture at the Thompson Forum at the University of Nebraska and to speak with students in Professor Kathleen Wilson's undergraduate elementary grade literacy methods class. I learned that she had been a graduate student of Professor Robert Calfee's. A little more than a year earlier, in December 2013, I had spent a few days with Bob and his wife, Suzanne Barchers, formerly of Leapfrog and a literacy expert as well, as part of a team conducting a workshop at the Beijing Academy, a new middle school intended to create a state-of-the-art model integrating technology for progressive education in China.

In the early 1980s, I was a Stanford graduate student in communication and encountered Professor Calfee's teaching and research through several fellow graduate students studying with him. A decade later, while working in educational media at the PBS station KQED in San Francisco, I became familiar with his leading role in the design team of Leapfrog's literacy software and devices. So it is both a professional and personal privilege to introduce this book as a way of honoring Dr. Calfee's lifetime of achievement in advancing the teaching of the language arts and Dr. Wilson's own impressive and creative teaching and scholarship.

Both of these authors understand that this is a pivotal time in our nation's history, when we can create a school system to educate our students to prosper in a global and uncertain future, or we can continue to carry the baggage of 20th-century school systems, curricula, and assessments into this future. If implementing the CCSS results is more of the same—students sitting in classrooms where teachers provide most of the information, perhaps with a nod to technology and students now reading digitized textbooks—then we will have failed. And the prospects for the United States will grow dimmer. Every important issue we face as a nation—the economy, jobs, health care, national security—relies on a more highly educated citizenry.

This book trumpets some good news for education and our future. It comes at a time of some controversy and confusion, to say the least. The changes needed by our schools—and our children—are dramatic, and the forces of politics at all levels are weighing in, from states rescinding commitments to the CCSS to parents marching on school boards, concerned that their children will fare worse on more challenging assessments. These disputes will dissipate when more educators work to show the path forward.

In this book, Calfee and Wilson act as our pathfinders, shining their lights on the multiple pathways now possible for students to achieve mastery in reading, writing, speaking, and listening. Everyone interested in understanding the CCSS and how they translate into the classroom—and that should include everyone interested in improving schools—should read their account.

In the history charted by the authors, the CCSS represent the most important blueprint developed for our nation's schools and perhaps our last, best chance to align what happens in classrooms to the future our students need. They ask us to understand the "big picture" of the CCSS and strive to meet its highest goals, rather than think narrowly and "dumb-down" ambitious standards, as we have done in the past. They want us to look up, not down, and reach higher, not lower. They ask all educators to peer to the further horizon of what today's 18-year-olds should know and be able to do and backward-map to the types of "deeper learning" activities 6- or 12-year-olds should be doing come Monday morning.

Calfee and Wilson present a clear and compelling—indeed exciting— view of the new learning landscape now made possible when every student has his or her own digital device connected to the rich resources of the Internet. While politicians have been arguing over who should control what happens in schools, the last decade has transformed how, when, where, and with whom powerful learning can happen. Technology has continued to get better, faster, and cheaper, changing every aspect of modern life. Those changes are now coming to the classroom. The world's digital resources are offering students novel, interactive, and engaging ways to learn to read, in English and other languages, as well as experiences not possible in the textbook-based era, such as visiting the world's greatest art museums, cultural sites, and science centers. Importantly, today's students can meet and learn from their peers around the world, as well as from authors, scientists, artists, and historians. The Internet had made learning "Internet-ional." It has also made it more personal, so that students can connect academic content to issues from their own lives, families, and communities.

In this new world of learning, Calfee and Wilson show how disciplinary silos should disappear and how interdisciplinary, project-based learning can move from the edges to the center. They also advocate for critical shifts in roles, where teachers can act as "conductors rather than soloists" and students become "collaborators in self- and peer assessment." These shifts mirror the modern workplace, where professionals collaborate in teams to create products and services much larger than any one individual can produce on his or her own.

In some ways, these changes may appear unprecedented and untried, but, in fact, this new learning landscape asks us to return to many aspects of childhood from the past, from an agrarian age when children knew where the food on their table came from and how to fix the radiator on their new Model T. Perhaps, when they needed more information, they might have ridden their bikes down to the local public library, thanks to Andrew Carnegie.

Now, a century later, enabled by a stunning array of new tools and community-based experiences, project-based learning asks children to again understand the phenomena of their daily lives and how their lives today are embedded in a much, much larger world. They can now compute the carbon footprint of blueberries that have traveled from Chile for their breakfast and how the climate changes they experience today may be related to events thousands of miles away.

Today's Maker Movement also asks children to again learn to use their hands to design and manufacture products, from a personalized iPhone case to a robot that runs on a lithium battery. The Shaker adage of education "[for] the head, heart, and hands" is a perfect motto for 21st-century schools. Today's students should know how the products they use were made, just as their great-grandparents knew these things when they were children.

One of my favorite vignettes from this book tells the story of John Anderson, a ninth-grade science teacher who asks his students to "build the battery of the future." Students who understand this problem will "do well by doing good" in designing tomorrow's vehicles. They will have exciting and well-paid jobs, while creating a sustainable future for their nation and the planet. In so doing, they will be learning at the higher levels of the

CCSS—not the simpler ones, but the more challenging ones. In our work creating the *Edutopia.org* website, we profiled the story of high school students from West Philadelphia who, led by their teacher, Simon Hauger, a former engineer, designed and built hybrid cars running on biodiesel fuel. They won prizes competing not just with their peers, but with college teams. Today we need to make what is now possible for some an educational reality for all.

Finally, you hold in your hands a book whose authors practice in their writing what they preach about literacy. Their use of language is clear and concise, inviting and encouraging. They eschew jargon in favor of clarity in a book that could be read by active parents as well as teachers, researchers, and policymakers. *Assessing the Common Core* is an inspiring collaboration across two generations of scholars: Dr. Wilson is "paying forward" the legacy of her mentor, Dr. Calfee. Their greatest achievement will be seen in the teachers who take this book to heart and whose students learn to love language and, through it, many other things.

MILTON CHEN, PHD
Senior Fellow and Executive Director, Emeritus
George Lucas Educational Foundation
(*www.edutopia.org*)

Preface

With the release in June 2010 of the *Common Core State Standards for English Language Arts and Literacy in History/Social Studies, Science, and Technical Subjects* (National Governors Association [NGA] & Council of Chief State School Officers [CCSSO], 2010), the opportunity has emerged for fundamental reform of American schools. The English language arts (ELA) Standards document calls for high school graduates to be college, career, and citizen ready and lays out a progression for reaching these goals that guides students through acquisition of *academic language and literacy,* the formal style of language found in school, but also the language of societal and workplace institutions around the world. Print literacy is an important component of this competence, but formal language pervades all aspects of communication and reflection that we associate with the educated person. It is essential for participation in the formal disciplines, it is the language of entrepreneurs, and it is critical for understanding and assuming our responsibilities as citizens of a democratic society.

As we completed this book, a flurry of activity surrounded implementation of the ELA Standards. It seems clear that, in order to respond to the challenges posed by the Common Core, teachers will need to move to a level of professional responsibility and authority that constitutes a major departure from the prescriptive trends imposed by its predecessors, No Child Left Behind (NCLB) and Reading First. In our reading of the Standards, teachers will provide the primary driving force for significant changes in curriculum, instruction, and assessment:

- *Curriculum.* Rather than following a linear sequence of piece-meal learning objectives, teachers will rely upon their understanding of an instructional progression for acquisition of academic language/literacy. From the earliest grades onward, students experience school as a series of project-based activities that are motivating and engaging, as well as educational. The curriculum is continuously adapted to the interests and capacities that students bring to the projects, and to the outcomes of their explorations of a wide variety of topics and themes. The literacy curriculum laid out in the ELA Standards serves as a rich tapestry that establishes coherence in the previous motley grouping of skills and facts.

- *Instruction.* A major shift for teachers under the ELA Standards will be the move toward managing learning rather than teaching by talking, toward a role as conductor rather than as soloist. For students, this means a shift toward learning as searching (and researching) rather than stashing away facts and completing prescribed assignments, a change most fully embodied in the capstone Writing Standard, *Research to Build and Present Knowledge.*

- *Assessment.* Another significant change in teachers' roles under the Common Core is the transformation from test-prep coaches into observers and commentators on student learning. The stimulus for this change has been the emergence of a new conceptualization of *formative assessment*, the practice of ongoing inquiry into students' learning paths along the instructional progressions laid out in the Standards. An especially important correlate of this practice is that students have emerged as collaborators in self- and peer assessment, supporting the development of traits such as independence and efficacy that are called for in the Standards.

The preceding descriptions reflect our reading of the ELA Standards. We are convinced that this vision provides the necessary ingredients to prepare today's graduates for tomorrow's worlds—to be college, career, and citizen ready. These images are presently imperiled, however, by alternative interpretations of the documents that focus on a few relatively undemanding standards, and by the pending imposition of summative testing programs that continue the policies of test-based accountability that have prevailed under NCLB. These two developments will continue current policies and practices that are failing students and frustrating teachers, while the worlds beyond school are moving forward with lightning speed.

We have written this book for everyone who shares our hopes and concerns about the public schools, to lay out the reasons for our distress, and to propose plans for moving implementation of the ELA Standards back on track. Two big problems were identified above: (1) a proliferation of packaged programs in which a few basic standards are taught as isolated objectives, to the neglect of the curriculum of student-based inquiries that is laid out in the Standards; and (2) the dominance of a program of year-end summative testing of student achievement, ignoring the critical importance of formative assessments as a means to monitor and guide student learning. These two issues are interrelated, and need to be addressed synergistically. The resolution of these issues cannot be resolved by the top-down activities that currently dominate implementation, but will require the engagement of educators and broad participation by other groups, including parents, business and industry, and policymakers. The Common Core State Standards reflect an effort to move our public schools away from federal controls that have resulted in an extreme version of test-based accountability, and a return to the traditions of local control that have served our nation well during past generations—"well," if not perfectly. The Standards offer a grand opportunity for substantial advances in the character and quality of public schools, if we can capture the vision laid out in the founding document, which surveys indicate has been read by very few people (Editorial Projects in Education, 2013).

This book is not—or not just—another addition to the considerable literature explaining how to successfully implement the ELA Standards in classrooms. Yet we see the practical implications of the book as potentially profound. We begin in Chapter 1 with images of a possible future, where classrooms embody the vision laid out in the Introduction to the ELA Standards (pp. 3–8). The images may seem familiar to readers who completed their schooling before the imposition of current policies and practices, including teachers and other educators whose experience reaches back to the 1980s. Quality instruction for the future will rely in part on practices that have been around for a long time. But the images also embody new features, some reflecting advances in learning science and digital technologies, and others springing from the concept of literacy in the ELA Standards, which takes shape as an all-encompassing fabric that expands the potential of the human mind from thinking to communicating.

Chapter 2 describes the state of public schools in 2014–2015, the year in which implementation of the Common Core hit its full stride, following a decade under NCLB. Many have characterized that decade as "no child left untested," reflecting the federal imposition of punitive test-based accountability upon the nation's schools (McGuinn, 2006, p. 195). Discontent is widespread as Congress struggles to develop new legislation. Our argument then takes an upbeat turn in Chapter 3, where we take a careful look at what the ELA Standards actually say. The primary document is relatively brief at 66 pages, but it appears that most educators have read the work piecemeal, if at all. The Introduction, at eight pages, is also very brief, but judging from current discussions of the Standards, it has not been read by anyone; most educators appear to have skipped to the grade-by-grade

(G × G) sections to find out "what to do on Monday." We give special emphasis to the Introduction, a truly remarkable tract. We then review the G × G standards, which comprise the bulk of the document, where we discover why current implementation activities are so misguided. By picking and choosing from grade-specific objectives, program developers have lost sight of the whole. The complete G × G standards are presented in the Appendices at the back of this book for easy reference. Because we examine the Introduction and the Anchor Standards in depth in Chapter 3, we haven't repeated them in an appendix. We encourage readers to study the full text of these remarkable documents on the Common Core website at *www.corestandards.org.*

Chapter 4 presents a survey of the current implementation activities, focusing on "shifts" that have guided professional development and production of curriculum materials, and on the work of assessment consortia that were established with federal funding shortly after the release of the ELA Standards. There are few villains in this account. Much of the work is reasonably sound by current criteria, but from our perspective it simply does not mesh with the vision promulgated in the Common Core.

In Chapter 5 we lay out an implementation framework that will seem provocative to some, but that we think is true to the Common Core vision. The curriculum framework is established upon the structural foundations of the ELA Standards. Current curricula follow a brick-by-brick approach. Building a scope-and-sequence curriculum proceeds step by step, with each new learning objective presented, practiced, and tested until mastery is reached. The ELA Standards, in contrast, start from the ultimate outcomes of the K–12 experience: What is to be expected of graduates from 13 years of public education? The standards are then *backward-mapped*; from kindergarten onward, the instructional progression is to be designed with the ultimate goals in mind. The Introduction is followed by an ensemble of Anchor Standards that remain in place from kindergarten through graduation. The Anchor Standards are then elaborated as G × G objectives— but these are best comprehended when considered in context. Rather than starting with kindergarten and moving up through the grades, the best way to read the Standards is to begin with grades 11 and 12 and work backward. The expectations for graduation are quite extraordinary!

Chapter 5 also advances the notion that some Anchor Standards are more demanding than others. The authors of the ELA Standards are explicit about *backward-mapping*, and emphasize the importance of *integrating* the literacy strands (reading, writing, speaking, listening, and language) addressed in the Standards, but are silent about priorities. It is the Anchor Standards themselves that speak to this matter. Some call for the acquisition of basic skills in individual strands, for example, Reading Literature 1—"Read closely to determine what the text says explicitly and to make logical inferences from it" (p. 10). Other standards are far more encompassing, for example, Writing 7—"Conduct short as well as more sustained research projects based on focused questions, demonstrating understanding of the subject under investigation" (p. 18). This Standard is even more daunting when taken in broader context, which calls for sustained inquiry around authentic themes and topics (p. 33), where the inquiry is integrated with the primary academic disciplines—literature, history and social studies, the sciences, and technical subjects. We think that these more demanding standards should serve as keystone requirements throughout the grades. If you study the entire collection of ELA Standards, you will realize the immensity of the changes called for in this initiative, and the implications it has for students and for teachers. For students, it means that by the time they graduate they will have accumulated records of their skills and knowledge, establishing their readiness for college, career, and citizenship. The evidence will come not from test scores of *any* sort, but from actual performances. For teachers, the changes in preparation, professional development, and assessment will be even more significant. To fulfill the responsibilities called for by the Standards, teachers will require a deep knowledge of the development of literacy skills and knowledge, and a rich understanding of instructional strategies that promote the capacity to use language as a tool for thinking and communicating—for all children. The institutional settings within schools will need to change, with professional development communities becoming common practice rather than an occasional rarity.

Chapter 6 serves as a summation and a plan for positive action. Following the challenges of Chapter 5, it discusses ways of moving from our current undertakings toward implementation activities that are more consonant with the Common Core vision. Our primary focus is on building a conceptual framework, which we have posed as a set of "big shifts," where the Common Core vision takes shape as a lighthouse guiding vessels toward the harbor. In this chapter, examples are shared of a variety of school settings in which implementation of the Standards has led to positive outcomes for schools, teachers, and students. These examples demonstrate the necessity, and the ultimate benefits, of embracing the new shifts entailed by the Standards. They are "bright spots" that point the way forward for us all.

Finally, our story unfolds in the future tense—it is a *story*, which we begin a decade hence. We are optimists, and believe that good things are going to happen as a result of the Standards. So let us begin, back to the future. . . .

Acknowledgments

Writing a scholarly book such as this one required the generosity of many people, including teachers, school and district administrators, graduate students, academics, and policymakers. They expressed their generosity by serving as sounding boards for ideas, reading drafts of chapters, pointing us to resources we may not have known about, and offering arguments that challenged our ideas. We are grateful in so many ways to all of them.

As far back as 2009, Bob Calfee and I had many conversations about writing a book advocating the use of formative reading assessment in the elementary grades to counter the narrowing influences of standardized testing on curricula that were occurring under No Child Left Behind (NCLB). General ideas would ebb and flow about the direction for our proposed book, but nothing was compelling enough to bring the manuscript to the forefront of our attention. It wasn't until November 2011, as we heard more and more about the Common Core State Standards (CCSS), that we began sifting through previous outlines for the book and discussing the Common Core as our new context. As Bob talked with individuals who were closely involved with the process at the national and state levels, he began developing a model for an integrated approach to assessment and instruction for Common Core implementation. All of these people were invaluable resources for us as the book developed. The promising potential for a widespread adoption of formative assessment became more of a reality in the spring of 2012, when plans for a digital library of resources, including formative assessments, were described in both the Partnership for Assessment of Readiness for College and Careers and Smarter Balanced assessment designs posted on the Educational Testing Service's K–12 Center website. Our interest in melding Common Core implementation and formative assessment of literacy learning deepened as we cowrote chapters in edited books and journal articles on formative assessment. To support the direction of our thinking, Bob decided that we needed to deeply examine, analyze, and consider what the writers of the CCSS actually espoused as learning goals for today's schools. We began to develop outlines, position papers, and PowerPoint presentations that we hoped would generate reactions and feedback. To augment our study of the CCSS, we had rich discussions with others in government, academia, and the schools that were associated with education policy and practical approaches to meeting the Standards. The ideal and the reality can be far apart, and we needed both views. We are grateful to all of these individuals for their willingness to share their ideas, points of view, and critiques along the way.

Several individuals are worthy of special acknowledgment for their support as we wrote this book. First, we thank our editor, Craig Thomas, and his predecessor, Chris Jennison, at The Guilford Press for their belief that we had a message worth sharing. Craig in particular kept us moving steadily toward our goal of finishing this book, even as we took on smaller projects. In actuality, these projects fine-tuned our thinking, but we needed his periodic shepherding to bring us back on track. Craig met with us at conferences, by phone, and through e-mail, offering his very helpful comments and suggestions for revisions that encouraged us and challenged our thinking in positive ways. We also thank Roger Bruning of the University of Nebraska–Lincoln for his reactions, probing questions, and practical on-point suggestions that aided us in honing our ideas from the earliest months of the book's creation. After Bob passed away in the fall of 2014, Roger was instrumental in helping me bring the manuscript to the point of submission for editorial review. For this help, I will be forever grateful. Along the way, Bob sent early drafts of chapters and ideas about an integrated approach to implementation to Barbara Kapinus, a coauthor on a related book chapter and a journal article, and Fritz Moser, a Senior Research Specialist at the Consortium for Policy Research in Education. Their suggestions enhanced our thinking about both formative assessment and the creation and implementation of the Common Core. Our conversations with David Pearson and Freddy Hiebert, as well as attending their conference presentations over the course of writing the book, helped us to refine our thinking and clarify our position on an integrated approach to implementation. Kim Norman at California State University, Fullerton, a longtime colleague and (like me) a former doctoral student of Bob's, added to our understanding of teachers' capacity to implement formative assessment when the CCSS were first adopted.

One group we want to recognize is the fall 2013 class of graduate students who enrolled in my course on the Common Core at the University of Nebraska–Lincoln. For the first half-hour of each week's class meeting, Bob posed questions and shared musings about teaching, formative assessment, and the students' take on the course readings and their research on the implementation of the CCSS in a sampling of states that had adopted the Standards. We thank them for frankly sharing their experiences, their findings, and the changes they were making in their own teaching. This experience was particularly remarkable because, as of this writing, Nebraska has not adopted the Common Core. These graduate students—future and current teacher educators, classroom teachers, professional development providers, community college instructors, and school administrators—recognized the potential and real impact the Standards were already having on their teaching and the materials they were using.

Finally, we want to thank our spouses, Suzanne and Jerry, for their enduring interest and forbearance over the years we worked on this book. They were partners in this project in so many ways. We are indebted to them for being generous hosts as we worked on the book at each other's homes, offering words of encouragement toward completion, and letting us know if we were making sense as they read the drafts and listened to ideas.

Thank you all. You are appreciated more than you know.

KATHLEEN M. WILSON

Contents

CHAPTER 1

The State of American Classrooms in 2024

Snapshots of a Possible Future

It is September 2024, 10 years after the Common Core State Standards (CCSS) actually became the "standard" in American schools with the administration of the first "test that counts." Classrooms have become "places of the imagination," filled with engagement and excitement. As your mind's eye moves from kindergarten through the grades to high school, you see students participating in challenging activities and projects directed toward significant topics and themes, during which they fashion tapestries of knowledge and experience woven on the looms of literacy. As they have moved through the grades, students have acquired increasing competence in using language and literacy to explore questions that really matter with powerful tools that support thinking and communication. In Kate's kindergarten you will see a rock transformed into a diamond in the rough. Nancy's gaggle of third- and fourth-grade misfits keeps you well beyond your allotted time showing you the stories of their lives, and you are entranced. The seventh graders in Bert's classes leave you persuaded that the "king tides" are real, that environmental change is happening, and that someone needs to do something about it. And then there is John and his ninth-grade team of packrat scientists. You had never heard of the "Baghdad battery," nor anything about zinc-air and nanotube power storage devices. As you leave in your 6-year-old Tesla automobile, you realize that you should wait for another year before buying a new car. These snap-shots of schooling have made a big impression on you.

A visit to classrooms almost anywhere in the United States at the start of the 2024–2025 school year demonstrates why our nation's public schools have become the envy of the world. International comparisons of test scores tell part of the story, but numbers cannot fully capture the experiences.

This chapter is an exercise in imagination, a venture into the future, and is admittedly risky. Our goal is to give our readers a concrete sense of the potential impact of the English language arts (ELA) Standards for students and teachers in classrooms a decade from now. We assume that most readers know something about the CCSS, but current surveys show that relatively few people have studied the actual documents (Editorial Projects in Education, 2013). Current reports offer mixed messages: "major reforms are taking place," "it is really life as usual," "the tests are much too tough," "there is not enough money," "there is too little time," and so on. Most states have adopted the CCSS, which means that these documents should lead to significant changes in public schools. What do the standards really say? Rather than relying on secondhand accounts, we will take you through a close look at the actual documents in Chapter 3.

You will probably be surprised by what you find in the Common Core documents. Graduates are to be college, career, and citizen ready. You may have heard that phrase, but have probably not heard *independent*, *responsible*, and *sensitive to other perspectives and cultures*. You may have heard about "close reading," which is what it sounds like, but not about *research to build and present knowledge, conducting sustained research projects to answer questions or solve problems across the disciplinary spectrum*—literature, history/social studies, and the sciences and technical subjects. These sound like expectations from advanced placement programs, but in the CCSS they are goals for all students, with teachers given the responsibility—and authority—for guiding students toward fulfilling these expectations.

The CCSS are abstractions. The snapshots, vignettes, and portraits that we present below are designed to provide concrete images that "clothe" these abstractions. You are well educated, and have spent a lot of time in classrooms, but you will also need to use your imagination along the way. We do not know what might have been on the mind of the ELA Standards writers; the framing of the standards was not entirely transparent. And so we have relied on our imaginations. Our illustrations include the old and the new. You will find realistic images of teachers and students in classrooms, generally not greatly different in some respects from today. We doubt that students a decade from now will be learning in the "cloud." You will find some ideas that, while not entirely new, have a different flavor. For example, inquiry-based activities appear in a few places in today's classrooms; examples from the Expeditionary Learning schools (*http://elschools.org/student-work*) seem rather amazing and well worth exploring. But schools and teachers in 2024 will confront many of the tensions found in schools for more than a century—control versus freedom, tradition versus exploration, work versus play. If the ELA Standards are implemented as intended, however, you will find much that is new, even extraordinary. Students are more engaged and motivated, largely because they are delving deeply into topics and problems that are important and "relevant." Their work is serious, and they can talk to you about what they are learning and why. They proudly show you their work products. Teachers are engaged and even inspired. They speak about the importance of being able to make decisions about what and how they teach, and display a firm understanding and commitment to ensuring that their students reach goals set by the CCSS. In the following vignettes we try to capture these issues, to illustrate what we see as the tremendous potential of the ELA Standards to transform schooling, while recognizing the ever-present inertia that can stifle any effort at change.

THE START OF KINDERGARTEN

Kate Hampton has taught kindergarten for more than 20 years, and her first week of class follows well-established routines. Fairmont School in Southern California is in a neighborhood afflicted by several decades of economic distress. The school, built in the late 1940s after World War II, is overcrowded, woefully in need of repair, and technologically "challenged." On the other hand, the campus is spread out, with a sense of park-like openness. Kate's classroom is inviting, the walls filled with brightly colored pictures, word and letter charts strung above the windows, activity centers located around the room (art, blocks, four computer stations), a rug laid with pillows for circle times, children's names posted on their cubbies, and a neighborhood map locating each child's home, along with a photograph of the student and his or her family (Kate had visited each home the week before). Books are everywhere—you recognize *Brian Wildsmith's ABC* (1962) and Leo Lionni's *Swimmy* (1963) as among your personal favorites. The door is open from Kate's arrival until her departure, except for those rare occasions when the temperature is on the cool side. Visitors are welcome, especially parents, many of whom are in the room on opening day.

The first day of class opens with introductions (children and parents), followed by a review of the daily schedule. Next, to settle things down, comes Kate's reading of Bill Martin Jr.'s classic, *Brown Bear, Brown Bear, What Do You See?* (1967). The remainder of the day—actually most of the first week—is dedicated to establishing Kate's classroom routines: the picture book center, the art table, the building block corner, and so on. Kate spends relatively little time in whole-class activities, preferring to work with small groups and individuals, listening and taking notes more than talking. By the end of the first week, she has developed a detailed portrait of each child, and of the class as a whole.

An especially important routine in Kate's class is *show-and-tell time*, a kindergarten commonplace since the beginning of time. Each child stands before the class for a few moments to present something of interest or importance to him or her. For the visitor, the experience can be wonderfully engaging; "Kids can say the darndest things." For Kate, though, the activity is an essential first step in the literacy curriculum. For most children, kindergarten is a strange experience, quite unlike preschool or Head Start, sometimes causing distress (and even tears). The idea of standing before strangers is uncomfortable, even when mothers are present. Show-and-tell topics are open-ended—anything a child offers is acceptable. In Kate's routine, however, the child must satisfy two requirements by the end of the first week: (1) every child must make a presentation, and (2) each child must "tell" three things about the "show" thing.

It is Friday morning, and Charlie's time has come—everyone else has presented. Charlie is somewhat shy, and several other children volunteer to go in his place. Kate thanks the volunteers, and then calls Charlie over to her side: "What is something that you can tell us about, something that you have seen or found?" Charlie, hands in his pocket, frowns for a second, and then brightens a bit. "I found a rock on the way to school!" Kate nods: "Charlie, that's great! Show us the rock and tell us about it—where did you find it, what does it look like, and what are you going to do with it?" After a moment's hesitation, Charlie proceeds to churn out responses. "It was in the dirt just by the porch steps—and it's grey with black spots and kinda rough and bumpy—and I'm gonna take it home and put it in my rock box. I've gotta lot of rocks and some other stuff there. The end!" The students applaud the presentation. Show-and-tell is over, and students move on to their centers. Later in the morning, Kate calls Charlie to her desk and has him repeat his "composition," which she writes down on one-quarter of the Daily Report, which Charlie will then illustrate. A copy of the Daily Report—three "student papers" and a note from Kate—is taken home by each child. Charlie has just published his first five-paragraph essay.

The morning is filled with a wide array of activities: painting, story reading, computer games, block building, the planting of radish seeds, and a report by a mother on her work as a dentist, including advice for brushing teeth and a toothbrush kit for every student. After lunch and a nap, Kate guides the children through a review of the events of the week. She also makes notes that will be the starting point for Monday. For Charlie, the favorite event was his rock report.

This brief anecdote is more unusual than may appear on first glance, both for what students are doing and from Kate's explanations. Every activity during the day, from *Brown Bear, Brown Bear* to planting radish seeds, is designed to promote the development of language and literacy, of thinking and problem solving, and of collaboration and independence. The basis for this claim lies in Kate's descriptions of what was going on and why. She begins with a crisp account of her expectations for what her students will be able to do by the end of the year:

> "A few years ago, I would have shown you a list of test scores, but now we emphasize student performance. The key is *academic language.* These children come to kindergarten with an incredible array of experiences; many have survived hard times. But their experiences with school language are not as rich as the children's from more advantaged backgrounds. They don't know as many words as children from more privileged backgrounds, and they haven't learned to 'think' about how they use language. I developed a project 2 years ago called 'My Kindergarten Story.' Each child keeps a record of his or her learning from September through June. They meet with me weekly, and tell me about 4 new words that they have learned, they assemble their show-and-tell reports to make a book, and so on.
>
> "I mentioned *school language*, and the ELA Standards are leading me to think more carefully about this idea. One of the Standards calls for kindergartners to sort common things into categories, which we have done forever. But it pushes the notion of helping the students to understand how concepts work. For example, most kindergartners— most ordinary people—can tell you about an apple. It is round and red and sweet. But it is also a fruit, and so can be put together with bananas and grapes and kiwis, which don't look or taste anything like an apple. Why do we put them together? What are other ways of clustering or sorting words? It's not just having more words, but what you can do with them.
>
> "I am also interested in biology, and we track students' body changes during the year! We measure height and weight, how much they can lift, their running times. Here are some samples from last year."

Kate describes connections to biology and mathematics, and the importance of the project to the individuals:

> "These are really research reports—each child is studying him- or herself. If you look at page 33 in the ELA Standards, you will find a very interesting example of building knowledge about your body. We use

our computers to turn out reports that look really professional. We only have four computers, and they're ancient, but we use them to search for information and to prepare presentations, just as called for in the ELA Standards. This work helps me document what every child is learning."

Kate focuses on Charlie:

"He is off to a slow start, but by the end of the year he will have completed a report on what he has learned—he will have an idea of where he is headed. Charlie has spent the last 2 years in a day-care setting, mostly child care with a few learning opportunities. He is from a single-parent family; his mother is a high school dropout who works part time. A few years ago I would have not expected too much of him, but now I have a clearer picture of where he needs to be heading—and how to help him get there. We used to devote the primary grades to basic skills—phonics and the like. And skills are important. But now it's really all about language, about using it to 'say his piece,' and to help him understand how to communicate. He talked about his rock, which may seem a small thing. With a little encouragement, he began to talk about the other things in his rock box. Other children were interested in what he had to say, and suddenly he was on a roll. Charlie has lots of stories to tell, and he has lots of reports to talk about. The radish garden is our next research project, and by next May who knows what we might be up to. As long as they show up in class, every one of these children will be reading and writing—about things that really matter to them for now and for the future. I know where they need to be going, and I'm making sure that they get there."

GRADE 3: "FAMILY ROOTS"

When Nancy King decided to become a teacher, her commitment was to especially needy students. Her younger brother had a serious physical disability, and Nancy knew firsthand about helping others. With 10 years of experience with third- and fourth-grade combination classes, she happily takes on all comers, including students with learning problems, third graders on the retention list, and overactive boys. Every student in her class covers the same curriculum, and everyone seems able to move ahead on track. Her current class is typical in its wide variations in backgrounds, interests, and achievement levels.

Nancy's routine this year has followed a pattern she established several years ago. September and early October are organized around "little projects," each centered on a short story or a familiar topic. For example, to review concepts of character and plot, she spent 2 weeks in early September on "movie reviews," during which students did projects on their favorite summer movies and television programs. The last half of September she shifted the focus to informational text, using "news reports" from newspapers or television news. Students prepared "News of the Day" reports, which they first presented in a television format, and then compiled as the "Weekly Badger" (Nancy had attended the University of Wisconsin), a newspaper that they published on the school website every Friday.

The fall was busy with holidays—Halloween, Thanksgiving, the winter celebrations—distractions that make it difficult to carry out extended projects. In late summer, though, as she was planning for the year ahead, Nancy mulled over an idea that she had heard during a spring convention, a research project in which students investigated their family genealogies. She was quite impressed with the presenter, who provided details about planning for the project, links to the Standards and to history, and cautions (modern families often bear no resemblance to "Dick and Jane"). She introduced the project to the class just before the Thanksgiving break, the prototypical "family" holiday. Her plan called for students to work on the project during the entire month of January, an assignment that would require considerable staying power for elementary students. But it was good preparation for middle school, when they would be expected to spend sustained amounts of time on even more demanding projects.

Nancy introduced the project by telling students that they will take on a really big job in January, following the winter break:

> "We have a lot on our agenda, but I think you are going to find this a very interesting project. There are lots of holidays ahead, and you'll be spending a lot of time with your family and friends. The project will be about your family history, your 'roots.' It's called *genealogy*. Each one of you will do research on your ancestors, and then write a book about what you discover."

Discussion of the project starts slowly—it is the first time that any of the students have taken on a project in which they planned the research on their own from start to finish. They had conducted small projects in earlier grades, but they always had a plan to follow. Nancy raises several starter questions that she had adapted from her notes: How can you find out about your family? What is a "family"? What would a family report look like? What would go into the book? A plan begins to take shape in the students' minds.

The project proceeds in phases. In the first week of December, Nancy's students watch selections from the television classic *Roots* (a

40th-anniversary DVD had been released in 2017), which leads to discussions about how to investigate the complexities of family histories. Nancy reminds the students of the similarities between histories and stories. Students have become familiar with the elements of a story map—characters, plot, setting, and theme—which are laid out in the ELA Standards beginning in kindergarten. Their assignment for the winter break is to talk with family members about their family histories, and to make notes along the way.

In January, the class goes to work in earnest. Nancy uses the story map to present her own genealogy, and to tell how she has uncovered missing information. Based on this model, students begin to sketch drafts of their own stories, filling in what they have learned and identifying missing pieces. The challenge is to construct a theme that captures the distinctive character of their family. Nancy recommends several autobiographies and biographies: Laura Ingalls Wilder's *Little House on the Prairie* series, biographies of Martin Luther King Jr., and so on. As the weeks move on, students work on organizing and analyzing the artifacts that they have collected—interviews, Bibles and genealogies, letters and photo albums. They conduct lengthy discussions with relatives, carry out computer searches from established sites, develop graphics to organize the information, and debate various ways in which they can frame their stories.

The final phase begins in late January, when the students complete the various parts of their "roots" books. The results turn out to be rather lengthy, 20 pages or more, developed using the computer packages, but with the addition of handmade artworks. Each book follows the same basic design: title page, table of contents, dedication ("To my parents, without whom this report would not be possible"), thematic overview (using *Roots* and biographies as resources), the results of their investigations of families and ancestors, and a "Forward to the Future" piece in which they imagine themselves at their high school graduation. Each book includes writing, artwork, graphics, and artifacts. The project has taken more than 3 weeks to complete, and every book is a work of art.

Nancy discusses the project with a colleague who visits the classroom in February. The entire collection is displayed on the window sills. Nancy comments, "*Roots* took a long time to complete, but it was clearly a worthwhile activity and consistent with the Common Core. Go through the ELA Standards for reading, writing, speaking/listening, and language/vocabulary, and you'll see that we covered them. But the students also fulfilled expectations from the standards that are hard to measure—independence and stick-to-itiveness. They used the content areas—literature and social studies, history and geography. Several students created maps and timelines to show their families' journeys. The kids developed a real sense of audience. They were highly motivated and determined to produce a quality product. And you can see, the proof of their learning is in these products. They are proud of what they have done, and so are their families. I can't imagine another year when I don't conduct something like this—and it's all about the Standards."

GRADE 7: "KING TIDES AND GLOBAL WARMING"

In 2012, newspapers up and down the California coast headlined the first appearance of a new threat to those living in low-lying areas: king tides. Homeowners and businesses suddenly had to deal with tides a foot or two higher than normal, which in combination with heavy winds meant that ocean water was flooding their buildings. This weather did not seem like big storms; there was no real warning, and no real danger. The water level gradually increased, and suddenly streets were impassable, underground power stations were disabled, and houses and businesses were flooded. The first few king tides were relatively minor, but by the end of 2023 they were becoming more frequent, and were attracting considerable attention.

Bert Bauer's seventh-grade social studies classes in Redwood View knew about king tides firsthand. Only a few of the students had been directly affected, but during a recent downpour, several school buses were delayed because of high water, and one actually stalled when its driver attempted to drive through a flooded intersection. In December, their school was one of several that closed for a day because of the threat of a king tide. The entire community was concerned. It was on the edge of San Francisco Bay, and was familiar with the high waters and flooding that might accompany Pacific storms. But king tides were different—like a thief in the night, they crept in, and then stole away. And they were becoming more frequent.

In January, Bauer decided that king tides might provide an opportunity for assigning an inquiry project to his middle schoolers. What was causing king tides (the label was a real attention-getter)? Were they really getting worse? What could be done about them? Some of these questions called for scientific research, but Bauer also saw the occasion as an opportunity to explore local history and geography. His classrooms, like others in the school, had limited Internet access (it was not tied in by optic fiber), but it was sufficient for basic searches: (1) high and low tide levels over the past 100 years; (2) changes in local Bay-front geography, mostly as a result of harbor dredging and landfills; and (3) data on the effects of paving large areas and redirecting creeks. The classes also obtained information from the Internet about land usage and property values; they were amazed to discover how much they could learn about variation in housing values from one neighborhood to another, and about the relationship between school test scores and property values.

Bauer got the ball rolling with a topic of immediate interest to the students: newscast reports on the likelihood of further increases in king tide heights in different locations throughout the city, many of which included students' homes and places where their parents worked. Each of his 6 classes started the project by recounting personal experiences with flooding, considering how to work out details about the investigations, and deciding what they needed to "produce." Bert assigned each class to a specific neighborhood (he used school attendance zones) for detailed investigations by small teams. The winter months, especially January and February, are stormy in the Bay Area, and there was a lot to talk about the tides. Bert arranged for visits by several local experts, including a meteorologist, several first responders, and the president of the city council. By the end of March, students had completed a series of PowerPoint report presentations that were featured at the school open house event; a reporter from the Redwood City/Woodside *Patch* even covered the project.

GRADE 9: THE ALL-ELECTRIC TESLA AND THE BAGHDAD BATTERY

John Anderson is the senior science teacher at Franklin High School, a large facility serving more than 1,500 students in a highly diverse community in the upper Midwest. Because of his seniority, Anderson can pick the classes he wants to teach, and he always chooses diversity. His specialties are physics and chemistry, and he teaches advanced classes in each subject, along with general science classes for grades nine and ten. Students in the advanced classes are college-bound, well prepared, and highly motivated. The general science classes generally attract lower-achieving students, including many who need to fulfill the state science requirement but are not really interested in technical subjects.

Anderson is a conscientious teacher, and when Franklin began full implementation of the Common Core ELA Standards in 2016, he attended the sessions for content-area teachers, and studied the Standards with some care. At first he was largely on his own; the other content-area teachers could not see how it affected them, and the ELA teachers were busy with their own duties and demands. Anderson, however, was something of a maverick. The Next Generation science standards called for separating the disciplines for the advanced classes, which Anderson thought was simply silly; he favored teaching "general science" across the board, focusing instead on "problems." He did applaud the attention given to the engineering side of science, to practical applications, which he thought was a good idea for a couple of reasons: (1) engineering was more interesting than pure science, and (2) there were more jobs in engineering. Unfortunately, the textbooks still offered little coverage of engineering. Over the years, John had found ways to "sprinkle" a little engineering into the general science classes, but the advanced classes were still driven by textbooks and tests.

In 2023, after considerable reflection and some small-scale trials, John decided to conduct an "experiment" with all of his general science classes. His justification for this move was the ELA Standards, which called for content-area teachers to conduct research projects as a means for helping students acquire content-related literacy skills. He reasoned that he had little to lose. His students currently had difficulty wrestling with the text-books, they did poorly on the tests, and they were generally disinterested in science.

He announces to the classes at the beginning of the school year that they are going to work on a *special project*: "building the battery of the future." His reasoning is that (1) battery technology is about engineering, (2) it draws upon science from chemistry and electronics, and (3) batteries have been hot topics in the newspaper and television news reports during the past 2 years. Lithium batteries were essential in the development of the Boeing *Dreamliner* and the all-electric Tesla automobile in the first part of the 21st century. Early problems with the batteries—fires and explosions— seemed to have been solved. As the years passed, however, new problems emerged, including the scarcity of lithium, the need for greater efficiency, and issues related to disposal. The costs of the batteries are increasing, cus-tomers are especially unhappy about recharging and "range" features, and safety concerns would not go away.

Anderson is not sure where the project might go. He introduces the project not with "batteries," which would probably seem boring, but with the Tesla, which had captured attention as the best-selling, all-electric car in the 2010s—and it still looked really cool! Notwithstanding its extreme popularity and its fantastic stylings, cost and range limitations have con-tinued to limit sales through 2024. In 2021, rumors had emerged that the company was working on a breakthrough in battery technology that would be announced "soon." Although nothing had appeared in the newspapers and newscasts since then, the previous summer John had read a science paper about a new battery that is made of zinc and air! The idea originated at Stanford in 2013, but ran into engineering problems. Now these prob-lems have apparently been solved, but everything is still hush-hush.

John decides to try out the idea of a research project on batteries, which he thinks will be a hit with his students, who are clearly interested in cars. They have probably not given much thought to batteries, but this topic is increasingly in the headlines. The shortage of lithium has become a prob-lem for cell phones, laptop computers, and tablets, all of which are essential for teenagers; China has the world's greatest deposits of the mineral, and has placed limits on production to increase value. Zinc, by contrast, is more common, less volatile, and cheaper. John thinks about the possibility of linking the project to a colleague in social studies—batteries have a long history, and are clearly connected to economic and trade issues. It occurs to him that, like many other technologies, batteries are pervasive but invisible—just the right topic to raise with his students.

John prepares for the introduction of the project at the next meetings of his general science classes. The main office has a recycling jug for used batteries; he empties the collection into a bag for distribution and discussion. While checking to see what Wikipedia has to say about batteries, John discovers the "Baghdad battery," an urn excavated near Damascus that might be the very earliest device for generating and storing electrical energy. He stops by the local Tesla dealer, who is happy to provide brochures and a couple of posters—and promises to pay a visit during lunchtime during the first week.

Batteries connect with most of the science disciplines: chemistry, physics, biology. They are the product of engineering. They work in invisible, almost magical ways; John makes a note to bring his voltmeter to the class, along with a couple of flashlights. The school librarian promises to collect a bunch of books, including those on "how things work." The social studies teacher is puzzled when John broaches the idea of a project on batteries, but then reflects on the economics of the topic—he was assigned to teach the economics course several years ago, and maybe this topic will provoke some much needed interest.

John feels prepared for the first class, but realizes with some apprehension that he is not entirely sure where the class will take the idea—if anywhere at all. The first-period students enter and begin to murmur among themselves when they see "BATTERY" written on the screen. There are also big posters for the newest Tesla, along with boxes of used batteries, including several C's and D's cut in half. What has any of this to do with science? John begins with a few words about the project plan, including mention of Stanford's research on battery engineering, and Martha raises her hand rather tentatively. John knows her from the year before. As usual, she is seated at the back of the room with friends, checking text messages, but she had apparently been listening. "Mr. Anderson, you said something about good jobs in engineering that pay good money. What is an engineer anyway, and what do they do?" John realizes that he may have touched a responsive nerve. The students may not know any engineers, but the phrase "good job and good money" has grabbed their attention. He promises to bring an engineer to class to answer their questions as soon as he can make arrangements.

As we noted in the Preface, the CCSS ELA Standards for *literacy* call for high school students to "conduct sustained research projects"—the Standards actually have a great deal to say about this matter, which we will discuss further in Chapter 3. When the Standards were released in 2010, high schools gave them little note, except for English teachers and special education instructors. English teachers seemed concerned that they were going to have to help students read the science and social studies textbooks; special education instructors worried that many of their students would fail to meet even more stringent requirements. For most other teachers, however, the Standards seemed irrelevant. John dutifully attended the district workshops, and left wondering what the fuss was all about. As the semester moved on, he began to connect some dots—he actually read the whole CCSS document to see what it had to say. One point that resonated is that reading and writing are supposed to be about important things to understand in the disciplines. A second is the emphasis on student-initiated projects in high school. Finally, John began to realize that the ELA Standards are not about standardized testing, which had been the source of many concerns in 2015, the year that the tests first "counted." He and his colleagues were on the sidelines during this time—testing was about reading and arithmetic, mostly in the elementary and middle school grades. They had nothing to worry about. He slowly realized that the Standards were really about educating students to deal with the interrelated world that seemed to be expanding every year. He began to "talk it up" with other teachers in the lunch room—to his surprise, he discovered that Terry Williams, the shop teacher, and Martha Taylor, who taught physical education and coached the women's teams, were becoming increasingly enthusiastic about pursuing these ideas. Taylor, who was finishing her doctorate at a local university, shared a phrase from her philosophy class—"We should be teaching a few things well."

GRADE 11: MANY PEOPLES, MANY VIEWS

Not long after the Common Core was widely adopted, the local state research university invited individuals and organizations to submit ideas that pushed the boundaries of traditional education and business. The university's new Innovation Campus was being developed to house high-technology companies and other local organizations with collaborative long- and short-term projects, providing a synergistic environment that became a beehive of activity that allowed for all manner of productive creativity. One of the now established projects is the Communication, Arts, and Technology School (CATS)—a collaborative endeavor of the university, the burgeoning high-tech business world, and the local public school district fashioned much like the highly successful Bay Area's Freestyle Academy in Mountain View, California (*http://freestyleacademy.rocks/map*) that came into existence in the mid-2000s. Unlike many public school magnet programs, CATS is not earmarked for high school students who are designated as gifted, nor is it necessarily for students who had a broad knowledge and experience with computer applications. On the contrary, the program designers' intent was to attract students who find traditional programs disengaging and are doing just enough to be on track for graduating. Although the program is open to any interested students in the district, priority is given to the closest two high schools, which serve students mainly from highly diverse, low socioeconomic status (SES) families. The students, who are accepted into this hybrid program, attend CATS courses in the morning and return to their neighborhood schools for their remaining coursework.

CATS creates project-based learning environments where students are immersed in interrelated English, social studies, arts, and technology courses that are grounded in real-world applications. Thinking outside the box is a goal of this half-day public school program as students learn to solve real problems by using the sophisticated technology of the Innovation Campus blended with the application of the arts and humanities. Because the courses address the learning needs created by the quarterly projects students design, learning tasks make sense; students see a clear purpose for them that make learning relevant and very engaging.

Alexandra Kagan is currently an English teacher at CATS, with 18 years of previous experience teaching in a wealthy neighborhood school as an advanced placement (AP) literature teacher there. Before joining the CATS faculty, she moved toward literature projects for junior–senior combinations—no entry conditions. The focus of her teaching has been on the analysis of contemporary novels that speak to important issues— political and social. She would start the year with Khaled Hosseini's *Kite Runner* (2003) and the Afghan war, and then move to the larger issues of Islam, and of the tensions that divide people. Interesting stuff, but she jumped at the chance to teach with CATS's project-based learning, where she believed that she could push herself and this new group of students to new levels.

Because the region is a long-standing refugee resettlement area with many rich cultures represented, Alexandra and the world geography teacher, Larry Carter, decided to explore the possibilities of students creating multimedia projects that could ultimately contribute to a television/ magazine series in the local public television and print media outlets. The Innovation Campus would provide the technology needed to create final products, local businesses the media expertise and community immigrant connections, and CATS faculty the foundational instruction to facilitate the projects.

Alexandra plans to open the winter quarter by having her students wrestle with the powerful ideas presented in Azar Nafizi's *Reading Lolita in Tehran* (2003) to develop a sense of why individuals are compelled to leave their homeland for political reasons. Larry is creating a corresponding companion unit examining geopolitical and historical aspects of the Middle East from the end of World War II to the present. In addition, students will be asked to look for similar geopolitical patterns in other hot spots around the world to compare and contrast experiences. By this point in the school year students have gained many of the advanced basics of multimedia applications. The students will now build upon those basics by learning even more complex media design and incorporating new multimedia equipment to support their individually designed projects. Because Alexandra and the other teachers believe that learning is most profound when it is socially constructed and purposeful, they structure interrelated mini-projects along the way where students will work in pairs and small groups to tackle tough ideas and solve the challenging demands of their projects. Students will also conduct research collaboratively on the cultural, political, historical, and geographical aspects they are identifying that will then inform their final presentations.

To add more depth and local interest in the project, the students—armed with newly acquired background knowledge—will soon be contacting local refugee families to create video interviews of them about their experiences. The students have already visited local community centers and churches that might prove to be resources for locating and contacting refugee families and for translators, if the context required one. Coinciding with all of the arrangements being made through phone calls, meetings, and e-mails, student teams work together to develop and test culturally sensitive, open-ended interview questions to see what types of responses they might gather. Timely revisions in the questions will be made to optimize the interview session.

As students progress through the project, they create scripts for the media segments and visuals to go into their finish presentations. All in all, the full spectrum of the literacy components is in the forefront of what students are accomplishing. The mini-projects lend themselves well to assessing students formatively along the way. The teachers are ready with rubrics for the mini-projects and the multimedia presentations that the students can use as guideposts for what is expected as they work. They are learning and applying a diverse set of knowledge and skills that would serve them well in the future. The expectations for the students are demanding, but they are embracing the challenges this quarter's work is presenting to them. The students are fully engaged and show pride in their work; an observer would not need to hunt long for examples of that engagement or for impressive learning going on. The students are looking forward to sharing their final projects with the rest of the CATS students, faculty, and families, and especially with the local community through real-world media.

BACK TO THE PRESENT

What do these stories mean? What are the differences between these snap-shots of 2024 and conditions in schools today? Teachers are still teaching students in classrooms about reading and arithmetic. Some schools and teachers and students are still doing better than others. Poverty is still an important factor. But, in our story, the decade since 2014 has seen a regrowth of confidence in public education, and a newfound respect for teachers.

We will take a look at current conditions in the following chapter. Meanwhile, here are our emerging principles behind the snapshots of 2024:

• End-of-year tests no longer dictate instruction—summative tests are administered in late May, two days covering language arts and mathematics with applications in science and social studies. The test data are used to monitor achievement trends. Teachers no longer feel pressured to teach to the tests.

• Teachers have no time to teach to tests. Students are intensely engaged in productive activities—in writing, in presentations, in research projects—that all take sustained amounts of time.

• Teachers manage student learning rather than lecturing. Students are actively learning rather than listening.

• Teachers vary widely in the topics and activities in which they engage students, but are united in their instructional goals, which they link to the Standards—they can explain their work, and they are clearly connected into a professional community.

• Student learning and achievement are continuously monitored by formative assessment of their performance, of the products that they create, and of the processes (and explanations) that they demonstrate. Teachers are primarily responsible for ensuring that student learning is evaluated and documented, but as students move through the grades, they take on increasing responsibility for self-assessment, and for taking on roles in peer assessment.

• Students are able to explain what they are working on, and to describe what they are learning. They appear motivated and engaged. As the Standards describe it, "Students who have met the Standards . . . readily undertake close, attentive reading . . . , [they] habitually perform the critical reading needed for the staggering amount of information available today . . . , they actively seek wide, deep, and thoughtful engagement with texts . . . , [and] they reflexively demonstrate the cogent reading and use of evidence that is essential . . . for responsible citizenship in a democratic republic" (p. 3). The students in the snapshots are deeply engaged in tasks that make strong demands on language and literacy—and they are finding purpose and value in these activities.

Each of these points represents fundamental shifts from current practice. None of these shifts will be easy. None of them can be packaged. All of them depend on changes in the ways that teachers conduct their professional practice, and on public trust and respect. Following more than a decade under a federal regime of test-based accountability, it is now difficult to imagine a time when teachers could actually recapture their status as professionals, to the point that they had the authority to take on the responsibilities of educating all students to their full potential. In 2014, the word on the street was about the remarkable accomplishments of teachers in Finland and Sweden, contrasting with the failures of the U.S. schools. The film *Waiting for Superman* had recently been a smash hit.

CHAPTER 2

No Child Left Untested

The Unrests of 2010

As a result of the No Child Left Behind Act (NCLB) of 2002, by 2014 virtually every school in the United States was dominated by year-end standardized tests. With the imposition of NCLB, the Right to Read (1970), an important feature of the Kennedy–Johnson War on Poverty, came to an end. NCLB offered the promise of a brighter future, but text-based accountability led to a much darker reality: a curriculum restructured around basic skills, pacing charts, and teacher-based recitations. In 2010, the release of the CCSS produced a revival of hope and enthusiasm, but the establishment of two large testing consortia soon overshadowed the CCSS, auguring "more of the same" and creating a mood of anxiety, uncertainty, and frustration.

This chapter describes the state of public schools in 2014–2015. More than a decade has passed since the implementation of NCLB. Congress continues to struggle with the development of new legislation. Implementation of the CCSS has approached fever pitch, largely focused on preparing for the new tests under development by the Smarter Balanced Assessment Consortium (SBAC) and the Partnership for Assessment of Readiness for College and Careers (PARCC), two consortia funded under President Obama's Race to the Top initiative, which are designed to continue federal policies of test-based accountability established under NCLB.

Testing of some sort has been part of school for as long as most of us can remember. There was the Friday spelling quiz, writing papers, history exams, and so on. These were teachers' doings; they decided what to test, when, and how. Students generally learned how they had done soon after they had completed the test. In mathematics, they had to show their work, and getting the right answer the wrong way was not the right way. But how did it come about that distant agencies captured the power to test, with such dire and Kafkaesque impact on the inhabitants of our public schools? Complaints of this sort have been voiced for a long time: "Educational tests that set the limits within which teachers must move will be reduced to their proper subordinate position in the teaching process" (Kilpatrick, 1933, p. 210). The story can be told in different ways, but the most important theme for our purposes centers on the changing federal influence in the conduct of K–12 public schooling.

We can tell only part of this story here; others have written in great detail from different perspectives (e.g., McGuinn, 2006; Ravitch, 2011; Rothman, 2011a, 2011b; Vinovskis, 2009). Vinovskis (2009) covers the span from *A Nation at Risk* (Gardner, Larsen, Baker, & Campbell, 1983) through the first years of NCLB. He recounts how Lyndon Johnson saw himself as the first "education president," and as part of the War on Poverty persuaded Congress to pass the landmark Elementary and Secondary Education Act of 1965. This legislation emphasized equal access to education, along with high standards and accountability, the last mentioned to be the responsibility of states and local education authorities. The idea of a federal mandate for test-based accountability was not given serious consideration. In the almost 50 years since the original authorization, the Act has undergone several major changes, many related to the allocation of funds (e.g., to individual students or to schools), but in the past two decades the program has served increasingly as a vehicle for federal mandates related to testing and accountability, most recently in the reauthorization of NCLB.

Vinovski's main story begins with the release in 1983 of *A Nation at Risk* by Reagan's National Commission on Excellence in Education. The commission certainly pulled no punches: "The educational foundations of our society are presently being eroded by a rising tide of mediocrity that threatens our very future as a Nation and a people. . . . If an unfriendly foreign power had attempted to impose on America the mediocre educational performance that exists today, we might well have viewed it as an act of war." Those claims have undergirded federal educational policy since their release: public schools are broken, and the federal government has got to fix them. The commission's recommendations comprised an interesting mix: (1) institution of a broad array of course requirements for high school graduation; (2) standardized testing at "major transition points," especially high school to college; (3) increases in school time (7-hour school days, a 200- to 220-day school year); (4) teacher salaries that were "professionally competitive, market-sensitive, and performance-based"; and (5) a federal role in ensuring that the needs of "key groups of students" were met, with special attention to "ensure compliance with civil rights." Reagan's later policy initiatives were quite different: voluntary prayer, voucher credits, and abolition of the Department of Education. As it turned out, federal funds were never authorized for any of the recommendations. But *A Nation at Risk* has had a lasting impact, according to Vinovski's analysis, as the progenitor of subsequent activities by the federal government, including the America 2000 initiative, Goals 2000, and NCLB. The driving force behind all of these activities was *A Nation at Risk*, and the claim that declines (multiple) in our public schools were a threat to the nation's social and economic well-being.

The various federal "goals" projects of the 1990s were clearly spinoffs from *A Nation at Risk*, reflecting the efforts of George H. W. Bush and then Bill Clinton to build their reputations as education presidents. Both Bush and Clinton involved the states and the governors in their discussions— schooling is not covered in the Constitution and so governance in education is reserved to the states. Clinton made a valiant effort to pick up the baton from Bush's 1989 Charlottesville Conference with governors, but in the end Congress would not pass the Goals 2000 legislation, although the recommendations were relatively modest: (1) all children will start school ready to learn; (2) high school graduation rates will reach 90%; (3) support for graduation requirements similar to those described in *A Nation at Risk*; (4) steps to ensure that U.S. students would have the highest achievement scores in mathematics and science of any nation in the world; (5) requirements that every teacher have access to high-quality professional development programs; and (6) a scattering of other items that were ancillary to achievement issues. Clinton also proposed several initiatives for improvement of the technological resources available in schools (the IBM personal computer first appeared in 1981, and the Apple Macintosh was released in 1984), but little came of these efforts.

The story line changed dramatically during the 2000 presidential campaign, when George W. Bush proposed substantial changes in ESEA reauthorization, and in a stroke of marketing genius labeled the new program No Child Left Behind (2002; McGuinn, 2006).When Bush signed the NCLB Act at Hamilton High School in Hamilton, Ohio, in January 2002, at his side were Senator Ted Kennedy and Representative George Miller—one could not find more ardent liberals in Congress. With this range of political perspectives providing support, it appeared that a new era might lie ahead. The major requirement was that each state establish standards for reading and mathematics, which were coupled to a testing system for grades 3–8. While the spotlight was on the "world-class standards," the main business centered on the tests. Each state could develop its own standards, decide on the tests, set cutpoints for judging "proficiency" (meeting the standards), and lay out a road map for improvement. But the legislation mandated some very important "stuff." Most significant was the API/AYP model—*academic performance indicator* and *adequate yearly progress*. The key requirement was that, by spring 2014, "no child would be left behind." Every student—100%—would meet the test-based proficiency requirements in reading and mathematics. The clock started ticking in 2002 and schools had a dozen years to meet the requirement.

The testing legislation was designed to ensure that no students were overlooked. Test reports had to provide *disaggregation*: a variety of target groups were identified for separate reporting, and AYP trends had to be reported for each of these groups. The NCLB disaggregation feature had widespread appeal; schools had to demonstrate that *all* students, including those on *free and reduced-price lunch*, the children of the poor, were doing well.

This requirement was strongly supported by advocates for equal education, who were concerned that their constituents might fall by the wayside. As time has gone by, however, this requirement has proved to be a major hurdle for virtually every school and district. If even one group failed to meet the trend requirements, the result could be a school's reclassification as "needing to improve."

Establishing and meeting the AYP trend-lines has proved to be a daunting challenge. As of January 2014, more than 90% of the nation's schools and districts had been identified as underperforming—as predicted at the outset by measurement experts such as Bob Linn (e.g., Linn, Baker, & Betebenner, 2002). Each state was required to develop a track for API scores assuring that, by spring 2014, every student in every school scored at the "proficient" level on the standardized tests—100% meant that no child was left behind at that point. Similarly, each school had to make *adequate progress* toward the 2014 goal on the AYP track—every group on both reading and mathematics.

This is where the hammer came into play—if *any group in either reading or mathematics* in a school failed to make adequate progress for 2 years in a row, then the school would be labeled *needs to improve* (NTI), which meant that it must accept "technical assistance" as directed by the appropriate state education agency. If any of the groups failed to make adequate progress for a third year, then the school would be subjected to "more serious corrective actions," or restructuring, which may entail replacing the principal and some or all of the teaching staff. Although being labeled as needing to improve is bad enough, the chaos caused by restructuring has been traumatic. With the passing of the years, administrators have resorted to a variety of strategies to avoid the NTI label. At the beginning, most schools and districts moved into a "test-prep" mode. Curriculum materials emphasized the basic skills, leading first to elimination of "frills" such as the arts and crafts, and then to reductions in such disciplines as the sciences and social studies. States developed techniques for handling disaggregation issues early in the process, largely by establishing sample-size limits; if there were only a few students in a target group, then the average would be unreliable. By setting the limits as high as possible, districts did not have to report the scores. A second strategy was the identification of "bubble students"; any student who was just below the proficiency cut score was identified for special assistance, the argument being that with a little bit of help, he or she could make it over the boundary. Students who were far below basic were unlikely to make the needed improvements, so they were triaged. Finally, there have been instances of outright cheating and fraud.

As an aside, during the writing of the NCLB legislation, the concept of *equal opportunity to learn* rose to the surface on a number of occasions (McGuinn, 2006, Ch. 5). It had been evident as far back as the Coleman Report (Coleman et al., 1966), *Equality of Educational Opportunity*, which documented the enormous differences in school resources available in schools serving predominately African American students, compared to schools in which white students were the majority. Coleman also reported that these differences were less important than differences in family background, leading many to conclude that investing in schools might not be worthwhile. The triage approach described above is a clear instance of a strategy that literally guarantees unequal opportunity, although in this instance the additional opportunity to practice basic skills may not be especially beneficial.

We will return to other ramifications of the AYP policy shortly, but first a few comments about two other issues that have greatly affected classroom teachers, issues with substantial impact but that have received little attention: the "highly qualified teacher" (HQT) requirement and Reading First. The HQT requirement was undoubtedly motivated by the best of intentions. For a variety of reasons, some teachers, especially in schools serving large proportions of at-risk children, were not "fully qualified." These teachers may have lacked credentials, or (more often) they were teaching out of their content area (e.g., teachers with no preparation in math or science were teaching courses in these areas). NCLB required that districts remedy this situation over a reasonable period of time. Subsequent problems have arisen not because the intent of the requirement was misguided, but because of heavy-handed top-down implementation, a recurring challenge with federal mandates. One situation, which affects a large number of teachers in the secondary grades, results because special education teachers generally have the same students for the entire day; they therefore are responsible for covering the full range of subject matters—math, science, social studies, and so on. These teachers are credentialed to handle students with a broad range of learning problems, from dyslexia to autism and beyond. The challenge for most of these students is to learn to learn, to deal with attention issues, self-discipline, and so on. They are often substantially behind their classmates in the scope-and-sequence chart. Many are still wrestling with the fundamentals of arithmetic, and if they are helped to understand the most basic essentials of a linear equation (e.g., "A car is going 50 miles per hour; how far will it travel in 2 hours?"), that is progress. But throughout the nation, many teachers now spend their summer months acquiring advanced certification across the full spectrum of content areas (literature, the sciences, history and geography, etc.). It is an enormous cost to the teachers, with little benefit to anyone else. Although such a requirement may seem reasonable on the surface, "on the ground" it is clearly an annoyance and in many instances a discouragement for teachers who are doing an excellent job helping students with serious problems move forward and are in fact "highly qualified" by this criterion.

READING FIRST

Reading First is an even more serious matter. The origins of this program are found in the National Reading Panel (NRP) Report, a project that began in 1997 at the request of Congress for the executive branch to "convene a national panel to assess the status of research-based knowledge . . . on the effectiveness of various approaches to teaching children to read" (NCLB, 2001). The NRP, the brainchild of Reid Lyon, chief of the National Institute of Child and Human Development (NICHD), released its report in 2000, almost simultaneously with the passage of NCLB. The report contained a number of recommendations based on its review of "scientific research," a review based on a definition that led the NRP to reject 99.5% of the studies that had been conducted in the previous three decades. The recommendations conformed to a "simple" view of reading (Gough & Tunmer, 1986), in which young students were taught sounds and letters (phoneme awareness), then letters and words (phonics), and finally words and the "good stuff" (comprehension, and so on). In the regular course of events, the NRP Report would have been presented by the panel, study reports would have been published, and so on. But with NCLB about to arrive on the scene, the report was ready-made to complement what became Reading First (RF), a $1 billion program for the primary grades conducted in 2002/2003 under NCLB. RF workshops and summer institutes trained teachers to use instructional materials incorporating five curriculum components featured in the NRP report: phoneme awareness, phonics, vocabulary, fluency, and comprehension. Implementation of RF was a condition for federal funding under NCLB, and so districts serving at-risk students had to participate in RF. The RF legislation also funded extensive evaluations of the program, showing that, although following the summer workshops teachers made earnest efforts to implement the program in their classrooms, Reading First did not produce a statistically significant impact on student reading comprehension test scores in grades one, two or three. (Gamse et al., 2008b, pp. 38–41). Moreover, "Findings based on exploratory analyses do not provide consistent or systematic insight into the pattern of observed impacts" (Gamse et al., 2008a, p. 8). The NRP recommendations, as implemented in RF, had no effect on student learning, and nothing was learned from the evaluation research about what might have been the problem. Phonemic awareness, the "secret ingredient" highlighted in the report, remains a central feature of today's reading programs, even though this skill is difficult to teach and a challenge to learn.

THE LESSONS OF NO CHILD LEFT BEHIND

The lessons learned thus far from NCLB seem rather distressing: policies and practices mandated by the federal government seem to be wasteful of time, with little positive effect on student learning (Goodman, Calfee, & Goodman, 2014). These consequences are actually of little consequence, however, compared with what is presently happening as a result of the AYP mandate—the "King Kong" of NCLB (McGuinn, 2006). RF did not solve the nation's "reading problems," but it probably did not make them any worse. In our view, however, AYP poses a serious systemic threat to our public schools by undermining public confidence and by sowing the seeds of disruption—not for schools "in general, " but for individual schools called out by name. More than half of the nation's schools were labeled "needs to improve" or worse by the beginning of the 2011–2012 school. The current Obama administration has offered "waivers" to selected urban districts to provide short-term relief from this state of affairs, but the long-term prospects are no less gloomy. By the end of the 2013–2014 school year, when "no child was to be left behind," an overwhelming preponderance of our schools not receiving "waivers" were being labeled as failing. Today this process continues to move inexorably forward as schools are encouraged to enter the bold new era of the CCSS. On the one hand, test-based accountability with dire consequences for failure to meet unreachable targets creates enormous pressure for strictly paced basic-skills instruction. On the other hand, teachers are being asked to foster the development of high-level understandings through project-based activities.

How has this bizarre state of affairs come about? Early warnings about AYP were actually in print almost before the ink was dry on the NCLB bill, thanks to the work of Linn and his colleagues. Linn and colleagues (2002) warned at the outset that "the accountability requirements [of NCLB] . . .

set ambitious objectives for rapid increases in student performance . . . for subgroups defined by race, ethnicity, and economic background. . . . The NCLB goals are laudable, but . . . pose substantial challenges for schools, districts, and states" (p. 15). Linn and colleagues then offered recommendations for alleviating some of these challenges, such as "the volatility in school-level results from year to year." Now, what has happened in the decade since Linn's analyses and recommendations? Figure 2.1 shows data from a 2012 report on the proportion of schools that have been designated as "needs to improve" from 2006 through 2011. The numbers stayed around 30% through 2009, and more recently jumped to 39% in 2010 and then to 48% in 2011. The trend is consistent with state plans that assumed an acceleration in improvement during the final years of NCLB, an acceleration that proved impossible to achieve.

As the 2015–2016 school year gets underway, NCLB remains the law of the land. The primary effects of the program are on elementary and, to a lesser extent, middle schools. The story is not a happy one. In the first years of the program, it was primarily the schools serving poor communities that fell prey to low API indices. But over the years, *needs to improve* spread throughout the country, slowly at first and then more rapidly, so that the label has now been placed on many "good schools." Predictions of a narrowing of the curriculum have come to pass; reading and mathematics are covered, largely through a skills-oriented, teach-to-the-test approach, using

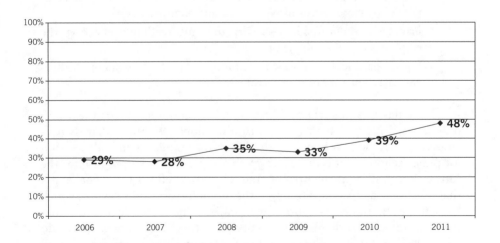

FIGURE 2.1. The percentage of schools that did not make AYP, 2006–2011. In 2006, 29% of the nation's schools did not make adequate yaerly progress. By 2011, this percentage had increased to 48%. From Center on Education Policy (2011). Copyright 2011 by the Center on Education Policy. Reprinted by permission.

interim benchmark tests to "direct instruction," and pacing charts to keep teachers in line. Art and music are gone, and history and science are diminished; science is "on the test," but generally only once from grades 3–8, and with little weight in the API. Writing is seldom tested, and so it is seldom taught. The primary grades are not tested (SBAC and PARRC), and so they receive less attention, but phonics is very important, with significant effects on first grade and, increasingly, on kindergarten. With the recession of 2008, resources were further diminished, leading to increases in class size and reductions in support services. An all-encompassing miasma has permeated schools all around the nation.

It is against this backdrop that the CCSS have continued to develop. At the point of their emergence in June 2010, the idea was that they would permit a clean break from the past. States rather than the federal government would call the shots. The CCSS would pursue a new vision and be grounded in the professional contributions of teachers. The hope was that the nation could quickly move beyond the unrests of NCLB. Unfortunately, as of 2015, images of the Standards are rather discouraging. The CCSS are seen (American Federation of Teachers, 2014; Rothman, 2011a, 2013) as being:

- A federal rather than state/local initiative.
- Mandatory rather than collaborative.
- For practical purposes, a new set of tests—really difficult tests (supported by experiences in New York and Kentucky).
- Primarily about reading—really difficult reading (reflecting the emphasis on text complexity).
- For all practical purposes, little more than NCLB in slightly different garb—just more of the same.

How has this happened? Were the initial enthusiasms for the CCSS only hollow rhetoric? Is there no reason for hope? We think that there is considerable reason for hope. We think that the Standards embody a vision for public schools that is quite remarkable and offers great promise for the future. We think that the present state of affairs reflects three challenges that need to be addressed. The first is the recent history under NCLB, which has left the nation's teaching force demoralized and fearful, convinced that the best course of action is to find out what "they" want done, and to do "it" as well as possible. Greater authority for curriculum should be shifted from external forces back into the classroom. The second is that actions by the federal government to continue policies and practices that sustain test-based accountability are focusing attention on tests rather than on education. We advocate for a greater balance between *assessment for learning* rather than *testing of achievement* (Calfee, Wilson, Flannery, & Kapinus, 2014). The third is that implementation proposals by national organizations are "stuck" on one side of the "bracketing" described in the previous chapter; they are emphasizing basic skills and linear scope-and-sequence instruction, while the Common Core vision begins with the ultimate goals of preparing graduates who are college-, career-, and citizen-ready, and then backward-maps from that point. To support these claims, we turn in the next chapter to the task of addressing a rather simple question: *What do the Common Core ELA Standards actually say?*

CHAPTER 3

The Common Core Standards

A New Vision for American Schools

This chapter presents the vision of American schools described in the Introduction to the CCSS ELA Standards (pp. 3–8). The introductory eight pages are a truly remarkable tract, and it is unfortunate that they have received so little attention by either advocates or opponents. We then describe the Anchor Standards, an unusual feature of the CCSS that has also received little notice. Finally, we look at the grade-by-grade (G x G) standards, which are easily (and mistakenly) interpreted as "specific objectives" like those found in today's scope and sequence charts. Most educators seem to have started with these detailed entries, overlooking the overarching, broad-based outcomes that are at the heart of the ELA Standards. By emphasizing the G x G objectives and ignoring the larger outcomes, implementation plans are replicating existing curriculum designs (Schmoker, 2012); students move through endless lists of disjointed, piecemeal, "sliced and diced" activities (e.g., McGraw-Hill, 2014), in which the teacher introduces an objective, students complete worksheets for practice, and are then tested (increasingly) by a computer to document their level of "mastery." This state of affairs is not what was envisioned by the framers of the CCSS, and it will *not* advance the quality of education for students. The ELA Standards call for students, from kindergarten onward, *to inquire into engaging themes and topics, to conduct research that is informed by the disciplines, where literacy is acquired as a set of skills and strategies that support thinking, problem solving, and communication.* This message is illustrated with particular clarity in an example on page 33 of the CCSS ELA document, which emphasizes "building knowledge systematically" through sustained engagement in significant topics, themes, and problems, both within and across grades.

We begin with a brief history of how the CCSS were developed, which is important for understanding where we are and where we need to go in implementing the Standards. Here is a synopsis of the story line (cf. Rothman, 2011b, 2013):

1. The CCSS were an effort by the states to regain authority over public schools—where it belongs, according to the Constitution. One team developed the Introduction, and a second team then prepared the detailed G × G standards.
2. The CCSS were about education, not about curriculum and not about tests.
3. Once the Standards were released, "federalization" emerged almost immediately.

Two testing consortia were established with Race to the Top funds. In addition, several national organizations responded to cries from practitioners— "What are we supposed to do? Where are materials? What is going to be on the tests?" After more than a decade of NCLB, educators were understandably hesitant to step forward and seize the opportunities provided by the CCSS, which were heralded by the *New York Times* on March 13, 2010: "The new Standards provide an excellent starting point for remaking public schooling in the United States."

Big changes plainly were afoot, but what were they? What were educators and publishers supposed to do? What resources were needed, and where would they come from? New, tougher tests were being developed, but what would they look like, and where was guidance for teachers and students? Few educators took time to read the Standards, and they seemingly did not need to—instructions were almost instantly available telling them what they were supposed to do.

A FULLER STORY OF THE COMMON CORE STATE STANDARDS

Once upon a time there was NCLB. . . . It is difficult to understand the CCSS without knowing about the previous two decades. Rothman's (2011, 2013) accounts of the emergence of the Standards open with the presentation of the final draft on June 2, 2010, at Peachtree Ridge High School in Suwanee, Georgia, by the governors of Georgia and Delaware, state superintendents from West Virginia and Florida, and leaders of the two national teacher organizations. Notably, there were no representatives from the federal government. This was a project of the states—of the National Governors Association (NGA) and the Council of Chief State School Officers (CCSSO)—with the concurrence of the teachers' organizations. The proposal for establishment of national education standards was a landmark event in its own right, but it is also possible to view it as a move by the states and local governments to return the public schools to their rightful owners.

After setting the stage with the release of the CCSS, Rothman flashes back to a meeting convened by North Carolina governor Jim Hunt in June 2006 in Raleigh, North Carolina, in which a "small group" talked about a "third rail issue," the issue of national education standards (Rothman, 2011b, p. 53). Three months later, the conversation continued in Washington, D.C., where the initial team was joined by representatives from educational policy groups (the Aspen Institute, the Education Trust, the Fordham Institute). The meetings were closed, but again it appears that the federal government did not participate. The organizers were mindful that, only 10 years prior, "President Clinton's proposal for voluntary national tests went down in flames" (Rothman, 2011b, p. 53). But the discussions were not about tests—they were about standards. The decision was to move ahead.

In 2007, the project was taken on by NGA and CCSSO, and the pace increased as leaders like Gene Wilhoit, executive director of the CCSSO, and Janet Napolitano, governor of Arizona, became involved. The working group enlisted support from a variety of sources, including the National Research Council (NRC), which released an analysis of key considerations in the development of state standards (NRC, 2008, in Rothman, 2011b). A forum in January 2009 expanded the basic ideas, and a group called Achieve joined the team (Rothman, 2011b, pp. 58–61). Achieve was a nonprofit organization founded by Sue Pimentel and David Coleman, which had completed the *American Diploma Project* in 2001. While the Project had little immediate effect on high school graduation requirements, it served as a starting point for the Standards, as the foundation for a backward-mapping strategy. In April 2009 at the Chicago Hilton, NGA and CCSSO drafted a memorandum laying out plans for developing state standards in literacy and mathematics, the job to be completed by December 2009 (a daunting timeline!). The standards were to be voluntary and could be adapted (within limits) by individual states. By June 2009, all but four states (Alabama, Michigan, South Carolina, and Texas) had signed a memorandum of support for the project.

The December deadline was too ambitious—and the team did not make it. The first part of the document was prepared behind closed doors by a "brain trust" including Achieve, ACT, and the College Board. Several prominent names from academia (Linn, Hakuta, Schmidt, and Snow) are mentioned by Rothman, along with representatives from several states whose standards had received positive reviews (California, Colorado, Florida, Georgia, Massachusetts, and Minnesota). The work was "shielded from the public eye" (p. 67) for the most part, but a leak occurred in July. Reactions to the draft were mostly positive, although Core Knowledge (Pondiscio, 2009) complained that there was not enough content. The team continued its work, and a second draft—which appears to have been the Introduction, was released in September 2009. This time Core Knowledge seemed to approve of the revision.

At about the same time, a second group began development of the anchor and grade-by-grade standards (Rothman, 2011b, pp. 70–72; 2013, p. 8). Pimentel and Coleman managed a writing team of 50 educators and a much larger group of reviewers in completing the work. A new draft was released for public review in March 2010, receiving generally positive reactions (cf. the *New York Times* response quoted above). Rothman lists three criticisms to the March release: (1) general opposition to the notion of any national standards, in this case most vocally by Tea Party members; (2) requests that nonacademic outcomes needed to be covered; and (3) a concern that too much was expected of young children. These reactions were considered in the revision, but changes were generally minor (Rothman, 2011b, pp. 73–74). The final draft was finally released in June 2010—despite the delays, a breakneck accomplishment!

Rothman (2011b, Ch. 5) describes the sometimes rocky road to adoption, partly reflecting pressures from the federal government—for example, award of funds from the $4.35 billion dollar Race to the Top program became contingent on adoption of the CCSS, and in September 2010 the Obama administration provided $330 million dollars for the establishment of two large assessment consortia, each assigned to develop national tests that would "count" in the June 2015 administration (Rothman, 2011, Ch. 7). By the end of 2010, 43 states had adopted and adapted the Standards. The tasks of implementation loomed large, but states were still in the throes of conforming to NCLB.

Meanwhile, an ongoing stream of headlines captured people's attention. New standards were in place, much more challenging, world class, tougher textbooks, and so on. And new tests were under development, also tougher, computer-based, no more mark-the-bubble. What were educators supposed to do? There were no new curriculum materials. There were no guidelines for implementation. There was no timeline. Who was in charge? When would the new tests be completed, and what would they be like? When would new curriculum materials be available? Meanwhile, the realities of NCLB testing, AYPs, and APIs were demanding immediate attention; teachers had no time to focus on the Standards.

WHAT DO "THE STANDARDS" SAY?

The Common Core ELA Standards are published in a 66-page primary document comprising four major sections: the Introduction; the Standards for ELA and Literacy in History/Social Studies, Science, and Technical Subjects for grades K–5; the ELA Standards for grades 6–12; and the Standards for Literacy in History/Social Studies, Science, and Technical Subjects for grades 6–12—along with three appendices. This section of the current chapter takes you through a careful reading of the primary document. The three appendices contain important supporting information, but are outside the intended focus of this book. Our goal is to set the stage for a review of the plans and programs that have emerged during the past several years. All of these purposes have been designed to help educators and publishers to implement the ELA Standards. Based on our analysis of the Standards, however, we are convinced that these efforts, well intended though they may be, are seriously off-course. We think that the reason for this state of affairs is a lack of a full understanding of the ELA Standards by both promoters and customers. Our analysis is divided into two parts: *structure* and *substance*. The CCSS are organized differently than earlier standards, and they embody a different vision of public schooling for the nation. As a result, they can be difficult to comprehend on a quick reading.

THE STRUCTURE OF THE ENGLISH LANGUAGE ARTS STANDARDS

The foundation document, *Common Core State Standards for English Language Arts and Literacy in History/Social Studies, Science, and Technical Subjects* (NGA & CCSSO, 2010), for brevity, the ELA Standards, comprises the Introduction (pp. 3–8) and the Anchor Standards with grade-by-grade (G × G) entries (pp. 9–66). The Introduction is a brief but pivotal document, and we examine it in some detail in the section on *substance*. The Anchor Standards and G × G state the specifics.

As you can see in the Table of Contents (Figure 3.1), the Standards themselves are divided into three parts: grades K–5 (pp. 9–33), grades 6–12 for English Language Arts (pp. 34–58), and grades 6–12 for the content areas (pp. 59–66). Each section is further subdivided by literacy domains: Reading, Writing, Speaking/Listening, Language, and Range/Quality. Reading is further divided into Literature and Informational Texts, and for the K–5 segment there is also a section on Foundational Skills. The Reading Standards for the grades 6–12 content areas are organized by disciplines, History/Social Studies and Science/Technical Subjects.

From one perspective, the most practical strategy for approaching the ELA Standards would be to decide on your purpose, and then proceed to

Table of Contents

FIGURE 3.1. Table of contents of the CCSS ELA. From NGA and CCSSO (2010). Copyright 2010 by the National Governors Association Center for Best Practices and Council of Chief State School Officers. All rights reserved. Reprinted by permission.

the directly relevant sections. For example, a fourth-grade teacher might head for Reading Standards K–5, while perhaps glancing at the Writing Standards K–5, the Language Standards K–5, and the Speaking and Listening Standards K–5. Reading has been the core of the elementary curriculum for the past two decades, with the basal reader the primary basis for instructional support. A first-grade teacher presumably would look at the Reading Standards K–5, but then will study the Foundational Skills, familiar territory covering phonological awareness, phonics, and fluency. Middle and high school English teachers will turn to the English Language Arts section for grades 6–12 (middle school is covered in a single segment), and will probably feel relief. Most content-area teachers might not give much attention at all to the ELA Standards because they do not see themselves as literacy experts.

The writers of the ELA Standards probably had a quite different idea about how readers would approach the document, assuming that readers would begin with the Introduction. But, following decades of experience with standards documents, what would be the point? But this Introduction is different—it turns out to describe a set of expectations considerably more challenging than previous state standards, and, more importantly, to present a view of classroom learning that calls for fundamental change in schools and schooling.

The writers hold up the College and Career Readiness Anchor Standards (based on the American Diploma Project) as an essential part of the design. The exact same set of 36 Anchor Standards are in place from kindergarten through graduation, reflecting the backward-mapping strategy used to create the Standards. The writers took seriously the advice from Whitehead (1927) to "teach a few things well." The idea was that every teacher would hold in mind an image of the entire learning progression, rather than relying on a limited view based on one particular grade. As a further way of simplifying the curriculum, the writers recommended the combining of multiple standards into clusters around complex projects. They expressed regret that they had to separate literacy into different domains, but emphasized the concept of an integrated literacy program in which reading, writing, speaking, and listening were combined.

Even though the Introduction recommends an integrated view of literacy, the divisions in the Table of Contents require significant efforts in order to reconnect the pieces. Unfortunately, if readers do not study the Introduction, and don't understand the concept of Anchor Standards, they will find themselves overwhelmed with the magnitude of the task: more than 80 standards per grade, for a total of almost 1,100 standards across the grades. Even if readers have read the Introduction, and understand the concept of clustering about large projects, there is substantial work to be done in transforming the lists into a coherent curriculum.

We will propose a plan for dealing with this "humpty-dumpty" collection in Chapter 5. In the meantime, in order to clarify the overall structure, we would suggest the following modification of the title: *The Common Core Standards for Literacy in English Language Arts, Social Studies (History, Geography, and Civics), Physical and Natural Sciences, and Technical Subjects (Engineering, Arts, and Crafts)*. This revision places literacy at the center, a critical and important placement. It emphasizes literacy in the service of the academic and professional disciplines, which we think captures the spirit of the ELA Standards. It expands entries for Social Studies to conform with the C3 Standards (C3, 2013), and includes candidates for Technical Subjects, which are presently orphans.

Turning back to the Table of Contents, the overall organization mirrors the key differences between the elementary and secondary grades, and in the secondary grades differences among the content areas. In the K–5 section, Reading Foundational Skills covers phonics, tied closely to the NRP Report (2000). Language is a complex domain, including sections on conventions such as grammar, punctuation, and spelling, but also vocabulary development, a more conceptual domain. Somewhat surprisingly, there are no "foundational skills" for Writing—even with the added emphasis on writing in several Anchor Standards, nor for Speaking/Listening. The English Language Arts 6–12, designed for middle and high school English teachers, covers both literary and expository materials. Some observers have concluded that these teachers must cover the literacy domain for the other content areas, but that interpretation is clearly mistaken, as is clear from the separate section for these areas. What is less clear is how teachers in science, social studies, and "technical subjects" are to respond to the standards. If content-area teachers do review the standards, going directly to the G × G sections, they are unlikely to see much relevance. For instance, *Reading 1, Grades 11–12*: "Cite specific textual evidence to support analysis of primary and secondary sources, connecting insights from specific details to understanding the text as a whole" (p. 61). This is a set of basic skills, and if a student has not acquired them before the last 2 years of high school, it is too late. And besides, a content-area teacher does not have the preparation for teaching these skills and has a lot of material to cover. There is no time for anything else. The other reading standards call for students to perform tasks that most are neither willing nor able to take on: "Provide an accurate summary that makes clear the relationships among the key ideas (R 2); Evaluate explanations for actions or events" (p. 61). Many content teachers are not likely to go as far as the Writing Standards, but if so, there they will discover even more challenging expectations: *Writing 7, Grades 11–12*, "Conduct short as well as more sustained research projects to answer a question (including a self-generated question) or solve a problem" (p. 66). The idea of project-based activities may resonate with some teachers, but what do these have to do with literacy? It is difficult to imagine most content-area secondary teachers linking to the Literacy Standards under these circumstances. Significant work is needed in the design and development of discipline-specific literacy skills required for the various disciplines (Norris & Phillips, 2003).

Another structural issue is the contrast in the ELA Standards between Literature and Informational Texts. Reading standards are laid out for both categories for the elementary grades, although the Anchor Standards are identical. For ELA in the secondary grades, both categories are also listed, but the other content areas are covered only by informational texts. For writing, the Anchor Standards for *Types of Writing* include argument, explanation, and narrative compositions. This arrangement is somewhat quirky. For example, the Anchor Standards for Reading are *not* subdivided, only the G × G objectives, while the Anchor Standards for Writing cover different categories. The Grade 6–12 Writing Standards for English Language Arts cover all three genres, but are not fully tailored to Literature (e.g., essays, reminiscences, and other genres typical of literary studies). The secondary standards for the other disciplines do cover narrative by means of a note. No explanation is given for these and other decisions, but here are some thoughts about this matter.

The ELA Standards stress the need for a better balance of literary and informational (or expository) texts, especially in the elementary grades, a point with which we strongly agree. But why apply this idea only to Reading, but to none of the other literacy domains? Expository writing is increasingly essential as students move through the grades. Another matter is that the two text types are actually representatives of a much larger collection of genres, and most texts of any length combine a variety of structural forms. The choice of genre depends on purpose. Expository texts are most frequent in the sciences, for describing, explaining, or arguing. But science also has numerous stories to tell. In literature, texts are often narratives—novels, short stories, poems, and plays. But essays and reminiscences are also part of this field—as are book reports. In social studies, there is wide variation between fields such as history and geography. Writers seldom start by saying to themselves, "I think I'll write a narrative"—except for school assignments. Rather, they begin with a topic or theme, and hopefully a sense of audience and purpose. Then they select combinations of genres needed for them to construct a passage with a given audience in mind—much like playing with Lego blocks.

Another structural issue in reading the ELA Standards is the distinction between the *anchor* and *grade-by-grade* (G × G) entries. The Anchor Standards, an unusual feature of the Standards, have received surprisingly little attention, even though they represent the ultimate goals of the

Standards. Most educators are familiar with the G × G format from earlier standards: "By the end of fifth grade, students should be able to identify features of the major character in relation to plot developments in short narratives." What is the purpose of the Anchor Standards? Why are they needed? Here is how the Introduction explains the two sets of entries:

> The Standards are an extension of a prior initiative led by CCSSO and NGA [the American Diploma Project] to develop College and Career Readiness (CCR) standards in reading, writing, speaking, listening, and language as well as in mathematics. The CCR Reading, Writing, and Speaking and Listening Standards, released in draft form in September 2009, serve, in revised form, as the backbone for the present document. Grade-specific K–12 standards in reading, writing, speaking, listening, and language translate the broad (and, for the earliest grades, seemingly distant) aims of the CCR standards into age- and attainment-appropriate terms. (p. 4)

The Anchor Standards provide critical foundations, and the G × G standards offer more specific guidance for each grade. The Anchor Standards embody the graduation expectations, and serve as the foundation for backward mapping. In creating the Standards, the writers began by spelling out the details for the high school years, and then worked backward to specify what students needed to achieve at each preceding year in order to meet the final expectations. The strands appear in the primary grades, including kindergarten, where the paths to graduation begin in developmentally appropriate expectations.

A careful reading of the G × G Standards reveals a characteristic that at first may seem quite puzzling. The Introduction states that "The K–12 grade-specific standards define end-of-year expectations and a cumulative progression designed to enable students to meet college and career readiness expectations" (p. 4). One might think that a "cumulative progression" would entail steady changes in the demands from one grade to another. But that is not what happens. In many instances the G × G entries remain unchanged for 2 or more years (Calfee, 2013)! For example, here are the G × G standards, kindergarten through second grade, for Reading Anchor 1: "Read closely to determine what the text says explicitly and to make logical inferences from it; cite specific textual evidence when writing or speaking to support conclusions drawn from the text:"

> *Kindergarten*: With prompting and support, ask and answer questions about key details in a text.
>
> *Grade 1*: Ask and answer questions about key details in a text.

Grade 2: Ask and answer such questions as *who, what, where, when, why*, and *how* to demonstrate understanding of key details in a text.

Grade 3: Ask and answer questions to demonstrate understanding of a text, referring explicitly to the text as the basis for the answers.

The Anchor Standards lay out broad domains of competency within literacy *to be achieved by the end of high school*, and the G x G entries provide sketches of learning progressions designed to lead students toward attainment of that competence. But unlike the writers of the detailed specifications found in today's scope-and-sequence plans, the Common Core writers have again followed the advice to "teach a few things well"—a laudable goal in our estimation. Learning to wrestle meaning from a text is an important achievement. The G x G standards recommend that teachers work with students on this objective from kindergarten through third grade. At grade 4, the G x G entries for Reading 1 add "inferences" to the collection, and this augmented objective stays in place for another 2 years. We cannot pretend to read the minds of the writers, but it appears that they were trying to identify a few important competencies, provide adequate time for students to develop expertise in each of these competencies across a variety of situations, leaving it to teachers to guide students through a broad array of texts and tasks to ensure that they attain a reasonable level of competence. In short, the Standards do not tell teachers what to do, but where to direct student learning.

The final structural issue that we think merits attention is the bringing together of related Anchor Standards into *ensembles* needed to perform a large task. For example, *Key Ideas and Details* comprises three Reading anchors: textual details (literal and inferential); central ideas and themes; and analysis of key features (individuals, events, and ideas). In Writing, an ensemble of extraordinary importance is *Research to Build and Present Knowledge*, which covers three Anchor Standards: conducting research projects; gathering, critiquing, and integrating information relevant to the topic under investigations; and using these activities to "support analysis, reflection, and research" (p. 18). The G x G standards in this ensemble lay out high expectations for students, making it clear that the Reading standards should be included in the projects. We suspect also, although it is not explicitly stated, that the relevant Speaking/Listening standards should also be included in the mix as part of the presentation of knowledge.

In summary, the conclusion from our structural review of the document is that the Standards are not intended as a list of isolated learning objectives to be taught in piecemeal fashion, but are a call for substantial projects that require the development of demanding competencies in contexts that provide coherence and purpose. We next turn to the substance of the Standards, where we will find the same theme.

THE SUBSTANCE OF THE ENGLISH LANGUAGE ARTS STANDARDS

The presentation of the CCSS on June 2, 2010, generated an enormous reaction throughout the nation that included (1) the adoption of the Standards by most states, (2) the establishment of two gigantic assessment consortia, (3) development of computer-based curriculum programs designed to replace current systems (Pearson/Gates, Education Week), and (4) frantic efforts by districts, schools, and teachers to prepare for enormous changes, changes of unknown character and magnitude (Gewitz, 2014a, 2014b, 2014c). The Standards clearly pose significant challenges to our educational systems, including (1) all students should be college- and career-ready (and prepared for civic responsibilities); (2) substantial increases in the complexity of instructional content; (3) high levels of student understanding; (4) the capacity of students to study and discuss important topics in the academic disciplines; and (5) the readiness of students to participate in the digital age.

What does the Introduction offer? These expectations obviously are worth serious attention. But what do the ELA Standards actually require of the nation's schools, students, and teachers? We think that the writers of the Standards answered these questions quite clearly in the six-page Introduction, but suspect that relatively few people have managed the time and effort needed to fully comprehend this passage. In an ideal world, everyone concerned with education of the nation's children should read the original document, but this requires searching the Web and then carrying out a close and critical reading. Here is our synopsis of the Introduction, which is presented to support several claims that follow. Our interpretation relies for the most part on material taken verbatim from the Introduction.

The following excerpt provides a clear and compelling statement about the goals of literacy instruction for future graduates:

> The Standards also lay out a vision of what it means to be a literate person in the twenty-first century. Indeed, the skills and understandings students are expected to demonstrate have wide applicability outside the classroom or workplace. Students who meet the Standards readily undertake the close, attentive reading that is at the heart of understanding and enjoying complex works of literature. They habitually perform the critical reading necessary to pick carefully through the staggering amount of information available today in print and digitally. They actively seek the wide, deep, and thoughtful engagement with high-quality literary and informational texts that builds knowledge, enlarges experience, and broadens worldviews. They reflexively demonstrate the cogent reasoning and use of evidence that is essential to both private deliberation and responsible citizenship in a democratic republic. In short, students who meet the Standards develop the skills in reading, writing, speaking, and

listening that are the foundation for any creative and purposeful expression in language. (p. 3)

Higher levels of literacy are clearly an important feature of the Standards agenda, but the writers also proceed to lay out ancillary facets of what it means to become fully literate:

> As students advance through the grades and master the standards in reading, writing, speaking, listening, and language, they are able to exhibit with increasing fullness and regularity these capacities of *the literate individual.* They demonstrate *independence.* . . . They build *strong content knowledge.* . . . They respond to the varying demands of *audience, task, purpose, and discipline.* . . . *They comprehend as well as critique.* . . . They *value evidence.* . . . They use *technology and digital media strategically and capably.* . . . They come to *understand other perspectives and cultures.* (p. 7; emphasis added)

Where did these ideas come from? The writers did not provide references, and so we can only conjecture about their thinking. They certainly go beyond the technical definition of literacy as the ability to read and write. Many of them will not take full form until long after a student has graduated. They cannot be easily tested with standardized methods. The writers also appear to have joined the concept of full and critical literacy with elements representing the values of American culture. These are the characteristics of a well-educated person, for whom literacy provides a foundation (Mioduser, Nachmias, & Forkosh-Baruch, 2008). A person cannot become well educated without the competencies laid out in the Literacy Standards, and these Standards are not complete in the absence of the full array of characteristics. The current focus on technical aspects of literacy to the neglect of the cultural elements is a serious shortcoming (Saracho & Spodek, 2002).

To our knowledge, no other standards document promulgated during the past two decades has laid out such a compelling portrayal of the characteristics of "the literate individual." But here, in the new Standards, the writers go even further, suggesting that these expectations are only the beginnings. There is no "top" to the Standards. The writers emphasize that (1) the document should be viewed as a work in progress, and that (2) their aim was to establish *fundamental* expectations for high school graduates, rather than chiseling in stone a collection of "world-class" standards to be exactly followed (NGA & CCSSO, 2010):

> The Standards are intended to be a living work: as new and better evidence emerges, the Standards will be revised accordingly. (p. 3)

While the Standards focus on what is most essential, they do not describe all that can or should be taught. A great deal is left to the discretion of teachers and curriculum developers. The aim of the Standards is to articulate the fundamentals, not to set out an exhaustive list or a set of restrictions that limits what can be taught beyond what is specified herein. (p. 6)

For educators who may be striving to "teach all the standards," the prospects from this analysis may be discouraging. For instance, the grade-by-grade lists are daunting when viewed as individual learning targets. These are only the beginning? They need to be continuously revised and amended with experience? As we hope to demonstrate, however, the writers never intended for the Standards to be implemented as piecemeal objectives, but as focal areas providing the contexts for developing independence, and so on. This idea has appeared before. Consider the expectations for the nation's students laid out six decades ago, when Carroll and Chall (1975), writing about President Johnson's War on Poverty, had the following to say:

[The nation] should ensure that every person arriving at adulthood will be able to read and understand the whole spectrum of printed materials that one is likely to encounter in daily life . . . , an individual cannot participate in modern society unless he can read, and by this we mean reading at a rather high level. (pp. 8–9)

Although such fundamental aspirations have similarities to the CCSS, "daily life" today is different from the 1970s in many ways. The CCSS set forth a literacy agenda for today's students embodying a bold image of inquiry-based projects coupled to the primary academic disciplines through an integrated literacy program, elements that might be found in some students literacy programs half a century ago, but now are essential for *all* students. From the Introduction (NGO & CCSSO, 2010):

An integrated model of literacy. Although the Standards are divided into Reading, Writing, Speaking and Listening, and Language strands for practical purposes, the processes of communication are closely connected, as reflected throughout this document. (p. 4)

Research and media skills blended into the Standards as a whole. To be ready for college, workforce training, and life in a technological society, students need the ability to gather, comprehend, evaluate, synthesize, and report on information and ideas, to conduct original research in order to answer questions or solve problems, and to analyze and create a high volume and extensive range of print and nonprint texts in media forms old and new. (p. 4)

The ELA Standards emphasize the tasks of conducting authentic research projects, using the digital media that are increasingly abundant throughout today's world. As a middle school teacher from Doolin, Kentucky, observed, "If you teach the way that we've taught for years and years, basically we're robbing our kids of the future" (Rich, 2013). The ELA Standards also provide *linkage to the academic disciplines*:

> Similarly, the Standards define literacy expectations in history/social studies, science, and technical subjects [and in ELA/Literature], but literacy standards in other areas, such as mathematics and health education, modeled on those in this document, are strongly encouraged to facilitate a comprehensive, school-wide literacy program. (p. 6)

> Part of the motivation behind the interdisciplinary approach to literacy promulgated by the Standards is extensive research establishing the need for college and career ready students to be proficient in reading complex informational text independently in a variety of content areas. (p. 4)

These features of the ELA Standards stand in sharp contrast to the behavioral objectives and scripted lessons that have populated teacher manuals during the NCLB era. In the NCLB model, which was at the core of Reading First, teachers were directed to keep pace and stay on the same page throughout the school year. Students who fell behind were retained and recycled. Under the ELA Standards, students are also to keep pace, but in a completely different way. The Standards recognize that students can differ greatly in where they begin and how quickly they learn, but expect every student to move through the same demanding set of activities and materials, with teachers providing adaptive instruction and scaffolding as necessary to assist students in staying with their cohorts (NGA & CCSSO, 2010; also see Amendum & Fitzgerald, 2013, on the detrimental effects of scripted lessons):

> Students advancing through the grades are expected to meet each year's grade specific standards, retain or further develop skills and understandings mastered in preceding grades, and work steadily toward meeting the more general expectations described by the Standards. (p. 5)

> The Standards should also be read as allowing for the widest possible range of students to participate fully from the outset and as permitting appropriate accommodations to ensure maximum participation of students with special education needs. (p. 6)

The proposal for teachers to adapt and scaffold instruction has substantial implications for intertwining a Standards-based curriculum and instruction with ongoing formative assessment. Equally important is the advice in the Introduction to the ELA Standards to amalgamate collections of Standards around particular tasks and, we would add, around substantial projects:

> While the Standards delineate specific expectations in reading, writing, speaking, listening, and language, each standard need not be a separate focus for instruction and assessment. Often, *several standards can be addressed by a single rich task*. For example, when editing writing, students address Writing standard 5 ("Develop and strengthen writing as needed by planning, revising, editing, rewriting, or trying a new approach") as well as Language standards 1–3 (which deal with conventions of standard English and knowledge of language). (NGA & CCSSO, 2010, p. 5; emphasis added)

Taken as a whole, but especially in the descriptions of scaffolding and the intertwining of curriculum, instruction, and assessment, the ELA Standards have implications for teachers' professional responsibilities quite unlike anything to be found in the NCLB model. The call is for teachers to teach to the Standards, through ongoing, lesson-by-lesson engagement and adaptation to ensure student learning of demanding skills and knowledge. In the elementary grades, the Standards explicitly connect literacy competence to the attainment by all students of the concepts and content of academic disciplines, a task for which the Standards writers propose that teachers should have primary responsibility:

> By emphasizing required achievements, the Standards leave room for teachers, curriculum developers, and states to determine how those goals should be reached and what additional topics should be addressed. (NGA & CCSSO, 2010, p. 4)

Taking on these responsibilities will require in turn that teachers develop deeper (but not broader) understandings of the content areas, including (1) the essential literacy skills within each academic discipline, (2) pedagogical content knowledge for literacy integration in each discipline, (3) learning progressions for each discipline, and (4) developmental expectations for students (Calfee & Wilson, 2013; Neuman, 2013). Knowledge of these curriculum components is not enough; teachers also need to know how to work *with* and *from* a steady stream of formative evidence about the learning progress of each of their students, in order to make strategic short-, medium-, and long-term instructional decisions along the way (Calfee, Wilson, Kapinus, & Flannery, 2014). The broad-spectrum views of learning represented in the Standards call for teachers to zoom-in and zoom-out, capturing both snapshots and motion pictures of student learning, using careful observations and probing questions to explore students' responses to increasingly complex and challenging texts and tasks, and to decide how best to adapt instruction and document student achievement. Assessment is even more challenging, but doable, when one considers the total package of characteristics of "the literate person" presented earlier. The latter are impossible to incorporate on a standardized test, once the target constructs have been elaborated.

In concluding this section on the substance of the ELA Standards, we want to emphasize once more the power of viewing literacy as a continuum that stretches from early attention to basic skills to the emergence of the fully literate person. Equally powerful is the idea of becoming literate while studying topics important for understanding the disciplines and for appreciating cultural expectations. These features of the ELA Standards allow us to think about literacy in a revolutionary way—as providing the looms for creating tapestries *that tie together the ideas and experiences of human beings over the ages.* Literacy from this vantage point is far more than a basic skill, far more than the "printed word." This new literacy uses language for thinking, for problem solving, and for communicating (Calfee & Patrick, 1996). This way of thinking about literacy is also consistent with Norris and Phillips's (2003) assertion that *"literacy* in its fundamental sense is fundamental to *scientific literacy"* (p. 224; emphasis added) and their argument that science can be constructed, reconstructed, transformed, and applied only through the tools of critical literacy, defined as the capacity to use language in various forms to think, analyze problems, and communicate. As Norris and Phillips have stated, "reading and writing are constitutive parts of science . . . essential parts of a whole" (p. 226). But similar claims can be made about a broad array of human endeavors. Much of history, for instance, depends on the written records. Likewise, engineering is recorded in structures and tools constructed centuries or millennia ago, but appreciation of these structures and tools is only complete when documents are available laying out the designers' thinking.

Literacy for the disciplines has differing implications for the elementary and secondary grades. For the elementary grades, where students spend the entire day with the same teacher, one can imagine how literacy might be seamlessly extended to science and social studies. Today's basal readers often include brief passages on science and history. But the ELA Standards make it clear that the writers have something much more extensive in mind than an occasional "science piece" during the reading period. By second grade, Reading Standard 10, *Range of Reading,* calls for students to read broadly across the disciplines. An even more compelling and explicit statement of intentions appears on page 33 in the section *Staying on Topic Within a Grade and Across Grades: How to Build Knowledge*

Systematically in English Language Arts K–5. The page begins, "Building knowledge systematically in English language arts is like giving children various pieces of a puzzle in each grade that, over time, will form one big picture. At a curricular or instructional level, texts—within and across grade levels—need to be selected around topics or themes that systematically develop the knowledge base of students" (p. 33). The quotation refers to English language arts, but the accompanying list of K–5 trade books on the human body is about biology. The goal is not only to learn about the human body—although that is a good idea—but to learn to read and write about science in general.

As noted earlier, the ELA Standards also cover the middle and high school years, but several barriers must be overcome. Teachers in the secondary grades are more typically disciplinary specialists—they typically teach literature, physics, history, biology, and so on. They usually do not teach reading, and most—except for ELA teachers—certainly do not teach writing. So how can the Standards be applied in these circumstances? Current plans call for increases in text difficulty, and for instruction in close reading. Neither of these ideas seems likely to do much to improve disciplinary literacy. A more promising alternative emerges from the call in the Writing Standards for *Research to Build and Present Knowledge.* Project-based activities are a natural setting for application and a broad range of discipline-based literacy skills. The challenge here is that programs supporting project-based activities tend to focus on the problem and/or the discipline, and give less attention to the literacy elements required for the project. There are numerous books on "reading in the content areas," but these assume that reading is taught as a skill set, separate and apart from deep engagement in the discipline. Learning to read a science textbook is not the same as learning to apply literacy skills in a physics project on inertia. Reliance on project-based activities has the potential to transform content-area courses from "mile-wide, inch-thick" coverage to deep engagement in fewer topics that are more coherent and meaningful experiences than the present jumbles of topics.

BOTTOM LINES

Unpacking the ELA Standards has been a very big job. In our effort at comprehension—wrapping our arms around the document—we have attempted to be comprehensive, close, and critical. The Standards call for substantial changes from current practice, in curriculum, in instruction, in assessment, in the role of teachers, and in the organization of schooling. Based on the preceding analysis here are five *big shifts* that we have identified as being clearly called for in the Standards:

- Integration of language and literacy, and linkage with disciplines.
- Engagement in "big tasks" covering multiple standards.
- Inquiry/project-based learning activities.
- Authentic student productions and performances.
- Formative assessment by teachers and students.

To prepare students to truly be college- and career-ready, the emphases must shift to the nature of ideas. For the digital-global world there is no need to memorize—to "cover"—huge amounts of information in a shallow manner—"mile wide and inch deep." Rather, the task for 21st-century students is to learn how to find and use the vast resources that are now available to, in the words of the ELA Standards, "build and present knowledge." Tomorrow's graduates need to prepare to be makers, inventors, and entrepreneurs (Zhao, 2012). Our analysis of the ELA Standards document, encapsulated in these five big shifts, demonstrates that the *CCSS for English Language Arts and Literacy in History/Social Studies, Science, and Technical Subjects* will position students well to assume these creative roles in the future.

CHAPTER 4

Implementing the Standards, Part I

Current Directions and Misdirections

Our story has taken us from NCLB in 2002 to the appearance of the Common Core ELA Standards in 2010. At the writing of this chapter it is now 2015. How are things going? The answer is, not very well (Gewertz, 2014a). Chapter 2 briefly foreshadowed the current discontents, and the mismatch between the vision and the realities of implementation. In this chapter we take a closer look at what has transpired since June 2010 as a preface to recommendations for getting the train back on track, topics covered in Chapters 5 and 6. The 2013–2014 school year was a critical time for the transition from NCLB to CCSS. As of this writing, NCLB remains the law of the land, implementation of the Standards still has a long way to go (Council of the Greater City Schools, 2013; Editorial Projects in Education [EPE], 2014; Gewertz, 2014a), and the clock has ticked down to the spring 2015 administration of year-end standardized tests constructed by the two test consortia—tests that "count." It is a time of considerable turmoil.

TALES OF WOES

To put a timestamp on this chapter's story, we begin with excerpts from a four-part series in *Education Week* that tells tales from the Washington, D.C., schools during the spring and summer of 2013. The writer of this series, Catherine Gewertz, is an accomplished reporter. Her story is believable, and consistent with other reports and our own observations. Gewertz's reports are engaging and compelling; they give readers a sense of "being there," partly because of Gewertz's obvious concerns for the people and events being described. These are stories worth reading.

Common Core, Spring–Summer 2013: A Steep Climb

Part I of the Gewertz series (2013a) places us in the classroom of Dowan McNair-Lee, a middle school English teacher at Stuart–Hobson School in Washington, D.C. It is April 2013. We enter her classroom quietly: "The big clock in McNair-Lee's eighth-grade classroom is silent, but she can hear the minutes ticking away nonetheless . . . , a constant reminder of how little time she has to prepare her students for spring tests, and for high school and all that lies beyond it" (p. 1). Later, in Part III, we come to understand the full import of this first encounter. April has turned to June, and the testing is over. Her students have moved on, and she is alone in her classroom, about to leave for a new assignment. "She wonders how her students will fare in the months and years ahead. She worked hard, did her best. And some students soared in her classes . . . , others struggled. How well Dowan served her students in these two years of full-tilt common-standards implementation is a story still being written . . . , a question that hovers over every building in the district, and over the central office, which is orchestrating these big shifts" (Gewertz, 2013c, p. 7).

From Gewertz's account of what happened between April and June, we learn a lot about how the Standards are being implemented, and about the problems arising from the current interpretation of the Standards. We also learn a lot about Dowan:

- She is totally dedicated to teaching and to her students.
- She has accumulated considerable expertise after only 11 years in the profession.
- She is wrestling with the right questions, about teaching in general and the Standards in particular.
- She has learned how to "see learning" and evaluate transfer, and eager to take on formative assessment (Elawar & Corno, 2008).
- She has "bought in" to certain aspects of the current system that limit her vision; we wonder what might happen if she sees a world with different possibilities. . . .

Another thread in Gewertz's story had already begun in December 2012, with heads spinning around how to prepare students for the end-of-year *District of Columbia Comprehensive Assessment System* (DC CAS) and the interim tests *Paced Interim Assessments* (PIAs). These assessments are district-developed tests of individual Common Core Anchor Standards, mostly covering the first ELA Reading Anchor Standard (Reading 1), and mostly using multiple-choice items, with a few brief essays. Teachers decided to focus on a few key topics from the *shifts* (Engage NY, n.d.): *close reading, text-based evidence,* and *informational texts.* The list of shifts from Engage NY represented changes of emphases from the more traditional topics of instruction prior to the adoption of the CCSS. As the weeks go by, teachers add other items from the Common Core Anchor Standards to the list: *author's tone, mood, connotation, denotation, allusions, simile,* and *metaphor.* These are being taught in the usual way as specific objectives using worksheet materials. It is slow going for her students, and Dowan is worried.

The District of Columbia School System is large, urban, and very much in the public view. Most students are minority and poor. As noted in Gewertz's (2013a) *Education Week* article, when the CCSS appeared in June 2010, the District leadership bought into them big time—Mike Casserley, head of the Council of Great City Schools, described the response as "full tilt, whole hog." Adoption and implementation of the Standards has been top-down and high priority. Stuart–Hobson is one of the highest-achieving of the District's middle schools, "blessed with extra staff for academic intervention and social-service support." It is small, with 415 students in sixth through eighth grade, and is a "Capitol Hill Cluster" school with art and museum programs. Over the past few years, million-dollar programs have allowed facilities upgrades and technology support. Many of the graduates enter the city's top public and private high schools.

Several characters thread their way through the article's episodes. Mikel, a young man struggling with circumstances outside of school, shows promise in one-on-one situations, but is failing because he does not complete his assignments. There is leadership: Brian Pick, director of teaching and learning for the District, and Assistant Principal Katie Franklin, who is quoted as saying, "My teachers are trying so hard, but some are just not there yet." Gewertz takes a snapshot of Dowan during a particularly disruptive class: "You all'd better get with this! Do you have any idea what's ahead for you next year?" What is Dowan talking about? What is the menace? What are the problems? Why is everyone so upset? It is the test.

Close Reading and the Adolescent Mind

Part II of Gewertz's series in the June 5, 2013, issue of *Education Week* fleshes out the instructional challenges attributed to the Standards. In a nutshell, despite earnest efforts to follow the scripts, students often just don't get it. And when they do, they don't keep it. Consider *close reading*, a specially prized activity related to Reading 1 (cf. Brown & Kappes, 2012; see *Achieving the Core*, 2014, Publishers Criteria for grades 3–12, for details). The technique begins with a relatively short text that is new to the students. The teacher reads it aloud, the students read it to themselves, and then the class "dives into" the text. The idea is to stay close to the text, to analyze in detail words, sentences, and paragraphs, to dig out the explicit, literal meaning. Teachers have been told that it is especially important that students *not* be introduced to the topic; there must be no preparation other than the assigned task, to *read closely*. In an episode at the beginning of Part II, the close-reading assignment is to extract the "main idea" of the passage, in this case an article about Cesar Chavez's grape boycott and hunger strike. The class is performing poorly on main-idea test items, hence the review. Dawon does her best to scaffold the students' efforts: "Study the title, captions, subheadings, first and last paragraphs . . . , anything that is repeated." No response. "What is it about the personal experience of injustice that makes some people decide to help others, while other people help only themselves? Injustice causes some people to act. That's an inference, right?" Silence. "What's an inference?" Silence. Dawon's frustration is understandable for anyone who has been in this situation. " 'Remember,' [she] tells the students, 'you can combine the text with your own knowledge to make inferences that lead to the main idea.' " She models it for them, pointing to the last paragraph, which reports on Mr. Chavez's funeral ". . . 50,000 people attended.—So I'm gonna make an inference here. . . . I think he made a difference. I know this way of doing things [close reading] takes a lot more effort . . . but you really need to know this' " (Gewertz, 2013b, p. 18). Dawon is doing her best—even breaking the rules about sticking only to the text.

Actually, the close-reading technique comes not from the ELA Standards but from Student Achievement Partners, one of the organizations that played a major role in developing implementation strategies for the Standards (*http://achievethecore.org/about-us*). One tenet of the technique is that the reader needs to stay close to the text, to rely on text-based evidence rather than relying on any personal experiences. Sometimes this strategy makes sense—for example, when setting up a new computer. Even then, personal experience can be quite helpful. For the Chavez article, though, the question that Dowan asked at the end of the activity seems like a great opening for the lesson for her students—"Now we are going to read a passage about Cesar Chavez and his experiences with discrimination and injustice. What comes into your mind when you hear those two words: discrimination and injustice? How do you think a person should deal with them?" Responses to these questions—and we suspect that there would be more than a few, if it had been asked at the beginning of the lesson—would have set the stage for reading the passage in a way that is entirely consonant with the Standards. But as it happened, these questions were not in the script.

Dawon continues the lesson with close reading of a passage on migrant strawberry pickers—from the students, *nada*, nothing, no learning, no transfer. She had planned to ask students to write a brief essay for homework, but there is no time—"The essay will have to wait." Gewertz describes Dawon's reaction: "Many of my kids haven't mastered the basics of getting a project done. . . . It's frustrating for me because *this* [a project] *is how I see what they know.* It worries me when I think about them in high school" (2013b, pp. 3–4). As an experienced teacher Dawon can "see what they know. . . . " This is a remarkable comment!

Close reading runs through the entire *Education Week* series. Part III (2013c), for example, presents an account of "a leadership academy run by Brian Pick [the district administrator] on close reading, 'a skill prized by the Standards.' He leads the administrators through a detailed explication, parsing words to plumb the meaning of a challenging 53-word sentence" (p. 4). Our advice: if as a reader you ever encounter a 53-word sentence, your first reaction should be to ask who is responsible for such wretched writing. Another example of instruction for close reading that in our thinking misses the mark from Part III and is even more heart-rending is a close reading of Wilfred Owen's *Dulce et decorum est* on the human cost of World War I! If you are familiar with Owen's poetry, the idea of picking it to pieces must cut to the quick.

Let us return to Part II (2013b), and to Gewertz's description of another professional development (PD) session on close reading. The PD director "reminds the teachers that the Standards are 'bracketed' by Standard R.1 [literal and inferred meaning], and Standard 10 [reading independently and proficiently]. 'That's the bear. How do we get them from R.1 to R.10. . . . how to take off the training wheels gradually'" (p. 4). This exchange no doubt makes more sense now that you have read Chapter 3 on what the ELA Standards actually say. For present purposes, Reading 1 (R.1) is the Anchor Standard for literal reading comprehension (close reading), while Reading 10 (R.10) calls for students to read across a wide range of literary and informational passages. The director's comment is interesting in several ways. First is the notion that R.1 is the starting point from which students will eventually become avid readers. Close reading as presently defined is both difficult and boring, and so it is understandable that teachers are concerned about student progress toward the long-term goal. The Standards actually are quite clear that the Anchor Standards are not intended as a "sequence," but are to be implemented in parallel. The idea is *not* that students must master a series of basic skills, after which they finally begin to read widely. Instead, the Standards call for wide reading to be encouraged and supported from the outset. Second, the PD director is clearly aware of the endpoints for reading, but does not seize the opportunity to bring Reading 2–9 into the discussion. The intervening G x G standards provide the means for getting from Reading 1 to Reading 10. Meanwhile, the "bracketing" is actually intended to *encompass* the full range of standards, including speaking/listening and writing—*and everything in between*. By middle school, *writing and research projects should be filling the day*. Dawon appreciates this possibility—but "there is no time."

The Summative Testing Frenzy

In Part III (2013c), Gewertz describes the year-end summative testing experience. Dawon returns to her classroom after spring vacation to find chairs arranged in rows rather than clusters. It is April, and the test is coming. For the next several weeks every day will be spent on "skills." *Connotation* and *denotation* are on the test, and despite several efforts, her kids still don't get it. "Dawon hates the emphasis on tests, but she sees them as one indicator of how well *she's* prepared her students for high school" (2013c, p. 2; emphasis added). Dawon has bought into the idea that the standardized tests are valid indictors of *her* teaching, and that *she* is responsible for student performance. After receiving the PIA interim test results ("a sea of red"), "Dawon has what she calls a 'meltdown.' 'I had to leave. . . . I just walked up and down the halls. I needed time. I felt rattled. I was feeling that I hadn't done *anything* this year'" (p. 3). She is not alone; the entire school is in a state of turmoil. "With less than two weeks before the test, [the test coordinator] is head-down reorganizing the school schedule, compressing classes and three lunch periods into the afternoon, after morning testing. When the materials are delivered, she'll supervise the unloading, and their placement under lock and key in her classroom. . . . A bright blue sticker over the door jamb alerts her to any unauthorized entry. Even bigger is her task of orchestrating dozens of teachers' duties during testing. . . . What if a student needs to blow his nose? Bring a box of tissues. What if someone falls asleep? Tap them on the shoulder."

The days of testing finally come and go. The test booklets are bundled and boxed up. Score results will not be available until the end of summer. The final staff meeting of the school year actually seems rather upbeat to Dawon and many others, with "discussions of writing, of other ways to assess performance, and of greater flexibility in dealing with individual differences."

To emphasize a point made earlier, the CCSS are *not* about testing, but current plans for implementing the Standards are nonetheless driven by test concerns. The federally funded consortium tests began to count in spring 2015. The CAS and PIA are district-made tests that are designed to prepare students for the real tests starting in spring 2015. They bear little resemblance to the learning experiences laid out in the Standards. They are mysterious artifacts hidden from public view, which will define success and failure, "proficient" or "below the standard," for students, for teachers, for schools, for districts. The entire package, including tests and accountability, is now equated with "the Standards." This is the view in the DC schools, but it is also how Secretary of Education Duncan sees it from his office on Maryland Avenue. On January 18, 2013, in response to increasing concerns from the field about the testing burden, Duncan issued a statement: "After listening to teachers and education leaders, we are providing additional flexibility to states. This decision ensures that the rollout of new, higher, state-selected *standards* will continue on pace [for spring 2015], but that states that need some flexibility will have it when they begin using student growth data for high-stakes decisions" (Homeroom, 2013). Note that "the rollout of . . . standards" actually refers to the consortium tests. The reference to "student growth data for high-stakes decisions" reflects Duncan's assumption that the spring 2015 administration of the tests will continue the present policy of test-based accountability. States did not choose this policy, and while they participated in the design and development of the tests, it is misleading to say that they "selected" these tests.

It is important to note that the summative tests, currently the focus of consortium activities for both PARCC and SBAC, will cover only a subset of the Standards (PARCC, 2015; SBAC, n. d.). Both consortia proposed an integrated system in which summative and interim tests would be balanced with formative tests, the latter designed to support learning, the former to serve accountability purposes. As it has turned out, the summative tests have been assigned the high priority, with limited attention to either interim or formative assessments. The original idea, however, was to also build assessments that would allow teachers to continuously monitor learning and to adjust instruction to meet student needs. This is not possible with the summative tests; they come at the end of the school year, when it is too late to do anything with the information. Even more problematic is the limited coverage of the Standards by the summative tests. The restrictions imposed on the summative tests are clear and understandable: "Time and testing technologies impose limits on what can be tested, and hence a deep analysis has been conducted to maximize the most critical aspects of the Standards. The development process has considered priorities for what to evaluate and how at each grade" (SBAC, 2013, p. 13). Only selected grades will be tested (3–8 and 11), and any standard that requires large amounts of time or other resources—e.g., Research to Build and Present Knowledge—will not be covered fully. The original plan included several "performance tasks," which would have required students to write lengthy essays in response to a significant problem. The time requirements were too great, and only one performance task will be included in the reduced version of SBAC, 2012. For the PARCC assessment, there are two tasks that require considering multiple texts and writing extended responses to a task. One of these involves literary analysis of two or three texts and an extended written response; the other requires gathering information for a research simulation and writing an extended response. A third task involves writing a narrative. The SBAC performance task is administered during the end-of-year summative assessment that increases the need to limit students' time on this task. The PARCC research simulation, literary analysis, and narrative writing tasks are administered 75% of the way through the school year and thus not as constrained by time. Because of the way this system is structured, teachers are almost compelled to "teach to the test," violating a basic principle of most educational measurement, that tests are meant to *sample* student learning. These changes in policies and practices have significant impact on the curriculum. The summative tests are constructed around isolated objectives, despite initial plans to integrate assessment clusters. The DC summative tests were modeled on released items from PARCC, and it shows.

Part IV of the Gewertz series (2013d) recounts how teachers and administrators spent their summer. Six weeks after graduation exercises, results of the district tests were announced by Mayor Gray and Chancellor Henderson. The proficiency rate had risen from 59 to 64%, cause for jubilation. Later as they return to school, just before the start of the 2013–2014 school year, teachers from the 111 district schools began digging into individual scores. As reported by Gewertz, "Emotional ups and downs permeate the mid-August dive into the data. . . . They're analyzing performance . . . by grade level, subject, student subgroup, right down to the academic standards. . . . Tiny detail by tiny detail, they completed the grid that would help guide the work of the coming year." Now as the schools enter the third year of the Common Core Standards, it seems that the year-end standardized tests are increasingly the focus of Standards-related activity. Remember that the tests only assessed a subset of the Standards, and not the Standards as a whole. Discussions are not about project-based activities but about close reading; the curriculum has been narrowed to easily testable objectives. These practices are actually out of line with the Standards and go against the advice of experts in the field of educational measurement. Test preparation activities, well intended though they may be, provide little more guidance for "the work of the coming year" than the August fireflies blinking on DC lawns.

Two other episodes in Gewertz's compelling narrative should capture our attention. One is a memo announcing that the district has identified writing as a priority for the coming year. On first glance this appears to be a welcome change in direction. But then we learn what writing is intended to mean: "front and center in a late August professional-development day, secondary teachers hunker down with instructional coaches to work on sentence composition. . . . [Session leader] Hawley guides her 6th grade teachers in an exercise about 'subordinating conjunctions.'" A second episode tells us that "Ms. McNair-Lee [will be] directing a new school-wide enrichment program that allows students to study through the lens of something that they're interested in." The juxtaposition of these two items is jarring. Most students will be working on close reading and subordinating conjunctions, while a few students will be allowed to work on "something that they're interested in." This is not a picture of equal opportunity to learn, nor is it consonant with the vision of the CCSS. This is not what was supposed to happen.

PLEADING FOR INSTRUCTIONS AND GUIDANCE

The CCSS were launched in June 2010. Year-end summative tests for the Standards are being conducted for the first time in spring 2015. We are writing these words at the beginning of 2015—approaching the end of the assessment development period. As noted in Chapter 2, the initial reactions to the Standards on release were little short of euphoria. As we entered the second half of the course, however, concerns are increasing, despite concerted efforts to keep spirits high (e.g., Achieve, 2014; NGA, 2014). The testing programs are sources of particular uneasiness (Gewertz, 2014a, 2014c). Let us take a closer look at what has happened during the past few years.

Simple Solutions: Alignments, Criteria, and Shifts

By the end of the 2010–2011 school year, many states and districts were wondering what they were supposed to be doing about the Standards. Unlike NCLB, which was garbed in regulations and mandates, the new standards left it to educators to figure out how to handle implementation. Nobody seemed to be in charge. There were no mandates, no guidelines. Publishers were also uncertain about how to proceed. The CCSS were proclaimed as "fewer, clearer, and higher" (Rothman, 2013). What did this mean for development of classroom materials? Curriculum developers fell back on *alignment*, a quick, off-the-shelf procedure that had been used with previous standards. Alignment was a bookkeeping strategy that began with the lists of G x G standards as the basic working pieces. These detailed objectives were short, fairly simple, and familiar. The longer, more complicated Standards at the end of each domain were put into "hold for later" folders. Publishers and state curriculum developers proceeded to review their existing materials looking for matches between lesson objectives and grade-by-grade Standards entries. Many matches were straightforward; every reading series covered basic comprehension objectives at every grade. Likewise for vocabulary objectives. Phonics programs, which had been labeled Foundational Skills in the ELA Standards, were easily aligned. By the beginning of the 2011–2012 school year, some publishers were claiming that 90% of their instructional materials were aligned with the Common Core (Sawchuk, 2012)! It appeared that implementation of the Standards was going to be easier than expected. To be sure, some teachers expressed concerns that, aligned or not, the revised reading materials did not conform to the Standards (e.g., Strauss, 2012).

Alignment met some basic needs, but several other questions remained unanswered. How were states and districts to communicate the Standards to practitioners? What about professional development programs? Preservice preparation? Guidelines for administrators? Someone needed to take charge, and someone did. The first year of the Standards saw the emergence of several consultant teams who appeared with guidelines, programs, and instructional materials to fill the vacuum. The most influential among these groups were Achieve, Student Achievement Partners (SAP), and spinoffs like the Edmodo store and Common Core.

Achieve launched the *Publishers' Criteria, K–2* (Coleman & Pimentel, 2011a, 2012) and *3–12* (Coleman & Pimentel, 2011b) only a few months after the Standards appeared. These criteria (hereafter referred to as "The Criteria") provided specific directions for the design and construction of instructional materials and programs that would fulfill the mandates of the Standards. The advice was quite definitive. For example, "In aligned materials, work in reading and writing (as well as speaking and listening) must center on the text" (p. 1). "The Common Core Standards place a high priority on the close, sustained reading of complex text" (p. 4). However, the Standards had been worded to avoid issuing such mandates, including a cautionary statement that "the standards are a living work, to be revised as new and better evidence emerges" (p. 3). The coauthors, David Coleman and Sue Pimentel, who had served as coauthors for the Standards, were also coauthors of the Criteria, and so spoke with a voice of authority. The Criteria were criticized by some, mostly academics but also teachers and literacy policy workers (e.g., Pearson, 2013), and slightly revised versions of the Criteria were released in spring 2012. Since then they have become the primary resources by virtually every group involved with implementation of the Standards (Samuels, 2012).

Because they have had such widespread impact, let us take a closer look at these documents. The *3–12 Criteria*, which cover the "testing grades," lay out several topics for special attention: *text complexity*, *close reading* of short texts, *text-based questions and evidence*, a *balance*

between literary and informational texts, text-based writing, and practice
with *short focused research projects.* The spotlight throughout is on *text.*
"The Criteria . . . concentrate on the most significant elements of the Standards. . . . In aligned materials, work in reading and writing (as well as
speaking and listening) must center on the text" (p. 1). A frequently voiced
rationale for the emphasis on text was that teachers were paying too much
attention to students' interests and opinions, following the lead opened
by the *Preparation for Reading* sections found in all basal readers, which
directed teachers to find out what students already know about a story or
topic before reading it. Whatever the pros and cons of the matter, when one
considers the practical implications of this mandate, it requires only slight
changes in existing practices. Publishers and curriculum developers simply
need to eliminate the "Preparation for Reading" segment in basal readers.
The combination of close reading and text-based questions do require fairly
significant changes in the questioning strategies typical of basals. The questions in current basals range quite widely, including many where "answers
may vary." *Close reading,* which is identified with Reading Anchor Standard 1—"Read closely to determine what the text says explicitly and to
make logical inferences from it; cite specific textual evidence when writing
or speaking to support conclusions drawn from the text" (p. 10)—is said to
spring from Adler and Van Doren's *How to Read a Book* (1972). The close-
reading procedure actually bears little resemblance to either Reading 1 or
to *How to Read a Book,* but apparently was initiated by a video of David
Coleman conducting a close reading of Martin Luther King, Jr.'s *Letter from
a Birmingham Jail* (*www.engageny.org/resource/middle-school-ela-curricu-
lum-video-close-reading-of-a-text-mlk-letter-from-birmingham-jail; www.
ascd.org/publications/educational-leadership/dec12/vol70/num04/Closing-
in-on-Close-Reading.aspx*). The technique as prescribed by the Criteria is
quite explicit: "The Standards place a high priority on the close reading of
complex text, beginning with Reading Standard 1. Such reading focuses
on what lies within the four corners of the text. It often requires compact,
short, self-contained texts that students can read and reread deliberately
and slowly to probe and ponder the meanings of individual words, the order
in which sentences unfold, and the development of ideas over the course of
the text" (Publishers Criteria, 2012, p. 4). The Criteria frequently mention
requirements of the Standards, but seldom are these claims connected to
specific standards; only Reading 1 (literal comprehension,) and Reading
10 (broad reading) are specifically cited. To us, the requirements seem to
have been imposed by the authors. *Text-based or text-dependent questions*
were introduced in the Criteria as a complement to close reading. The idea
was to ensure that questions posed by the teacher during the reading lesson
should be answerable by explicit reference to evidence from in the text, not
from personal opinions or experiences. The text-based close-reading model

is the centerpiece of projects developed by Edmodo (Basal Alignment Program [BAP]) and CommonCore.com, and is featured in numerous instructional materials and professional development packages.

Three matters at the heart of the *3–12 Criteria* seem problematic to us: (1) the claim that all facets of literacy must "center on the text," (2) the positioning of the close-reading procedure as a critical first step in acquiring literacy, and (3) the notion that the choice of texts for virtually any purpose should be based in part or whole on text complexity, which for practical purposes is equivalent to readability. The Standards do mention texts and text complexity, but they also say that "students need the ability to gather, comprehend, evaluate, synthesize, and report on *information and ideas . . . , and to analyze a high volume and extensive range of print and nonprint texts in media forms old and new*" (p. 6; emphasis added). They state that literate students "set and adjust purpose for reading, writing, speaking, listening, and language *as warranted by the task*" [p. 7; emphasis added]. Students should learn to read closely, but also carefully, broadly, and strategically. On rare occasions, purpose may require reading and rereading a text, but more often the reader's purpose can be better met by quick reading, by skimming a broad array of sources, often digital, attending to graphics, to snapshots, and to moving pictures. Well done graphics may be more comprehensible than "words," but readability is not defined. Purpose and interest should surely be considerations in advising students what they should read, and what they are to do as the result of reading. The recurring theme throughout the Standards is that students should be allowed and encouraged to read broadly, as a way of increasing their knowledge. They also need to write broadly, to learn to express themselves and to discover and practice effective communication in situations that go beyond texting. They need to learn to hold their own in academic conversations (Zwiers & Crawford, 2011). And they need to immerse themselves in such activities not because they are assigned, but because they meet intrinsic needs and interests. Publishers and curriculum developers should rely on the Standards as their primary source.

Here we will look only briefly at *Publishers' Criteria Grades K–2* (Coleman & Pimentel, 2011a, 2011b); this document appeared shortly after the Grades 3–12 document, with a revision in 2012. The *K–2 Criteria* opens with an extended section on Foundational Skills, the phonics strand of the Standards. The remainder of the document is a condensed version of the *3–12* version. The *K–2 Criteria* emphasize at the outset that these recommendations "concentrate on the most significant elements of the . . . Standards" (p. 1). The first third of the document covers Foundational Skills, or phonics, implying an importance for this topic in the primary grades that seems at odds with what the Standards say: "These foundational skills are not an end in and of themselves; rather, they are necessary and important components of an effective, comprehensive reading program designed to develop proficient readers" (p. 15).

A complement to the *Publishers' Criteria*, the *instructional shifts*, has perhaps been even more influential than the *Criteria* themselves for implementation planning. In November 2011, in response to repeated calls for guidance in setting priorities, Achieve released a set of *three shifts*: (1) practice regular reading with increasingly complex texts; (2) ground comprehension in text-based evidence, rather than prior knowledge or experience; and (3) build knowledge through content-rich nonfiction (Achieve, 2011; Achieve the Core, n.d.). These three shifts were presented as high-priority items for implementation of the Standards. A second set of six shifts was released by the New York State Department of Education/*EngageNY* in 2012, and appears to be equally important. The *six shifts* provide somewhat broader coverage of the Standards, and the elaborations that accompany the list provide important details for interpreting each shift (see Table 4.1). Annotations for the *three shifts* are also available on the Achieve website.

On first glance, the shifts appear simple enough; they recommend that students do a lot of reading and writing. But the annotations convey a rather different message. Like the *Criteria*, the annotated shifts emphasize text materials, they focus on reading, and they give limited attention

---

TABLE 4.1. Instructional Shifts in ELA/Literacy According to EngageNY

- Shift 1: Balancing Informational and Literary Text
  Students read a true balance of informational and literary text.

- Shift 2: Knowledge in the Disciplines
  Students build knowledge about the world (domains/content areas) through TEXT rather than through the teacher or activities.

- Shift 3: Staircase of Complexity
  Students read the central, grade-appropriate text around which instruction is centered. Teachers are patient, create more time and space and support in the curriculum for close reading.

- Shift 4: Text-Based Answers
  Students engage in rich and rigorous evidence-based conversations about text.

- Shift 5: Writing from Sources
  Writing emphasizes use of evidence from sources to inform or make an argument.

- Shift 6: Academic Vocabulary
  Students constantly build the transferable vocabulary they need to access grade-level complex texts. This can be done effectively by spiraling like content in increasingly complex texts.

to writing and to speaking/listening. They do not mention the more difficult clusters, such as research. The shifts were quickly welcomed by many educators because they set priorities, identifying some standards as more important than others. They could also be easily linked to existing practices and could be easily assessed. For instance, *Balancing Informational and Literary Text* is a simple task for publishers. *Knowledge in the Disciplines*—coverage of the content areas has been limited in recent years and the emphasis is on informational *text*, so the mention of discipline is likely to be overlooked. *Staircase of Complexity* is complex, and you should read the document for yourself—its main point is that current textbooks are too easy. Close reading, which is covered in Shift 4, has received the most attention. *Writing from Sources* remains a rare event, as does *Vocabulary*. For elementary teachers, the message seems to be that they can proceed with business as usual for the most part, as long as they pay more attention to texts (Shanahan, 2013). In the secondary grades, ELA teachers should continue to be concerned about teaching reading and writing in the other content areas, while content area teachers should continue to cover their content.

What Should Students Read?

A continuing theme in both the *Publishers' Criteria* and the *Shifts* is the emphasis on complex text materials. For example, here is the extended explanation of Shift 1, *Practice regular reading with increasingly complex texts*, from the *three-shift* set:

> Rather than focusing solely on the skills of reading and writing, the Standards highlight the growing complexity of the texts students must read to prepare for college and careers. The Standards build a staircase of text complexity so that all students are ready for the demands of college- and career-level reading by the end of high school. (Achieve the Core, n.d., p. 1)

The emphasis on complex textual material seems reasonable on first glance. The Standards do indeed refer to *text complexity* in several places:

- page 3: "Students readily undertake the close, attentive reading that is at the heart of understanding and enjoying *complex* works of literature."
- page 4: "Students need to be proficient in reading *complex* informational texts . . . independently in a variety of content areas."
- page 8: "Key features of the Standards: The Reading standards place

equal emphasis on the *sophistication* of what students read and the skill with which they read."

- page 10: "Anchor Standard 10—Read and comprehend *complex* literary and informational texts independently and proficiently."

From these excerpts, the Standards are not focusing on text complexity, but on independent and proficient reading of increasingly more demanding material, for enjoyment and understanding, and for sophistication. *Skills*—proficiency—are part of the mix. But so are the content areas—the disciplines. If the curriculum leads students through the disciplines, then text complexity will accompany increases in "idea" complexity. The *shift* paragraph does not mention the disciplines.

Reading Shift 2 continues the text theme with a call for "reading, writing, and speaking [to be] grounded in evidence from the text, both literary and informational." The exposition of this point is quite lengthy, but the point is that "the text" is the primary source of knowledge for schooling under the Standards. Shift 2 does mention Writing and Speaking, which are also to be text-based. In contrast, the Standards repeatedly note the importance of worlds that go beyond "the text," the worlds of the digital age, and graphic and imaginal experiences that range across time and space. The section on *Research and media skills blended into the Standards as a whole* (p. 4) is a powerful call for literacy instruction that goes far beyond the "four corners of the text."

Reading Shift 3, *Building knowledge through content-rich nonfiction*, also sends a message about reading materials, but the message is unfortunately muddled. One muddle is the reference to *Content-rich nonfiction*. This term is not found in the Standards, but probably refers to the distinction between literary and informational texts, a contrast that conflates several textual features: fact versus fiction; stories/narratives versus reports/expositions; literary versus informational writing; simple versus complex text structures; and, perhaps most importantly, the discipline of Literature versus Science, Social Studies, and technical disciplines like Engineering and the Arts. The problem is the attempt to sort all textual materials into two buckets, overlooking the fact that (1) several dimensions and categories are needed to define text genre, (2) these genres should conform to the purpose and style needed in a given writing situation, and (3) the "new rhetoric" provides a toolkit of textual building blocks for students who discover that they have something to say (Rose, 1981).

Our starting point for unraveling this snarl is literary versus informational texts. In the ELA Standards, this means not only the difference between stories and reports, but also between fiction and fact, and perhaps between more or less interesting materials. Stories can be factual, fictional, or variations in between, and likewise for reports (Story Craft). The literature teacher focuses on narratives—novels, short stories, folk tales—but may also introduce students to essays, memoirs, opinion pieces, and so on. The science teacher emphasizes laboratory reports and descriptions of scientific phenomena, which are mostly expository texts, dealing with factual matters. But science also has stories to tell—biographies, of course, but also stories of discovery. For example, Stephen Hawking's *A Brief History of Time* (1998) could be characterized as a scientific narrative.

The ELA Standards propose a balance of literary and informational materials in the elementary grades; "the Standards follow NAEP's lead in balancing the reading of literature with the reading of informational texts, including texts in history/social studies, science, and technical subjects" (p. 5). Balance is defined here by reference to the disciplines. The Criteria (Coleman & Pimentel, 2012) tighten the requirements:

> The Standards call for elementary curriculum materials to be recalibrated to reflect a mix of 50 percent literary and 50 percent informational text, including reading in ELA, science, social studies, and the arts. Achieving the appropriate balance between literary and informational text in the next generation of materials requires a significant shift in early literacy materials and instructional time so that scientific and historical text are given the same time and weight as literary text. (p. 5)

Where the Standards call for balance, the Criteria mandate a 50/50 mix, with equal time and weight given to scientific and literary texts. How is this prescription to be enforced? What should be counted? Texts? Paragraphs? Sentences? Words? Time and weight? How to deal with complex texts, which often mix literary and information genres? A passage on sensory organs begins with a quick story (a toddler's discovery of her ear canal), followed by a descriptive exposition on the various sensory systems, and then sequential paragraphs on how the primary sense organs operate. To comprehend (or compose) texts of this sort—by no means unusual in their complexity—requires thinking about text complexity as akin to working with Lego blocks. To clarify the term *text complexity*, the CCSS define it as "the inherent difficulty of reading and comprehending a text combined with consideration of reader and task variables" (NGACBP & CCSSO, 2010, Appendix A, Glossary of Key Terms, p. 43).

The 50/50 recommendation detracts from the more fundamental issue of providing students with a balanced diet of reading materials driven by content and coverage of the disciplines, which we think is a main message from the Standards. Since the arrival of *Sally, Dick, and Jane* (Gray, Baruch, & Montgomery, 1940a) and *We Look and See* (Gray, Baruch, &

Montgomery, 1940b), basal readers have relied on stories as the vehicle for reading instruction. In the primary grades, the stories are simple and short, and unfortunately often repetitive and dull. In the upper elementary grades, publishers use excerpts from longer works, which can be quite exceptional, including winners of the Newbury Award. But they are nonetheless literary works, and the other disciplines are missing. It is this imbalance that has led many to plead for more expository and informational material.

The Gorilla in the Classroom: From Texts to Tests

The CCSS do not mention tests, but in surveys of practitioners, in reviews of concerns, and in efforts to prepare for the Standards, the year-end summative tests developed by two consortia, the Smarter Balanced Assessment Consortium (SBAC, or just Smarter Balanced) and the Partnership for Assessment of Readiness for College and Careers (PARCC), consistently emerged as the greatest sources of concern (EPE, 2014). Educators, parents, and citizens have limited knowledge about the tests, but they knew that they were coming, that they would use different formats than today's multiple-choice instruments, that they were likely to be difficult, and that they would be taken on computers. Beginning in spring 2015, the administered tests now count in many schools for accountability purposes. And anxiety is on the rise.

In the Obama administration, both President Obama and Secretary of Education Arne Duncan kept tabs on the Hunt committee as it worked on the Standards. When the Standards were finally released, proposals appeared almost immediately for establishment of two state-based assessment consortia. In 2010 the U.S. Department of Education awarded SBAC $150 million in a partnership with the California Test Bureau (CTB), and PARCC received $186 million for a collaboration with the Educational Testing Service (ETS) (Rothman, 2013). The K–12 Center at ETS was established shortly afterward to handle documentation and publicity. ETS K–12 is an autonomous group affiliated with ETS that handles primary-grade testing programs.

The ETS K–12 website provides excellent accounts of the history of the assessment consortia, including the *Coming Together* (K–12 Center at ETS, 2011) snapshots. To provide a sense of trends in test development for the Standards, we have chosen selections from the startup in February 2011 and the status at the end of 2013. The SBAC profiles are used here for illustration; PARCC is slightly different. Figures 4.1 and 4.2 show the Tables of Contents from the 2011 and 2013 ETS K–12 reports. The 2013 report is longer and more complicated. Since then, four additional consortia have been added along the way, two for English language learners and two for learners with special needs.

FIGURE 4.1. Table of contents from the 2011 ETS K–12 report. From Educational Testing Service (2011). Copyright 2011 by the Educational Testing Service. Reprinted by permission.

The substance of the reports has also changed over time. The 2011 *Coming Together* report addressed the question of what the "assessments were supposed to measure," which assumed numerical outcomes; if an outcome is not (easily) measured, then it is not included. The section on Literacy in 2011 discussed several key features of the Standards: "the new CCSS will shift literacy instruction toward empowering students . . . , directly engaging them in ways that are critical to their future success . . . , as *rhetors*, people who can speak and write effectively to communicate with others" (Frangos, 2011, p. 6). These words command attention, but the challenge is to bring them to life. The final section, *Finding Solutions, Moving Forward*, addressed two other issues of substantial importance—the task of connecting various parts of the system, including the summative and formative components, and the roles of technology for conducting the assessments and reporting the findings as illustrated in the Table of Contents.

The 2013 *Coming Together* (K12 Center at ETS, 2013) report opens with some cheerleading. In answer to the question, "Will Common Core and new assessments lead to improved student achievement?," the answer is a resounding "Yes!" "The standards are better, the tests will be better, and 'going digital' will open new doors" (p. 3). The final section of the report deals directly with a question on the minds of many school administrators: "Will schools be 'technology-ready' to administer next-generation assessments?" The conclusion, actually quite honest, is that the answer "hangs in the balance."

What do the systems look like? Figure 4.3 shows the SBAC operational systems from the 2011 and 2013 ETS K–12 reports. The differences between 2011 and 2013 may seem relatively modest, but changed priorities

Table of Contents

Welcome to Our 4th Edition of Coming Together

Will the Common Core and New Assessments Lead to Improved Student Achievement?

COMPREHENSIVE ASSESSMENT CONSORTIA

Comprehensive Assessment Consortia: System Designs, Work to Date and Future Plans

PARCC—Partnership for the Assessment of Readiness for College and Careers

Smarter Balanced—Smarter Balanced Assessment Consortium

Key Similarities and Differences of PARCC and Smarter Balanced (Table 1)

ALTERNATE ASSESSMENT CONSORTIA

Alternate Assessment Consortia: System Designs, Work to Date and Future Plans

DLM—Dynamic Learning Maps

NCSC—National Center and State Collaborative

Side-by-Side Comparisons of Assessment Systems (Table 2)

ENGLISH LANGUAGE PROFICIENCY ASSESSMENT CONSORTIA

English Language Proficiency Assessment Consortia: System Designs, Work to Date and Future Plans

ASSETS—Assessment Services Supporting English Learners through Technology Systems

ELPA21—English Language Proficiency Assessment for the 21st Century

GETTING TO THE CLASSROOM

Will Schools be "Technology-Ready" to Administer Next Generation Assessments?

As We Ask Our Educators to Step Up, Will We?

ADDITIONAL RESOURCES

More Resources from the K–12 Center

Consortia Timelines at a Glance

State Memberships in Assessment Consortia (Table 3)

FIGURE 4.2. Table of contents from the 2013 ETS K–12 report. From Educational Testing Service (2013). Copyright 2013 by the Educational Testing Service. Reprinted by permission.

can be seen if you know what to look for. Let us take you on a tour, starting with 2011 in the top panel. The topmost bar shows the yearly schedule. The blue box on the right shows that the last 12 weeks of the school year have been designated for year-end summative testing. The middle band, the *Digital Clearinghouse*, lists a collection of "goodies" that will be available to schools and teachers to assist in various aspects of implementation, including formative and interim assessments.

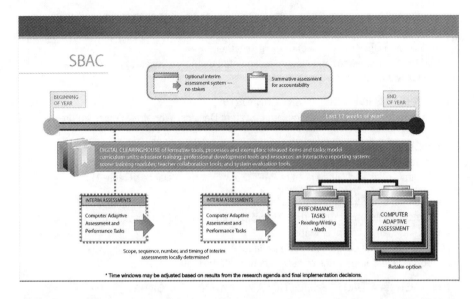

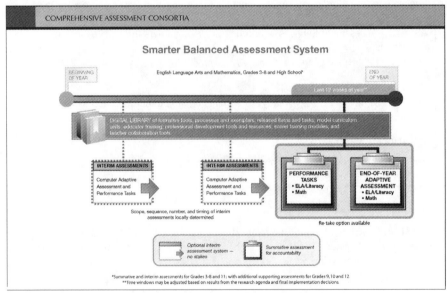

FIGURE 4.3. SBAC operational systems from 2011 (top) and 2013 (bottom). From Educational Testing Service (2011, 2013). Copyright 2011 and 2013 by the Educational Testing Service. Reprinted by permission.

The bottom row shows two segments, interim and year-end assessments. The year-end assessments include both Performance Tasks and Adaptive Assessments. These are both standardized tests, which means that they are performed under controlled conditions, and that students work individually in response to specific instructions, with limited time and resources. SBAC designed these tests around specifications for a restricted subset of Standards (SBAC, 2013, ELA Content Specs). For example, the year-end tests clearly could not cover Standard 10—"Broad reading and writing." Nor could students be tested on the Writing cluster, *Research to build and present knowledge*, which calls for students to generate research questions on their own, gather and evaluate information, and prepare a presentation. Adaptive Assessments were to use a selective-response mode, a variation on the multiple-choice method. Performance Tasks required students to write essays based on short passages. The (optional) Interim tests were to provide information to administrators and teachers about how well students were prepared for the year-end tests.

The middle box, the *Digital Clearinghouse/Library*, was to be the centerpiece of the "balance" promised in the Smarter Balanced and PARCC proposals. The Digital Library would provide a variety of resources, featuring formative assessment strategies to complement year-end summative tests. One-time, year-end, high-stakes standardized tests would be provided as measures of status, while classroom-based formative assessment offered ongoing information for feedback and guidance in instructional decisions. Formative assessment has undergone substantial developments in recent years, and, as will be discussed in Chapter 5, is an essential part of the integrated curriculum called for by the Standards. The original proposal called for establishing the Digital Library as a "repository" for materials and programs to be contributed by states, districts, schools and teachers, to be reviewed according to criteria established by practitioner collectives, and then made available to all comers. Practical and political realities such as the need to allocate resources to development of the summative tests that are to serve for accountability have altered these priorities. An advisory committee was convened by SBAC in spring 2013 to establish criteria for reviewing contributions to the Digital Library, and during the 2013–2014 school year, partner states took steps to solicit materials and programs. If all went according to plan, schools and teachers would have had access to these resources for the 2014–2015 school year, but these resources do not yet exist, so they would not have had the chance to impact on the spring 2015 year-end assessments. In the meantime, many districts have developed prototypes for the year-end summative tests that were given during spring 2015. As we entered 2014, the Smarter Balanced Digital Library still had yet to be populated. On the other hand, PARCC has a space on its website dedicated to educator information and resources and has held several Twitter sessions for teachers. To attempt to address the need for lessons and formative materials PARRC also has links to other sites that produce classroom resources and is planning to develop more in the future. These initial efforts by Smarter Balanced and PARCC to provide usable materials for teachers are slowly moving in the right direction.

TAKING STOCK: TIME FOR MIDCOURSE CORRECTIONS

The current uneasiness with the Standards has arisen for many reasons, including libertarian objectives to any programs that smack of federalism, an unhappiness with standardized tests generally, and simple inertia. Whatever the reasons, it seems important to take another, closer look at the Standards, and how they are being implemented. We have offered our interpretation of what has or is currently being done, which differs significantly from current implementation plans. It seems clear that classroom practices are not experiencing the radical transformations called for in the Standards. Most eyes are on the tests. Most curriculum packages make the claim to be Standards-based, but are instead incorporating the isolated objectives mandated under NCLB. Instruction continues to be teacher-directed, following basal scripts that have been in place for decades, with pacing charts to ensure that all classrooms march to the same beat. The close reading prohibition against connecting with prior knowledge and interests before and during the reading of a passage is being attempted by many teachers and publishers, but seems likely to fall of its own weight. Text-based questions have been created by a large corps of teachers who have volunteered their time to ensure that basal readers conform to the Criteria. By June 2015, administration of the end-of-year tests moved toward center stage. By the time you have read this, it is almost guaranteed that scores have dropped because of the novelty of the test content, procedures, and testing platform, and that the nation's schools, teachers, and students have been subjected to increased criticism and ridicule.

We have three suggestions about how to address this state of affairs. The first is to resolve the issue of what the Standards really say. Table 4.2 lays out the "little shifts" and the "big shifts" for comparison. As you can see, the basic set of problems is that they are not comparable. The little shifts are about texts, and the big shifts are about learning. The little shifts are mostly about reading, and the big shifts are about literacy in the service of problem-solving and communication. The little shifts address a limited set of the Standards, while the big shifts build upon a more comprehensive perspective on the document, including attention to the introductory material. Finally, the little shifts seem a much closer match than the big ones to

TABLE 4.2. Comparison of Little Shifts and Big Shifts

Little shifts	Big shifts
• Balance informational and literary text	• Integration of language and literacy, and linkage with disciplines
• Knowledge in the disciplines through texts	• Engagement in "big tasks" covering multiple standards
• Staircase of text complexity	• Inquiry/project-based learning activities
• Text-based answers	• Authentic student productions and performances
• Writing from text-based sources	• Formative assessment by teachers and students
• Academic vocabulary from increasingly complex texts	

what are covered on the summative tests. The little shifts have certainly captured the headlines, but only a few have begun to raise concerns—not about the tests—but about the substance of the Standards.

The differences between these two perspectives on the Standards seem so great that it is difficult to imagine a reconciliation. However, we can imagine various ways in which our interpretation might be called into question. The first objection might be that we have simply misread and misunderstood the documents. We are willing to submit to a comparison of our "close readings" to the "close readings" of others, as long as there is agreement that the task is to comprehend the whole of the documents. Another position might be that the Standards do indeed call for significant and substantial changes, but for practical reasons the schools must start with small steps, and then, over time, move toward the larger challenges. The problem here is that small steps tend to remain small, and generations might pass before any significant change begins to take place. A third position is that, on closer examination, the Standards are actually not workable because they demand too much of students and teachers. Perhaps, over time, a new generation of teachers must be prepared for the challenges of the Standards, but not anytime soon. We are more optimistic about the potential of the teachers and students who now occupy classrooms and school houses, and can see many "points of light" through the NCLB gloom.

Here is our sentiment. If, based on a more careful reading of the Standards, significant numbers of individuals and groups could reach similar conclusions as ours about what the Standards say and what the schools should do, then major efforts could be taken to implement a program quite different from that now moving forward. In our view, efforts are needed to implement a program that is quite different from what is now moving forward, one that builds upon an extended effort at professional *re*development. The need is not for better "aligned" materials, but for more knowledgeable teachers, not for close reading but for deep learning, not for waiting to see what will be on the year-end test, but for finding out what students know and need to learn. These are issues that we will explore in the next chapter.

CHAPTER 5

Implementing the Standards, Part II
A Curriculum Framework for Success

> Standards can be raised only by changes that are put into direct
> effect by teachers and pupils in classrooms. There is a body of firm
> evidence that formative assessment is an essential component of
> classroom work and that its development can raise standards of
> achievement. We know of no other way of raising standards for such
> a strong prima facie case to be made. Our plea is that national and
> state policy makers will grasp this opportunity and take the lead in
> this direction.
>
> —BLACK AND WILIAM, 1998b, p. 148

One of us (KMW) was reviewing the coming week's readings in preparation for her graduate course on teaching and learning. The topic for the
week was the role of assessment in teaching and learning, so she included
Black and Wiliam's (1998b) much-cited article summarizing their earlier meta-analysis (1998b), which was conducted on a range of formative
assessment research studies. It struck her, when reading the final paragraph
in their article quoted above, that here we are 17 years later and a few years
into the implementation of the CCSS writing a similar argument for the
need to integrate assessment *for* learning (e.g., Black, Harrison, Lee, Marshall, & Wiliam, 2003; Heritage, 2010; Stiggins, 2002) into the tapestry of
instruction and learning. Why has the formative process (Popham, 2008)
not become a commonplace occurrence in today's classrooms?

A survey of the literature suggests that most teachers "may have limited knowledge of formative assessment strategies and may think about assessment as being primarily for the purpose of grading" (Shepard et al., 2005). In the golden age of NCLB, school districts often required teachers to administer periodic benchmarking assessments like the Dynamic Indicators for Basic Early Literacy Skills (DIBELS; Good & Kaminski, 1996) that were created by sources outside the classroom, as opposed to classroom teachers. There are pros and cons to this approach. For instance, assessment systems like DIBELS allow teachers to compare the rate and level at which their students are learning basic skills compared to other students taking these assessments. What prepackaged assessment systems are not designed to do is to gain a sense of the higher-level thinking (metalinguistic knowledge) students used when applying those skills. These assessments gauged only easily measurable basic foundational reading skills and not the complex thinking required to comprehend well. It is the access to these deeper processes acquired through skillful formative process questions that aids teachers in uncovering the root of problems in students' thinking. Teachers may also become dependent on prepackaged assessment systems without exploring more flexible formative assessment strategies like focused observations, quality questioning, and short-term projects that are more directly tied to the enacted curriculum in their classrooms.

Another consideration that may be overshadowing widespread and enthusiastic adoption of formative assessment is that summative assessments of Common Core instruction are currently being piloted by PARCC and Smarter Balanced. Although both consortia originally planned digital libraries of lesson plans and formative assessment materials, those plans appear to have fallen by the wayside. Instead, teachers' attention is focused on the content and format of the summative assessments. They are concerned with how the assessment results will impact their schools, the instructional requirements they will have to meet based on the results, and their own professional evaluations as teachers. Because summative assessments are assessments *of* learning, they will have little or no practical influence in what teachers are currently teaching or on students' adjusting their approach to studying—no assessment *for* learning.

An ongoing assessment and instruction cycle grounded in teacher inquiry can profoundly influence student academic learning. But several factors may make or break the success of this cycle. The depth of teacher content knowledge; general knowledge of and self-efficacy for providing effective pedagogy and more specific pedagogical content knowledge; skill at forming questions to tap into student knowledge and application of learning; working knowledge of formative assessment strategies and how to evaluate the evidence gathered in an informative fashion; teachers' entrenchment in their current assessment and instruction choices; and finally their understanding of the CCSS can each be a factor inhibiting teachers from embracing the formative process. Teachers enter the work-force with varying degrees of exposure to formative assessment in their coursework. Preservice teachers may observe their cooperating teachers integrating formative assessment on a continuum from expertly across the school day to minimally (if at all!) and, in turn, enter their own classrooms with varying degrees of mentored practice in making the formative process a standard operating procedure in their professional practice. Although ongoing professional development is essential to establish and nurture the formative process habits of mind in new and current teachers, that com-ponent is not enough. We call for a concurrent change in the education climate itself.

Teachers and schools as a whole need to be in the forefront of changing the tone and the message of the Common Core narrative that has developed in the last few years within and outside of the school walls. In place of the present political tone and the misinformation put forth by some media outlets, the narrative should instead focus on the local successes in stu-dent achievement that are now emerging, reflecting the effectiveness of the changing instruction and formative assessment teachers are designing to meet these more demanding standards. Indeed, the Introduction section of the ELA Standards document is explicit about the professionalism of teach-ers in making instructional and assessment choices that are bringing about these successes when stating, "Teachers are thus free to provide students with whatever tools and knowledge their professional judgment and experi-ence identify as most helpful for meeting the goals set out in the Standards" (NGA & CCSSO, 2010, p. 4). It is when teachers share with their com-munities evidence of significant numbers of their students showing more engagement in learning and validated increased performance at complex learning tasks that teachers will be viewed as trusted educated profession-als guided by the theme of high-quality implementation of the Standards.

Thus, it is valid for our readers to ask: *What steps are being taken at the state and local levels to support teachers in affecting the transition to effective Standards implementation?* and *How are these changes being enacted in K–8 classrooms to engage students in learning at different lev-els?* This chapter attempts to respond to these two questions by advocating for embedding a formative assessment cycle within project-based instruc-tion for all students.

SUPPORTING THE TRANSITION

To allow the wholesale changes needed for a full formative assessment cycle implementation in K–12 classrooms to come to fruition in a project-based environment on a large scale, both new and current inservice teachers will benefit from sustained support in developing clear conceptions of how to facilitate engaging and worthwhile projects that address the Standards in complex ways. Teachers must understand deeply the formative/summative assessment continuum and how the utilization of evidence gathered from these assessments can support learning. Teachers must be given adequate time and support to plan, implement, assess, discuss, and reflect upon their students' learning. They require time to fine-tune their practice to fit it to the individual students in their classes. We believe that by supporting teachers in becoming proficient with the formative process, students will exit high school college-, career-, and citizen-ready. Several options for ongoing professional development should be available to teachers, including coaching, communities of practice, professional reading and self-study, and websites developed by state departments of education.

Coaching

Support can come through working directly with an *instructional coach*. One advantage of employing a coaching model is that literacy coaches are expected to be well versed in Standards integration within and across the academic disciplines by staying current with best practice literacy research. Literacy coaches have the know-how and availability to provide sustained professional development at district- and schoolwide gatherings or smaller groupings of interested teachers. Through these events literacy coaches become known to teachers as an easily accessed resource for teachers as they try out or fine-tune newly learned aspects of the formative process. Coaches have the advantage of understanding the local context, individual teachers' strengths and needs, and the potential for grade-level, content-area, and cross-grade collaborations that offer the needed synergy for furthering schools' efforts in embracing the formative process. Coaches offer "fresh eyes" on one's practice through observations; the feedback, modeling, and suggestions from a coach before, during, and after observations can be invaluable to teachers who want to become more effective. Finally, coaches are instrumental in supporting teachers in (1) formulating questions about student learning, (2) making decisions about tasks that best contribute to answering those questions, (3) analyzing the products for evidence of learning (or not), (4) recognizing learning trends and needs, and (5) acting upon them through the next formative cycle.

Communities of Practice

Another option for growing professionally is available to teachers to address effective adoption of the Common Core. Groups of professionals interested in collaboratively exploring their teaching and student learning in depth across the academic year can create *Common Core professional communities of practice.* Communities of practice can be formed within a school or, for teachers in rural communities, online across similar contexts. Teacher groupings may be organized around grade levels or academic disciplines. Professional communities of practice can decide to make the formative assessment strategies embedded in project-based learning a focus of their work. One avenue for common talk, action, and reflection is through reading books by expert researchers. For instance, researchers (e.g., Heritage, 2013; Popham, 2008; Wiliam, 2011) in the field of formative assessment have written books for practitioners that provide a stimulus for small-group discussion, sharing, and implementation. Another set of excellent resources for individual teachers and professional communities of practice to explore, discuss, and enact are ideas on websites like the Buck Institute's Project Based Learning site (*http://bie.org*), TextProject's resources (*www.textproject.org*), and the Teaching Channel's Common Core and Common Core for ELLs series and the Deeper Learning series (*www.teachingchannel.org*). These online resources offer teachers books, articles, formative assessment rubrics, and blogs to learn about formative assessment and project-based learning. An advantage of credible websites such as those listed above is the videos that show formative assessment and instruction in action in real classrooms and webinars with experts offering learning communities more in-depth information that support local conversations and implementation.

Professional communities of practice can take advantage of other modes of professional development available in their schools. Teachers can arrange to meet with and observe colleagues who are known to be skilled in using formative assessment and/or facilitating project-based learning to become aware of the intersections with their own teaching practices. Looking outside the school, long-term alliances with higher education faculty benefits both the teachers and the education researchers in multiple ways. For example, teachers can learn about the latest formative assessment research findings, while both groups partner in studying aspects of the enactment of the formative process that warrant a closer look.

Professional Reading and Self-Study

When professional communities of practice are not available, reflective reading on Common Core-based instruction, augmented with self-study through audiotaping or videotaping of one's attempts at implementation, can support instructional change. Recently published books, such as the fifth edition of *Best Practices in Literacy Instruction* (Gambrell & Morrow, 2014), report recent research and offer practical suggestions for implementing findings to meet the CCSS. Professional reading provides a starting point for teachers who lack professional communities of practice. Coupling professional reading with the critical analysis of one's own instructional practice helps teachers identify points in their teaching where they can begin to use formative assessment within a project-based learning framework.

State Departments of Education Options

Although the available resources for teacher professional development on Common Core-based instruction and formative assessment vary widely from state to state, a final professional development option for teachers is accessing individual states' departments of education and large school district websites dedicated to supporting the implementation of Common Core-based instruction. Most states' resources are accessible for in-state or out-of-state teachers and the public in general to download. For example, state departments of education's Common Core websites in Florida, Colorado, Hawaii, and Connecticut among others yield a range of videos, materials, lesson plans, and formative assessment tasks, although formative assessment suggestions are not as abundant as other resources offered. We found in an informal search of 16 state websites that some states have organized materials under the title Common Core, where others are located through a set of links under the state's personalized Standards title. Perseverance, selectivity, and a critical review can pay off.

In some ways, these state and district websites form a less convenient digital library like the one envisioned in the initial plans for Common Core implementation (e.g., *www.k12center.org*) by the PARCC and Smarter Balanced consortia. The intention of the digital library was to create an online repository for teachers and schools of a full range of curriculum frameworks, and instructional, assessment, and professional development materials. At the point of writing this book, the idea of a common digital library has not come to fruition.

A Final Word on Transitioning

We believe in the promise of the Common Core to guide high-quality instructional choices aimed at the goal of college, career, and citizen readiness. For this goal to be realized, all teachers need focused and sustained professional development to make the large-scale changes practical and less intimidating. We suggest a combination of coaching, the implementation of communities of practice, and individual teacher inquiry to facilitate an effective and efficient transition to the more complex teaching needed for the deeper learning called for in the CCSS. Examples of schools transitioning to project-based learning for *all* their students, not just high-performing students, already exist. The key is to start with the organizational structures inherent in schools that naturally complement the ways school function already. By this we mean facilitating schoolwide involvement in elementary schools and working interdisciplinary teams in middle and high schools.

NOW, BACK TO THE FUTURE

The chapter now shifts ahead in years for a glimpse into the classrooms described briefly in Chapter 1. The teachers you met at the beginning of the book have been enthusiastically implementing project-based learning to meet the Common Core goals for a few years. Their enthusiasm for teaching with this approach to addressing the Common Core is based on the consistently high levels of complex learning they observe in their students in comparison to the degree of learning teachers found during the years when the NCLB/RF (2001) implementation placed more of an emphasis on literacy skills acquisitions. Now, students are more motivated than in previous years to come to school to work on interesting projects on topics worth knowing. Working collaboratively and with individual explorations of topics of interest contribute strongly to students' motivation (Guthrie et al., 2007; Wigfield et al., 2004). Engagement is high; students increase their literacy competence while working on relevant tasks during which they make choices about the reading and writing connected to their projects. Students enjoy their work; their needs are being met for competence, autonomy, and connectedness (Deci & Ryan, 1985; Ryan & Deci, 2000), and the classrooms are humming.

Through participating in the variety of professional development structures described above, in addition to their own experiential learning in their classrooms over the last few years, teachers developed practical knowledge of how project-based instruction can easily integrate with formative assessment to achieve the goals of the Common Core Standards. Furthermore, new teachers do not start from scratch with this approach once they in are their own classroom. Instructional methods for facilitating a project-based learning approach are woven into literacy courses as well as methodology courses in the other disciplines in teacher education program courses. Education faculty arrange for preservice teachers to have practicum experiences in classrooms with cooperating teachers highly skilled in facilitating project-based learning and the formative process into instruction.

Teachers are more expert "kid watchers" (Goodman, 1978) than ever before, embracing an inquiry model to determine the depth of their students' learning. They know which learning tasks produce usable evidence of new knowledge being applied and what to look for in the evidence, based in part on their focus on a mix of planned and moment-to-moment formative assessment. Assessment during observation is more efficient due to the added focus on specific aspects of student learning and offers more complete information than in the early 21st century. Teachers are in a better position than previously to fine-tune their teaching because of ongoing analysis of evidence; they have developed into skillful facilitators of student learning.

DRIVING FORCES FOR CHANGE

Four factors emerged between the beginning years of Common Core implementation and our classroom snapshots that made sense to teachers and proved significant in propelling the change to widespread implementation of the formative process. The first factor was the choice by school districts and teachers to place an emphasis on the Common Core's Anchor Standards as the key organizing goals guiding the design of formative assessments. Formative assessment embodied the standards (Shepard et al., 2005) because teachers mapped backward from the Standards to inform their assessment decisions (Wiggins & McTighe, 2005). The Anchor Standards allowed for a logical, recursive ebb and flow of information between teachers and students that guided a flexible organization of curriculum, instruction, and formative assessment to respond to the needs of the students. Teachers shared with each student the assessment evidence relative to the Anchor Standard(s). Students knew the purpose of each lesson as being a step to achieving one or more of the Standards. They also knew they would be expected to demonstrate their new learning. When students understood how the current unit of study fit within the learning goals and that their learning would also be advantageous knowledge for the future, they bought into the endeavor. Thus, teachers and students worked as learning teams. Early in the Standards implementation, teachers and students noted that this teamwork approach of coordinated effort proved quite productive. Both teachers and students assumed ownership of student learning.

This sense of teamwork was not built overnight. Prior to widespread use of the formative process, students were rarely considered in this manner. School was generally a mandatory experience in which they had little choice, and where learning goals were clear for their teachers but tended to be murky for them. At the end of a 2014 summer program for secondary students who had experienced difficulties with academic literacy for years, one of us (KMW) had a conversation with a group of the students. One 11th grader shared her view of school prior to the summer program:

"Yeah, school is where teachers make you read books that bore you out of your mind . . . you are not interested in." These students experienced the formative process within a project-based approach for the first time during the summer program. As a group, they began as very tentative, disengaged learners and progressed over the 5 weeks of the program to full engagement. Their interests were honored, and they were reading and writing with a real purpose and a real audience in mind—all project-based learning characteristics. And, they had the ongoing formative evidence to prove to themselves and others that they were indeed learning. When asked to describe learning with this approach at the end of the summer session, they used the terms: "creative," "hands-on," "fun," and "we learned things!" Even though they were not reading leveled informational materials, the words "hard" or "boring" did not enter their conversation. Unfortunately, this framework, enacted in the summer program and that we are proposing in this book, had not yet been adopted widely. That was for the future!

The second factor supporting the successful implementation of the Common Core Standards in K–12 classrooms was a widespread shift to using formative assessments across the curriculum, a shift from measuring isolated skills in contrived and unauthentic test items. The teachers in our 2024 snapshots interweave a range of formative assessments in their instructional plans, keeping each student's progression in mind. Plus, teachers are able to observe students apply their knowledge and skills in more authentic contexts—a big change from decontextualized test items. The evidence of student progress gathered across complex project activities enables teachers to effectively pinpoint where the direction of instruction should go next. Teaching has become more targeted and efficient. For instance, before the shift to formative assessments, students would be asked to select the meanings of words in vocabulary test items unrelated to the reading and writing in the text they were assigned. After the shift teachers examined assessment evidence for the presence and correct usage of new disciplinary words in students' written and oral language related to the projects they were pursuing. Within a targeted formative process, teachers can more accurately gauge if students use the new words and the concepts they represent appropriately and with precision or if students only had an initial gist of a word's meaning that needs to be fine-tuned. High-quality evidence also yields more useful, targeted, and timely feedback from the teacher, so misconceptions can be addressed early in the learning process. The change away from decontextualized assessment practices to formative assessment prioritizes assessment *for* learning—assessment that informs teachers and students of their progress so they can adjust their learning tactics, as opposed to emphasis on assessment *of* learning—the summative norms of the years leading up to the implementation of the Common Core (Heincke, 2013).

By embracing an assessment *for* learning perspective, the third factor responsible for significant growth in student learning came into play. Teachers now employ an inquiry stance to frame and interpret their understanding of students' learning. Keeping close tabs on individual student learning is treated by teachers as iterative action research. By this we mean that teachers combine their knowledge of the Common Core Standards, observational evidence from students' oral and written performances, and their understanding of expected learning progressions in the disciplines to formulate questions about the depth and breadth of their students' learning. Because teachers in 2024 are asking specific questions about each student's learning, evaluating student products and oral discourse is not overwhelming. They have also found that they can create tasks within a project that address progress toward more than one standard. This change allows for efficient teaching and assessment and gives a richer view of student learning than in earlier years. For instance, the Anchor Standard *Research to Build and Present Knowledge* requires a more complex mix of literacy tasks that will, in turn, demonstrate one or more of the indicators of other Anchor Standards. In this case, students need to be well versed in reading, writing, and speaking to meet this goal, offering a range of formative assessment opportunities that can be triangulated to guide instruction. Additionally, to meet this multilayered goal, students must also possess New Literacies skills for locating information, determining credibility, and using online aids to comprehend the text and visuals available to them on the Web. To demonstrate their presentation ability, students must acquire a working knowledge of computer programs like Prezi, PowerPoint, and Glogster to share their research findings within and outside of their classrooms. Project-based learning is a learning environment well suited for complex learning and a range of formative assessment opportunities.

KATE HAMPTON'S KINDERGARTEN

To illustrate, Kate Hampton, the kindergarten teacher introduced in Chapter 1, wants to be sure that her student Charlie is on track in his development of language and writing to meet expectations for the end of kindergarten. It is now the beginning of February. Kate has observed Charlie growing in his early writing skills relevant to the Anchor Standards for Writing, but is concerned about his progress in applying his growing phonics knowledge—knowledge delineated in the Foundational Skills needed for reading and writing. Charlie participates orally in whole-class instruction, using the WordWork program's large alphabet cards to show how sounds and letters are related and how this relationship works in words. He is also very engaged in the class projects that include some early applications of individual written work. Kate used the formative spelling assessment for kindergarten from *Words Their Way* (Bear, Templeton, Invernizzi, & Johnston, 2011) and determined that Charlie is in an emergent reading stage (Bear et al., 2011). Based on the assessment findings, Charlie is engaged in learning individual letter–sound relationships. Many students in his class are starting to include correct letters representing the initial word sound, some are even including the correct final letter. The accuracy of Charlie's attempts at word writing is spotty. Other formative assessments, including teacher observation, show that Charlie has a handle on phonemic awareness and identifying individual sounds in consonant–vowel–consonant words; but he still appears to struggle with connecting many sounds with letters. As the basis of her inquiry regarding Charlie's foundational skills, Kate asks: "In what ways and to what extent is Charlie applying his phonics knowledge as he writes during his project work?"

The end of the school year kindergarten writing expectations for the *Text Types and Purposes* Anchor Standard include, "Use a combination of drawing, dictating, and writing to narrate a single event or several loosely linked events, tell about the events in the order in which they occurred, and provide a reaction to what happened" (NGA & CCSSO, 2010, p. 19). Related to this standard was another kindergarten indicator found under the Anchor Standard *Research to Build and Present Knowledge*: "With guidance and support from adults, recall information from experiences or gather information from provided sources to answer a question" (NGA & CCSSO, 2010, p. 19). The questions that Kate asks about Charlie's learning are related to transferring his learning from the language arts phonics lessons to his writing in the work connected to the project in which they are currently engaged. Charlie had entered kindergarten with little foundational phonics knowledge, but with Kate's support he is making headway. What learning tasks would yield the information she required to answer her questions? What evidence could she triangulate to determine where Charlie is on this initial segment of his development toward independence?

Kate's class begins their biology project as part of their study of growth during the second half of the year. As a form of pretesting, Kate opens the project by asking her students what food names pop into their minds when she says the word *dinner*. She uses the classroom smart board to record students' responses with a picture. After they exhaust their ideas for the brainstorm, Kate asks the students to repeat the name of each food and isolate its initial sound. She then writes the word or words next to a picture of the food, asking the students as a group what sound each word begins with. Then she writes the name of the food. Kate notes that Charlie is doing well at isolating the first sounds of the words *green beans*, but listens to his classmates name the letters that make the two initial sounds. She records her observations about Charlie and the other students for whom she has similar concerns following this brainstorming session to use as evidence of their phonemic awareness and early sound–symbol knowledge.

Next, Kate and the students organize the list using a topical web with the term *dinner foods* in the center and *protein foods, vegetables and fruits, grains,* and *dairy* as offshoots from the center of the web—a review of learning in their health unit from earlier in the year. This task is easy to do visually using the smart board. Kate enhances their thinking by first modeling her thinking aloud about where and why to add a food to a topical web. Then, Kate asks students to follow her lead as she scaffolds students' explanations of where each of the foods should be placed. Then, she asks her students to think about where these foods come from. Some students shout out their kitchen; others say the grocery store. After asking them to think quietly for a minute about where else their food comes from, Charlie shares that his mom had big blue pots on the balcony of their apartment where she grew tomatoes last summer. And, they were really good! This response opens the door to a conversation about growing vegetables and other plants in gardens and on farms, giving Kate the opportunity to gauge their current knowledge about plant growth. This information gives her an indication of what topics may warrant additional time and which appear to already be known. With a full curriculum to cover, there is no sense in spending a significant amount of instructional time on topics that students have a fairly good handle on. She tells the class they will be reading, writing, and reporting about things that grow, including themselves, in their new project, and closes the lesson with students excited about starting a new project that would include talking about their own growth at the end.

From this lesson, Kate gathers evidence of her students' knowledge on several fronts—about foods and where they come from, as well as information about their phonemic awareness and early phonics learning. Since the class had previously begun studying consonant letters and sounds grouped logically by how they are articulated—a key concept in the WordWork program, they had already had a few weeks of studying the letter-sound relationships of *p, t, k,* and their voiced pairs *b, d,* and *g.* The initial sounds of *green* and *beans,* /g/ and /b/, had been taught and practiced. Although the pacing on her WordWork lessons is on target for the majority of her students, Kate now knows that Charlie and four other students needed additional small-group lessons to better solidify their learning. She plans to meet with them tomorrow to begin a short series of mini-lessons to address this identified need. The students require a firm foundation in letter–sounds relationships to achieve the goals expressed in the Standards indicators for kindergarten.

As the class immerses themselves in learning about how things grow, Kate and the children read the classic Ruth Krauss's *The Carrot Seed* (1945), along with Helen J. Jordan's *How a Seed Grows* (1960), Gail Gibbons's *The*

Vegetables We Eat (2008), and Grace Lin's *The Ugly Vegetables* (1999), to gather information on how vegetables grow. They will be recording their research information gleaned from these books in their Grow Journals. These tasks address the Writing Anchor Standards for Kindergarten. Reading this set of books also gives Kate a variety of authentic opportunities to check students' letter–sound knowledge and application. She is familiar with the body of research on concept-oriented reading instruction (CORI; e.g., Wigfield et al., 2004) approach to teaching for motivated reading in the disciplines. In line with this approach, each table grouping has a tub of narrative and informational books about plants and seeds that Kate assembled from her own collection and with the help of the school librarian. She rotates the tubs and displays books around the room for students to use in their research. They watch videos like the Sesame Street YouTube video *Desperate Houseplants (Plants Need Sun and Water)* (*www.youtube.com/watch?v=HgM6NSqi98c*) and compare and contrast what they learn from the videos to what the books said. When they meet as a group to complete the compare and contrast activity with a large, interactive, class-size Venn diagram, Kate listens to each student's contributions on what to add and where they should look to confirm the information.

As mentioned earlier, an ongoing task that allows Kate to monitor her students' literacy and science learning is their Grow Journals, where the students record their observations of their radish seed's germination and growth. Because one of Kate's goals is to move them toward becoming independent learners, she teaches the students how to write the date on the page of each new journal entry, using the class calendar as their resource. Kate checks their journals for this notation early in the project, so that she could give them feedback on their accuracy. The journals include pictures students drew based on their observations, and Kate directs them to write an important word or phrase to accompany it. Many of the students are able to write the letters representing the beginning sounds of the word with a series of random letters following it to represent the rest of the word. They are gaining a concept of word, along with early phonics. Some students also include the letter that represents the last sound, showing they were farther along in the phonics knowledge. A few use the books or the materials on the walls around the room as resources to copy words that are posted as the project progresses. As they complete their journal entries each day, Kate makes a point to ask each student about his or her entry, writes notes about what they draw and write, and who asks for the spelling of a word. That request is an invitation for another quick assessment. Because each entry is dated, she could zoom-in on the evidence of exactly which letter–sound pairings each of her students has acquired and when the learning began appearing. Alternatively, to answer other questions she posed, Kate could zoom-out her lens a bit to determine where her students are on the whole word-spelling continuum. Kate uses these formative opportunities to make sure that Charlie and his classmates are now on track to meet grade-level goals. Those few additional mini-lessons on letter–sound relationships and all of the opportunities to practice this new learning have worked for Charlie. He is proud of his accomplishments, which show in his participation and engagement each day. And, he is able to present his learning to others with confidence, using his Grow Journal as a prompt.

Over the years since the implementation of the CCSS, teachers like Kate Hampton developed the know-how to plan and conduct mini-studies of student learning in the short, medium, and long term as opposed to waiting for externally authored assessments. They fine-tuned their question-asking skills to take advantage of moment-to-moment opportunities to probe for misconceptions and address them in a timely manner. Employing inquiry within the formative process noticeably accelerated students' progress from where it was 20 years before. Teachers in 2024 now gain a more holistic understanding of student progress than previously was the norm because they analyze students' application of new knowledge within practical projects. They don't make the assumption that all students have learned what was taught and move on, and they keep students apprised of their performance.

NUTS AND BOLTS

As illustrated above, the instructional practices in 2024 are equivalent to scientists asking questions based on observations, forming hypotheses that need testing, and developing an action plan to gather data and analyze the information based on the original questions. It is at this point where well-reasoned lesson and unit planning—the fourth factor—come into play. Through ongoing school-sponsored professional development like professional communities of learning and online venues, teachers learned to think systematically about where and how they plan to gather evidence of student literacy and content learning within and across projects. Just as the Standards were developed through a process of backward mapping (Wiggins & McTighe, 1998, 2005) from the 12th-grade indicators (Rothman, 2011b, 2013), backward mapping from the grade-by-grade and Anchor Standards is critical to successful classroom implementation and has become a commonplace lesson planning strategy. Cultivating this approach to thinking about curriculum has led to 2024 teachers possessing deep understandings of the goals they want their students to achieve by the end of the year and how to get them there in optimal and engaging ways. Over the years since 2010 research on literacy learning progressions has also become a trusted guide for teachers to gauge student performance as it naturally ebbs and flows across a school year. Multiple experiences evaluating formative evidence of learning (or not) led teachers to develop expertise in determining the extent of scaffolded practice students need to apply literacy skills and strategies in different disciplines. Transfer was not assumed, but was explicitly taught! Teachers included notes in their lesson plans of the most advantageous times to ask students when, for example, they themselves might use a story graph similar to the one they just completed to aid in analyzing a narrative plot. As students offer ideas, the teacher guides their thinking to include employing the graphic organizer as a planning mechanism for their own narratives. In similar fashion, Nancy King plans a set of transfer questions to ask in the final days of her third-grade *Family Roots* project aimed to generate a transfer discussion about extending her students' work to studying the history of their community. Nancy will ask, "Based on the research methods [project vocabulary] you used to uncover your own family history, what documentation [more project vocabulary] and methods might you and other historians use to learn about what life was like when our community was founded? How might you uncover more interesting information about the people who lived here long ago than what you might find by only reading a timeline or a history book?" In addition to piquing her students' interest in local history, Nancy plans to use the discussion to establish the depth of her students' new knowledge about the usefulness of primary source documents in learning about local history. Would her third graders know to transfer their research methodologies to a wider application? If not, she plans on incorporating a discussion to encourage transfer possibilities.

Now in 2024, teachers purposely plan opportunities for formative assessment. During the lesson-planning phase, they strategically include a mix of basic- and higher-level questions to monitor learning as lessons progress. Teachers found that if they plan questions ahead of time, they are more likely to limit low-level questions that only tap into surface understanding. Even small wording changes can make all the difference between a minimal response and one that encourages deeper thinking. After taking part in professional development and deliberately including a range of questions in their lessons plans, teachers developed high-quality questioning habits that took advantage of moment-to-moment opportunities to probe student understanding. Lesson plan formats, like the CORE lesson model (Chambliss & Calfee, 1998), support this instructional focus on questioning. Additionally, because teachers now have access to the learning progressions in each academic discipline, the formative information they gather from quality questioning allows for reasoned next steps.

An important element in curriculum planning is the inclusion of collaborative work time during projects. Students now are more used to working in research teams. They are apprenticed into collaboration from kindergarten on. As teachers facilitate group work, one aim is to purpose-fully eavesdrop on the interactions to note project vocabulary usage, mis-conceptions and misunderstandings expressed that need to be addressed, growing understanding of key concepts, and "aha" moments when shared information clicks as students talk among themselves. This type of infor-mal assessment allows teachers to zoom-in for a small-grain-sized view of learning progress. Instruction may then occur on the spot to clarify con-cepts or call attention to something the team may have missed. On the other hand, observing more widespread confusion would indicate the topic needs to be covered in the next whole-class mini-lesson in order for the class to move forward. Bert Bauer, one of the teachers from Chapter 1, assumed that his seventh-grade class possessed a basic understanding of tides in general that they could apply to learning about king tides. After all, their community was situated on the San Francisco Bay and the Pacific Ocean was on the other side of the peninsula. But, as he listens to small-group conversations that appear to be a mix of experiential knowledge and some initial information from the first readings they did, Bert knows that he has work to do to address their misconceptions about tides in general. He had to consider what approach to take that would take advantage of active learning for his students.

We now take a closer look at a model for pairing formative assess-ment with teacher inquiry. We will describe why better differentiation and deeper learning should occur when teachers view formative assessment *cycle time* and assess learning *grain-size* as key considerations in planning.

THE TEACHER INQUIRY MODEL

Figure 5.1 illustrates how embedding formative assessment into instruc-tion serves as a driver for planning fine-tuned and differentiated instruc-tion to address students' learning needs to achieve the G × G guidelines in the Standards. It is important to note the arrows within the outer circle indicate Common Core Literacy Standards framing the inquiry model. In many ways the teacher inquiry process parallels the more formal inquiry conducted by education researchers. The teacher begins by detecting and defining a learning problem. Problems may concern how best to approach the next step in a particular learning progression with this particular class, small group, or individual student. Or, a problem may emerge from evi-dence gathered that student learning may not have occurred, or is present but not to the desired extent. Misconceptions may also come to light in class discussions that are more widespread than expected and need to be rectified.

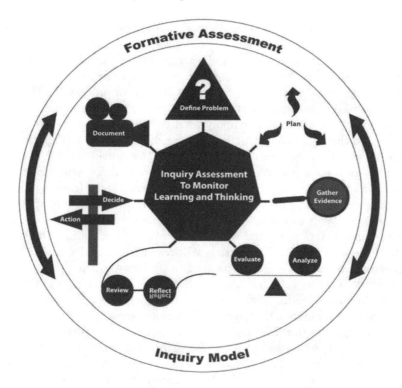

FIGURE 5.1. An inquiry model for formative assessment for instruction based on the Common Core Literacy Standards. From Calfee, Wilson, Flannery, and Kapinus (2014). Copyright 2014 by Teachers College, Columbia University. Reprinted by permission.

Once a problem is identified, the teacher plans instruction to generate evidence of learning along a grain-size continuum (see Figure 5.2) from moment-by-moment interactions that may focus on one piece of the learning puzzle to more complex and in-depth demonstrations of learning within and across clusters of learning tasks. Teachers then put their evidence collection plan into action. But collection of the evidence is not enough. The greater challenge for teachers is to analyze students' work products, assessments, and discussion responses to determine students' application within the immediate context being studied as well as their near and far transfer of learning. The teacher must organize and evaluate the evidence and triangulate the findings. Once this work is completed, it is time to review and reflect upon the evidence. At this point the teacher must call upon all of her resources to contribute to the decision-making process—her knowledge of the Standards, her evaluation of the data, her knowledge of learning progressions in one or more areas of interest, and her practical knowledge developed over time from working with previous students who had difficulty or soared ahead with this particular content or process. Do students appear to have gained only surface knowledge of newly introduced content or processes, but are unable to apply what they are learning to any deeper extent? Do they need an instructional nudge to move them farther along in their individual zones of proximal development (Vygotsky, 1978)? Are they ready for new information or do they need more practice with application tasks in a variety of contexts? Which students have just not learned the concept as presented and need reteaching with a new instructional approach to the topic? Who would benefit from enrichment at this point to deepen their learning even more, and what exactly would that entail to make the time spent worthwhile? This process will result in focused action that the teacher will document to determine if learning is now moving forward. She will decide whether more sampling is needed or if it is time to take new action. Another iteration of the Inquiry Model begins.

Group and individual project presentations, written products, website creations, and interim tests and quizzes offer more structured opportunities than observations and Q & A discussions for students to show what they know and for teachers to zoom-out for a larger-grain size of sampling student learning (see Figure 5.2). More details about grain size in a bit. Teachers study their notes on their own written feedback and rubric ratings in place of grades to inform their next steps in instruction. These dynamic indicators allow for a more nuanced understanding for teachers, students, and parents of learning than fixed grades. In each case the feedback is purposefully related back to the Standards to establish and review clear goals for the learning in each grade.

In 2024 teachers routinely share their findings with the school's literacy coach, administrators, and other teachers on their grade level or in discipline-based teams as a way to brainstorm instructional moves and calibrate growth in a low-stakes atmosphere within the school. Professional communities of practice can offer suggestions for instruction that have worked well in the past with students performing similarly. If several teachers are finding similar patterns in their own students, the group may decide to make this problem a focus for further study through readings from books and professional journal articles on the topic, viewing online resources, and discussions with teacher leaders to find effective options for instruction. This high level of professional collaboration has resulted in increasing the reliability and consistency of evaluations. Through problem-solving discussions of student learning, teachers widened the impact of instruction and assessment in beneficial ways.

Grain Size		Cycle Time
	Quarter/Annual Weeks - Months Portfolio Review Parent, Teacher, & Student Meeting	
	Project/Unit Days - Weeks Problem, Process, Product. Build and Present	
	Lesson Minutes - Class Period Episodic: Beginning, Middle and End. Set Outcomes Review Learning	
	Moment by Moment Seconds - Few Minutes Interactions, Questions, Discourse and Instant Action	

FIGURE 5.2. Cycle-time and grain-size dimensions for conducting formative assessment. From Calfee, Wilson, Flannery, and Kapinus (2014). Copyright 2014 by Teachers College, Columbia University. Reprinted by permission.

A Word on Documentation

It is important that teachers document their findings. Documentation in 2024 is accomplished with either a digital or hardcopy logbook in a way that makes student progress clear (Wilson & Calfee, 2007) to all constituents. The logbook facilitates the feedback process for teachers regarding the effectiveness of their teaching, for the student in how well his or her approach to learning is going, and for parents on the progress their child is making in relation to grade-level Standards expectations. For example, some teachers organize a framework in the logbook by child, dedicated to each of the Anchor Standards with notations for particular grade-level indicator. Alternatively, the logbooks of other teachers are organized for each child by the projects for the academic year and the student's progress toward achieving his or her goals. Pages or print can be color-coded to indicate if students are "in progress" or have achieved an indicator to aid in deciding on the next steps to take. When teachers create an online log-book in Word or in Google Docs, the "Find" function in those programs allows teachers quick and easy access to notations regarding an individual student. Teachers' mobile digital devices have streamlined adding notes on student learning as teachers observe students in action, working indi-vidually and in collaborative groups, or when meeting individually to dis-cuss works-in-progress during mini-conferences. Teachers have found the logbook to be an efficient, convenient tool for keeping track of student progress in relation to end-of-year targets and as a resource for informing instructional choices.

Students and Parents

As with their teachers, 2024 students are now more skilled at self-assess-ment, determining if change is called for in their approach to their school work. Some teachers use kid-friendly rubrics; others create rubrics with their students. Either way, students understand better the expectations teachers have for their work within and tangential to the projects they are engaged in. Teachers and students analyze assignment models, so that the students can visualize how detailed their work needs to be to demonstrate their learning. Along with having the Standards posted, teachers talk with students about how the work they are completing on each project fits with the Standards. For instance, tasks directed at meeting Anchor Standard 4 for Speaking and Listening—*Presentation of Knowledge and Ideas*—call for students to "Present information, findings, and supporting evidence such that listeners can follow the line of reasoning and the organization, development, and style are appropriate to task, purpose, and audience" (NGS & CCSSO, 2010, p. 22). This Standard has been particularly helpful in contributing to student self-assessment during project-based learning. As they listen to other students present ideas in elaborated responses to teachers' or students' questions or listen to others' research findings from projects during group work or formal presentations, students have mul-tiple opportunities to gauge their own understanding related to what they are hearing and to the rubrics. They know if they are on track or need to modify their learning strategies. They have the option of taking an active role in their approach to learning.

Communication with parents about their child's performance promotes the home–school connection. The schools make a concerted effort to keep parents informed of students' progress in achieving the grade level indicators for the Standards. Teachers use the Standards to frame parent–teacher conferences throughout the school year. By monitoring the formative information about their child's learning supplied by teachers on a regular basis, parents in 2024 find that they are actively supporting their child's learning—whether with praise for school accomplishments, encouragement to persevere with challenging homework, or facilitating homework completion by providing an environment conducive to learning. The strong lines of communication between teachers and parents allow for parents to talk with their children using consistent language, and this consistency enhances learning (Christenson, Rounds, & Gorney, 1992). Students received the explicit message that their efforts were valued within and outside of school. Motivation continues to be high because the students know that the important people in their lives care about their success and those people are working to build their academic competence (Deci & Ryan, 1985).

GRAIN-SIZE AND CYCLE-TIME RELATIONSHIPS

We now return to the classroom and take a closer look at two factors that are important as teachers plan for implementing the formative–summative assessment continuum: grain size and cycle time. Although some formative assessment occurs "in the moment" that is many times unplanned within whole-class and small-group discussions and while monitoring collaborative project work groups, teachers in 2024 design formative assessment activities within lessons and projects, and across quarters and semesters more systematically than ever before. As stated earlier, the purpose of the formative assessment process is to customize instruction to meet the learning needs of students on the way to meeting specific learning goals. Figure 5.2 lays out a visual depiction of how teachers are thinking now about multiple opportunities for students to show their teachers and others what they know. By planning more than one opportunity to triangulate the "what" and the "how well" of student understanding, teachers developed rationales for what needs instructional attention as instruction progressed. When teachers deeply understand the content of the discipline(s) they teach, they also have a strong sense of the progression of learning that needs to take place across a semester or an academic year. This depth of teacher knowledge is developed through ongoing professional development—especially in grade-level or disciplinary-professional communities of practice. Teachers are prepared to anticipate where misconceptions of more challenging concepts have a higher probability of occurring, so they know the critical points during the instructional units to plan for assessing for them. Because teachers understand students' learning paths as well as the instructional progressions needed to meet the learning goals set forth in the Standards, they chart out the year of instruction and assessment, modifying the plan as the year progresses (see Figure 5.3).

In Chapter 1 we learned that Nancy King, a seasoned teacher who took advantage of professional development opportunities, got the seed of an idea for her *Family Roots* unit. She had received a small stipend from her school allowing her to attend the May 2023 International Reading Association annual meeting. After listening to several presentations describing successful project ideas for integrating elementary grade literacy across the disciplines and talking with other third grade teachers from other Common Core states, she came back energized and excited to try one or more of them in the coming year. She could envision potential project tasks really propelling her students toward achieving the third-grade Common Core indicators. Nancy is well aware, though, that she will need to make several planning moves to create a blueprint for the year to decide where to place the *Family Roots* project even before the students first arrive at her classroom door. When in the year will she teach the literacy skills, strategies, and processes the students will need prior to the start of the project? Where in the project will students practice already-learned literacy components and when will new ones be introduced within this social studies project?

Having this leverage with curriculum decision making now in 2024 is very different from the restrictions found in many districts—especially the larger urban districts—10 years earlier. Although there were a few school districts and private schools scattered across the country that incorporated project-based learning in its various forms, literacy instruction in elementary schools tended to be dependent primarily on prescribed basal series. Publishers offered sets of materials that they advertised as aligned with the Common Core that had an impact on Common Core states as well as the few states that had decided not to adopt the Standards. Many school districts in non-Common Core states also used the same popular basal series as the rest of the country. The basal series like McGraw-Hill's Reading Wonders series (2014) offered a range of materials that districts or individual schools could purchase, including hard-copy and online-leveled readers, a Response to Intervention books, a handbook with worksheets to practice Common Core skills, and a lesson planner for each grade. The series also included an assessment package to monitor progress quickly. What these series did not do is support project-based learning that gives students choice in the topic they would research. Students are not given

Grain Size	Cycle Time			
	Moment	Lesson	Unit	Quarter/Year
Identify Question				
Develop Plan				
Collect Evidence				
Analyze and Evaluate				
Review and Reflect				
Take Action				
Review, Document				

FIGURE 5.3. Matrix for combining inquiry methods with the cycle-time/grain-size dimensions of formative assessment. From Calfee, Wilson, Flannery, and Kapinus (2014). Copyright 2014 by Teachers College, Columbia University. Reprinted by permission.

a chance to show that they can apply their discipline knowledge and literacy skills and strategies in the authentic reading and writing tasks of the research and creative work inherent in projects. Instead, teachers were given a scope and sequence to follow with very little choice in when and how they would teach and assess the material addressing the Standards. Project-based learning is more fluid in when and how the Standards are addressed, making the scope-and-sequence approach impractical and out of date. Formative assessments—the most frequent form of assessments in 2024—accommodate the fluidity of project-based learning, while effectively informing teachers, students, and parents of progress toward meeting grade-level Standards indicators.

The importance now placed on formative assessments within project-based learning illustrates yet another example of the change to local control indicated in the CCSS Introduction back in 2010 (NGA & CCSSO, 2010):

> Teachers are thus free to provide students with whatever tools and knowledge their professional judgment and experience identify as most helpful for meeting the goals set out in the Standards. (p. 4)

While the Standards delineate specific expectations in reading, writing, speaking, listening, and language, each standard need not be a separate focus for instruction and assessment. Often, several standards can be addressed by a single rich task. (p. 5)

While the Standards focus on what is most essential, they do not describe all that can or should be taught. A great deal is left to the discretion of teachers and curriculum developers. (p. 6)

Teachers in 2024 are viewed as professionals, who understand their students and know the learning to be accomplished at particular grade levels for students to be college- and career-ready and ready to be contributing citizens by the time they finish high school. Teachers receive the comprehensive instruction they need to become competent in implementing a project-based learning model infused with formative assessment based on teacher inquiry. This instruction begins in their preservice courses and continues in multiple formats during their professional lives. In short, teachers understand the CCSS and know how to achieve these goals with all their students.

We will now turn to the concepts of cycle time and grain size to understand considerations framing Nancy King's assessment and instruction decisions.

Cycle Time

Wiliam and Thompson (2006) highlighted three assessment cycles that should occur across a school year. Cycles in the assessment context are the intervals between assessments, including long-, medium-, and short-term cycles (see Figures 5.2 and 5.3). An end-of-project research report about the water cycle would be considered a long-term assessment by Nancy because she would not have her current third graders involved with the same summative assessment for that particular project again. For instance, she is not planning to assess students' understanding of local ecosystems' relationship to water during this school year. But she will note in the class logbook section dedicated to "Changes for Next Year" for how she will refine the assessment tasks for the next school year when she includes the project in her yearly cycle. Nancy wants to be sure to collect a wider range of evidence of the depth of student understanding of the interrelationships of local biosystems next time she teaches it. This fine-tuning occurs each year for every content area as Nancy reflects upon her students' assessment responses in all their forms. Her logbooks are a treasure trove of ideas that she revisits late each summer as she prepares for the new school year.

Figure 5.3 includes three cycle times that fall within Wiliam and Thompson's (2006) medium cycles. The size of the block of time between assessment and instructional change is decidedly less than the year or more in a long cycle, so instructional change based on formative assessment impacts Nancy's present class. Evidence of student literacy learning from individual lessons within projects or instructional units in various content areas and the projects or units as a whole should inform instruction for the next day, the next unit, or the next quarter and, therefore, would not fall into a long cycle. In Nancy's case, she would not plan to assess local biosystem relationships again this year, but she is interested in her students' growing understanding of the interrelationships among extended family members noted in their *Roots* research and the individual students. Would this broad concept of relationships transfer in some form to their *Family Roots* project? Information from the students' *Roots* journals, their personal timelines, and their family trees would be formative sources for Nancy of evidence of students' growth in understanding the concept of relationships and the interactions among them that would fall into a medium assessment cycle.

On a shorter cycle but still in the medium range, Nancy poses an inquiry question about her students' understanding of sequencing over time. She is especially interested in monitoring how Max, Josh, and Kirsten—three students with learning disabilities—do with the concept in a social studies context. The *Family Roots* project will give these students and the rest of the class time to reflect upon and practice sequencing events in authentic ways. From past experiences, she found that graphic organizers combining visual and written tasks could help cement the concept into their knowledge base. Nancy taught a lesson yesterday on creating and reading timelines using her life as an example. She included an oral think-aloud in her lesson to model which events she wanted to include, why to include them, and how to think about the placement of events. She projected the ReadWriteThink website mobile app titled Timeline (*www.readwritethink.org/classroom-resources/mobile-apps/timeline-b-31047.html*) from her iPad. By the end of the lesson, students including Kirsten, Max, and Josh were coming to Nancy's iPad helping to complete the timeline. Today, Nancy wants to see if they understand how timelines work and can apply the process they learned yesterday. The students start their own timelines using the iPads from the classroom cart, so it was important that she first connects them to yesterday's work. Then, she assesses their progress, giving her students specific feedback on what they are doing well and what they might try differently. She wants them to have a successful start, as they would be adding to their timelines as they continue with the research about their families. The timelines will be an important addition to their *Family Roots* reports. She is pleased to see that all three of her focus students are engaged and progressing well on their timelines today, needing minimal support.

A short cycle includes formative assessment within a lesson that is acted upon by the teacher during that lesson. Assessment can be moment by moment or at previously planned points in the lesson. Examples of a short cycle would include adjustments made in student thinking when misconceptions arise during a class discussion, a student–teacher mini-conference during writer's workshop where the teacher may model more specific content vocabulary for a student to use in a report, or during small-group observations. After modeling the story map of her own personal narrative, as mentioned in Chapter 1, Nancy brings up a story map on the smart board. She and the class begin to complete a story map for Laura and her family in Laura Ingalls Wilder's *Little House in the Big Woods* (1932), a chapter book the class just completed. Partway through the whole-class activity, she divides the class into small groups and has them collaboratively complete the story map, including sections on plot, characters, setting, and theme. The students' personal narratives will have a similar flavor. As the students work, Nancy circulates around the room observing each group and listens closely to monitor their discussions, asks clarifying questions, and addresses students' confusions. She is able to give immediate feedback on their efforts and get them back on track, if needed. Nancy finds that short cycles are effective because her feedback avoids misconceptions settling in early. The students would be ready to start a story map outlining their personal narrative tomorrow.

Grain Size

The grain size of a formative assessment (Heritage, 2010) refers to the purpose for the assessment and the size of the knowledge chunk being assessed to meet that purpose. Specifically, in a teacher inquiry framework, grain size is directly connected to the questions teachers ask regarding student learning. Assessments embedded in project work have the potential to give teachers the flexibility to gather multiple grain-size chunks of information within project tasks to answer a variety of questions about individual students, small groups, and the class as a whole.

Because instructional planning and an inquiry approach to the formative assessment process go hand-in-hand, we will gain insights into how Nancy purposefully weaves formative assessment at various levels of grain size throughout the unit to keep tabs on her students' learning. Nancy uses teacher inquiry to determine what she needs to learn about her third-grade students' growing social studies knowledge, their literacy skill and strategy application needed for that particular academic discipline, and how she will gather evidence just prior to and across her *Family Roots* genealogy project. The project is intended to be a focus on addressing several third-grade Literacy Standards. The *Family Roots* project will include formative assessment of the major literacy components: reading comprehension of literature and informational text, writing in several modes as they gather information and report their findings in their *Roots* books, listening and speaking during the oral presentations and their research interviews and as students work collaboratively, and using language that is appropriate to topics related to their genealogy in a manner that is communicated clearly.

Nancy starts planning her formative assessment opportunities with the end goals—the third-grade indicators for the Anchor Standards in each of the literacy components. She creates open-ended tasks that will take into account several goals for the year. Nancy starts with the third-grade indicators, including but not limited to:

1. Reading indicator 3 related to the Anchor Standard *Key Ideas and Details*—"Describe the relationship between a series of historical events, scientific ideas or concepts, or steps in technical procedures in a text, using language that pertains to time, sequence, and cause/effect" (NGA & CCSSO, 2010, p. 14).

2. Writing indicator 3 for the Anchor Standard *Text Types and Purposes*—"Use a combination of drawing, dictating, and writing to narrate a single event or several loosely linked events, tell about the events in the order in which they occurred, and provide a reaction to what happened" (NGA & CCSSO, 2010, p. 19).

3. Writing indicator 6 for the Anchor Standard *Production and Distribution of Writing*—"With guidance and support from adults, explore a variety of digital tools to produce and publish writing, including in collaboration with peers" (NGA & CCSSO, 2010, p. 19).

4. Writing indicator 8 for Anchor Standard *Research to Build and Present Knowledge*—"With guidance and support from adults, recall information from experiences or gather information from provided sources to answer a question (NGA & CCSSO, 2010, p. 19).

5. Language indicator 3 for Anchor Standard *Knowledge of Language*—"Use knowledge of language and its conventions when writing, speaking, reading, or listening.
   a. "Choose words and phrases for effect."
   b. "Recognize and observe differences between the conventions of spoken and written standard English" (NGA & CCSSO, 2010, p. 29).

These third-grade indicators and several others help Nancy assess student learning at differing grain sizes. She has decided to create analytic rubrics for each of the *Family Roots* products that students produce as one category of evidence of learning. Because Nancy wants her students to grow in their ability to self-monitor learning, she decides to coauthor some of the rubrics with the students. She will develop the remaining rubrics, but will set the stage by discussing the rationale for the work and how the task will be scored prior to having students embark on it. By choosing to include the students in building the rubrics, Nancy believes they will become more invested in their work on the project. The rubrics are versatile enough to assess small chunks of knowledge like "decoding multisyllable words" (third-grade Foundational Phonics and Word Recognition; NGA & CCSS, 2010, p. 17), as well as larger chunks such as "telling events in order." Rubrics are also excellent sources for her to give individual, specific feedback. In addition to utilizing rubrics, Nancy will triangulate evidence from the students' journals, drawings, graphic organizers, and of course the final e-book they create using the *Book Creator* app to answer her questions about each student's progress.

One of Nancy's goals that overlap social studies and literacy learning is to acquire the vocabulary related to the tools of the field. For example, she wants her students to learn, read, write and talk knowledgeably about the terms: *primary documents*, *timelines*, *family trees*, *interviews*, and *ancestors*. She notes in her logbook instances and artifacts to document student technical vocabulary use and their level of accuracy. As she prepped for the unit, Nancy found e-resources like the family tree graphic organizer and more from the National Archives website (*http://docsteach.org/tools*), where her students can experience authentic practice with these terms that will solidify their understanding. The artifacts they create from them can also be easily incorporated into the book they are creating. Nancy will give similar authentic practice with relevant literacy terms like *book dedication*, *table of contents*, *hyperlinks*, and *glossary* and will observe how they incorporate these components in their reports. She will determine the level of texts they are reading in order to learn more about their birthplaces or neighborhoods and how well they understand what they read. A combination of growing prior knowledge from interviewing relatives over the holidays and talking about the ancestors they find in family photo albums, along with their excitement and engagement in what they are learning, has set the stage for comprehending more advanced levels of texts and for more detailed writing. They are telling their stories well, and they are proud of their accomplishments. And, the literacy and social studies knowledge they are gaining is giving them a solid base for future learning.

Nancy makes a point of recording the evidence she is collecting each day. She set up charts in her online logbook with her goals delineated for each child where she can check off a concept or process learned and easily view a student's strengths and areas needing additional instruction. She had the idea this year of noting misconceptions and misunderstandings in red, growing knowledge in blue, and multiple evidence of working knowledge in green, which has added to her efficiency. Because she created her logbook in Word, it is simple to add columns or rows when needed. She reflects on what she is seeing to adjust for tomorrow's mini-lessons. She is impressed with how quickly and how much the students are learning, and decides that this project is a keeper for next year.

SOME FINAL THOUGHTS ABOUT THIS REALITY

It is our belief that this view into the future is not a fairytale, but will be a doable outcome if modifications in addressing the CCSS are made at the national, state, district, and classroom levels. The first change would begin in preservice teacher education programs. Teacher educators in all programs will need to be well versed in the Standards, the multiple forms of project-based learning, how projects can address learning in several academic disciplines concurrently, and the integration of a balanced approach to the summative–formative continuum.

Next, national and state officials, school districts administrators, and the public in general will need to view teachers as professionals who are capable producers of curriculum and assessment, and facilitators of student learning, and treat them as such. Basal texts should become only one of several tools available for teachers and students, not the focal point of instruction they are in many localities.

Finally, for broad and lasting change to come about, schools need to provide high-quality, sustained professional development for inservice and new teachers. We advocate for a mix of multiple formats of professional development to take place. Schools should establish and support the formation of professional communities of practice who come together to explore the most recent research on effective instruction. Topics studied should focus on effective instruction to meet students' learning needs that the teachers have identified through the formative process. As professionals, these groups should spend their limited time together on active learning and not as data teams on accountability requirements imposed by districts. Depending on the topics of interest, the professional communities of practice should jointly analyze and discuss student products to calibrate their efforts and to offer next-step suggestions. They can gather, read, and discuss books, edited book chapters, and research journal articles of common interest. These communities of practice can watch videos of each other's teaching, asking questions about choices and rationales, and giving focused feedback. High-quality websites, like Text Project (*http//:textproject.org*) and Teaching Channel (*www.teachingchannel.org*), as well as app shares can also offer jumping-off points for discussion and reflection. Another professional development option is to create partnerships with higher education institutions. Interactions should occur regularly and can take place in face-to-face contexts or through synchronous online connections. Finally, we recommend that schools should seriously consider hiring instructional coaches with advanced endorsements, who are very knowledgeable in literacy and technology integration, to work with all interested teachers in a nonevaluative role to fine-tune instruction.

All of the recommendations in this chapter are doable and are called for to effect substantive change. It is only when a shift from "business as usual" in our schools is enacted that students across the board will achieve college, career, and citizen readiness from the present reform efforts.

CHAPTER 6

Moving toward the Common Core Vision

Big Shifts and Bright Spots

In this final chapter, we step outside the classrooms of the future for a quick look at current events elsewhere around the nation, including several other "bright spots" like Nancy's classroom. As the spring progressed in 2015, the news about the ELA Standards returned to the front page, with the administration of the year-end summative tests. This is the first time that the Standards "count." Scores are likely to be disappointing. This outcome is not surprising when one considers the large-scale instructional changes that are called for to realize the Standards. There will continue to be a great deal of grumbling. Most schools and classrooms will meanwhile continue with business as usual. The question is whether the bright spots will begin to attract attention. Comparable examples of "good teaching" have been with us for a long time (Danielson, 2011), and we will share some of those stories in this chapter. The question is whether the Standards will provide the impetus for a major increase in "really good teaching"—and even more. What can be done to increase the likelihood of this turn of events?

STATUS REPORT 2015

After the initial exuberance that greeted the release of the Standards in 2010, implementation has been tumultuous, with continuous ups and downs. Different perspectives led to different positions. Views from the top tend to be quite positive and optimistic. Forty-three states and the District of Columbia currently remain committed to the Common Core, although Indiana, Oklahoma, and South Carolina reversed their Standards adoption decisions and are in the process of writing their own. Discontent in a few other state legislatures triggered calls for moving away from the Common Core, but those attempts lacked the requisite votes to make the change (Ujifusa, 2014, 2015).

Although most of the Common Core states chose to begin administering their statewide assessments from mid-March on, February 16, 2015, marked the opening of the testing windows for the performance-based assessments in a few states in the PARCC and Smarter Balanced consortiums. The pressure now was on at the school level (Gewertz, 2015). Children in 28 states are taking these new tests; 22 other states opted to use a variety of tests to measure student performance. The recently piloted and subsequently revised assessments from the PARCC and Smarter Balanced consortiums are having state impact for the first time in more than half of the Common Core states. In spring 2014, more than 1.1 million students took part in the field tests, with students reporting the tests as "challenging" and "really hard" (*Education Week* Report Roundup, November 11, 2014). The results contributed to the views from the bottom that were less favorable than those of the policymakers. Comments tended to fall into categories like "we are not prepared, we don't have the right materials, the computers don't work, we are doing the same thing, things are getting tougher and almost impossible"—from teachers, parents, and students. The view from organizations, including publishers and the test consortia, since the field tests ended was somewhere in the middle. Although there were some pockets with problems, reports suggested that the field testing went more smoothly than many had anticipated (Gewirtz, 2014b). It was a tough job, but steady progress with the revisions led to assessments that were ready in time for the spring 2015 tests.

BOTTOM LINES: WHERE ARE WE NOW, AND HOW CAN WE GET TO WHERE WE NEED TO BE?

Prediction is a risky business, but here are some hunches.

• *The Standards at present.* The success of the year-end tests is still unknown territory at the time of this writing, even after the large-scale tests in spring 2014. Support for tests is unsteady, with widespread uneasiness, across the board, including whole states, districts, and individual teachers. Some large districts like Los Angeles and Chicago have asked that the results not be used as accountability measures for this school year. Some schools in those districts do not yet have the requisite technology in place nor have the students had sufficient practice with the technology to allow for an accurate assessment of student learning. But, adoption seems to be holding—without clear ideas of what the Standards *mean* to many people, other than tests.

• *Curriculum.* The focus appears to be on the grade-by-grade entries, especially in Basic Reading. Little attention is being given to Writing, with practically none to Research. We view the Writing and Research Standards as espousing the synthesis and application of students' learning in achieving the other Standards. Unless there is a shift away from the current overemphasis of teaching to meet the Basic Reading Standards to a more balanced emphasis across the Common Core Anchor Standards, the promise of the Common Core Standards will never be fully achieved.

• *Materials.* Everything is now aligned, and "formative assessments" come in standardized packages, including "digital libraries." High-quality sources, like the Innovation Lab Network (*www.ccsso.org/What_We_Do/Innovation_Lab_Network.html*), are coming on the scene with resource banks of tasks, portfolio frameworks, rubrics, benchmarks, and protocols for schools to access in support of significant changes from "business as usual" (Darling-Hammond, 2014).

• *Professional learning opportunities.* These are a burgeoning cottage industry, but generally of the "late afternoon" variety. In an interview, Charlotte Danielson, a respected voice in instructional practice, stated

> The Common Core rests on the view of teaching as complex decision making, as opposed to something more routine or drill-based. . . . So I see the Common Core as a fertile and rich opportunity for really important learning by teachers, because—I don't know how to say this nicely—well, not all teachers have been prepared to teach this way. I see that as one of the enormous challenges facing the Common Core rollout. (Rebora, in *Education Week Teacher*, March 13, 2013, pp. 1–2)

• *Graduate schools of education.* These potentially influential professional learning providers have lagged behind in taking a leadership role in offering high-quality professional development for both inservice and preservice teachers. But innovative models for providing research-grounded professional learning opportunities are beginning to appear. They are committed to fostering complex instructional decision making in teachers, as Danielson advises, and can hold the greatest potential for needed change at the classroom level.

- *Baby steps.* Advancing in small steps has been the norm, but there have also been some giant steps and exceptional "bright spots"—exceptional in part because of the potential of emerging technology to transform research, sustained study, and engagement with real-world schools and classrooms, as the next section illustrates.

In the previous chapters we have laid out the components that we believe are important for schools to include in their instructional designs. All of the pieces of the puzzle have been available since the 1980s in one form or another. The challenge for the age of the Common Core is to connect the dots for educators; for the states, federal government, and other policymakers; for the public—businesses, the media, higher education, and concerned citizens—and especially for families. The critical job is to focus on the ultimate goal: readiness for college, career, and citizenship in the 21st-century "flat world" that lies ahead (Darling-Hammond, 2010). Education in the United States during the first years of this century turned increasingly to preparation for multiple-choice tests of basic skills and to instruction following scripted activities, thus narrowing the curriculum. With the CCSS, schools have the opportunity to reverse this trend by recognizing the classroom teacher as the most critical factor for promoting quality schooling. We turn now to the "bright spots" in schools across the country currently and in the past where teachers and schools have connected the pieces of the puzzle to create effective and engaging learning environments for students.

BRIGHT SPOTS PAST AND PRESENT, WITH PROMISE FOR THE FUTURE

Compelling examples exist of the instructional components we believe are necessary for the promise of the Common Core to come to fruition. The programs that we describe in this chapter weave a compelling tapestry of successful implementations with many common elements that emerge, including project-based learning, ongoing formative assessment built seamlessly into hands-on activities, and motivated students engaged in worthwhile explorations of relevant topics spanning from science to social studies to the arts that incorporate sophisticated use of technology. In every story, teachers are viewed as the linchpins for student success. We describe programs implemented prior to the creation of the Common Core as well as current collaborations between schools and universities or schools and business. Some K–12 programs are housed in public schools and others are private-school enterprises. Some focus on student learning where others spotlight models of teacher professional learning. The shared characteristics across the examples we present include real-world experiences, problem solving, critical thinking and decision making, collaboration, curiosity, and opportunities for communication—elements fostering deeper learning for all students that have been called essential survival skills for the 21st century (Wagner, 2008).

The Explorers Program

We begin in 1996, long before the CCSS were developed. The successful Explorers Program was a summer collaboration between the University of Nebraska–Lincoln's Center for Instructional Innovation and the Omaha Public Schools designed to meet the learning needs of students in low socioeconomic-status schools. The summer experience was developed to be an alternative choice for the district's regular summer school for upper elementary students. The goals for students in the program were to connect science and literacy expertise through experiential learning with nature, to develop motivation for literacy and science learning, and to learn how to work cooperatively in a project-based learning environment. To achieve this goal, reading and writing informational text for authentic reasons was woven into students' planned encounters with the natural world.

> Explorers spend one of the half-days per week in a nature area to learn observational skills and identify topics of interest. In the classroom students use expository books and other resource materials in long-term explorations on their topics. They work on their projects individually and in groups. They also read literature for pleasure and, to help build connections between science and literacy, take part in whole class and small group discussions, make oral presentations, and write frequently throughout the summer. (Bruning & Schweiger, 1997, p. 150)

Formative assessment was an integral part of the framework of the program. Teachers gauged student learning through student products such as semantic maps completed at the beginning and end of the program; summary writing of the content from texts student read; forms that guided students' reflections on their observations, readings, learning, planning, and strategies they used during the week; and a wide variety of writing samples from the day-to-day work of projects. Present-day readers will recognize the acknowledged influence of ideas from Concept-Oriented Reading Instruction (CORI; Guthrie et al., 1996) and Project Read/Inquiring Schools (Calfee & Patrick, 1995) to create their design.

The teachers from the 1996 summer program described the program's success and the growth of students and themselves, as evidenced in the following teacher comments (unpublished materials) collected after the 1996

program ended. They were novices at project-based learning when they
started the summer school, but the day-to-day experiences supported their
self-efficacy and enjoyment for teaching in the open-ended atmosphere.

"Fun! Students enjoyed working on a project they got to choose. Seeing the progress of the students was good. Definitions improved after
seeing so many different items. I enjoyed the change of pace and doing
something totally different. I was worried at the beginning with no
plans, but after first week this was not a problem. Explorer meetings
were great when we exchanged ideas—gave us new things to do." (L)

"I really enjoyed teaching Explorers. I think the most advantageous
benefit that resulted from the experience from the standpoint of the
students was that they really seemed to love coming to school. Many
positive comments have been made by parents that their kids were
anxious each day to come to school. One said her son was ready early
each day and was perturbed when someone caused a delay in coming.
She said last year she had to fight getting him to summer school. For
myself, it renewed my faith in my ability to teach and have it be fun
for *myself* and *my students*. I had been feeling pretty burned out prior
to starting." (G)

"At first I was worried about using trade books and no set curriculum to
follow. I was concerned that I would not know what to do. However,
once summer school began I found it was much easier—the students
lead (sic) a lot of the things we wanted to learn. I can see a lot of
changes in the students' quality of work and the questions they ask.
Also now whenever a student asks a question, many of the students
run over to the Jr. Eyewitness books to find the answer." (P)

"I learned a lot about nature and was excited to pass this along to my
students. I was impressed with the progress they made in being able to
summarize information from several sources. Using the same process
(locating important words and listing them, then highlighting the most
important, and finally using them in sentences), over and over, with
different topics really made an impact in their ability to summarize
independently. I also was impressed with the vocabulary development
that took place. For example, students would excitedly come up to me
with a book and say, 'Look at that butterfly's long proboscis.' My main
difficulty was keeping four of 15 students busy during independent
work time (on projects). Even though they could tell me what they were
going to do, they didn't follow through but played instead." (O)

Three challenges emerged from the Explorers Program research. First, if teachers are not experienced in child-centered classrooms, they need much support with how to initiate and provide different organizational schemes. Classroom management that allows for student autonomy, collaborative groupings, and individualized texts to support student research is difficult for teachers but is achievable through extended experiences with a project-based learning model. The last comment, from teacher (O), alluded to a classroom management issue that she was encountering. Short weekly or biweekly meetings with other teachers to see how they were approaching similar challenges can be useful resources for other program teachers, as well as having regular meetings with the reading specialist tied to the project.

Second, it is not just the teachers who are new to the processes required for project-based learning. The students are used to their teachers traditionally choosing what is read, written about, and presented in the classroom. Because project-based learning is student-centered, students must also learn how self-regulation works. As students first encounter project-based learning, scaffolding their initial efforts with open-ended frameworks can provide needed support without squelching choice. Having discussions about how productive and respectful group-work functions are important for setting up the classroom environment for success, when first implementing project-based learning. Taking the time across the first weeks of project-based learning to teach students the characteristics that support fruitful discussions might appear too costly in instructional time, but in the long run will prove to be beneficial for the process to run smoothly as well as promote a lifelong skill for the students.

Finally, the Explorers Program found that, even though the projects were student-centered, the teachers needed to teach them the reading and writing strategies necessary to complete their research and demonstrate their new learning. Because the instruction was directly related to their work, it was very relevant to the students. Students understood why they were fine-tuning their literacy knowledge and application and were more likely to attend to what they were being taught. This engagement thus contributed to the students' learning in ways not observed in them previously.

What becomes apparent in reading about the Explorers Program is that teachers viewed the exciting work they did as "summer work," not as a model for instruction throughout the regular academic year. There appears to be no evidence of plans or trials to continue the model in any form during the school year. This compartmentalized view of project-based learning in 1996 may be due to the deeply ingrained instructional configuration of traditional schooling (Zhao, 2012). Creative thinking would be needed to extend the model to a 9-month implementation. Weekly fieldtrips would not be feasible, but some accommodations could be made. If this program were to take place in 2016, students and teachers now have access to the Internet to allow for "digital field trips." Textual resources for students have also expanded because of the Internet. What we see, though, as the underlying driving force that was not present then, is the Common Core and the vision for learning described in its Introduction. In essence, if states wholeheartedly adopted the Common Core, they must also open the door to implementation of the *New Shifts*—the integration of language and literacy across the disciplines, students engaged in "big tasks" that address multiple Standards, project-based learning activities, authentic student products and presentations, and formative assessment by teachers and students.

Amazing Grace/Renton Prep Christian Schools

Amazing Grace Christian School and Renton Prep Christian School (*www. agcschool.org*) are current examples of how project-based learning is being implemented in engaging ways to address the ELA Standards vision for nurturing deeper thinking in children. The PreK–12 school complex has built their student-centered curriculum around themes that are explored through STE(A)M integration—Science, Technology, Engineering, Art, and Mathematics. Broad important questions are posed—some within grade levels and others across grades. Students at all levels (including preschool!) research problems and their possible solutions collaboratively, demonstrating the kinds of high-level problem-solving skills needed for the creative and entrepreneurial thinking that will be expected of them as adults of the 21st century. Students have a voice in their learning, which adds to their engagement in the projects. They work on projects to answer questions like:

> *How can you build a boat that will stay afloat when carrying heavy loads?*
>
> *What makes you stay and move? Inertia!*
>
> *What would be necessary to build bridges, towers, and other earthquake-proof structures to withstand small and large earthquakes?*

Students work in teams during the school day to pose hypotheses based on reading various sources and from observation. They plan possible solutions, create intentional designs/drawings/blueprints, and develop methods for testing their designs. Failure is not viewed negatively; it is seen as a challenge to explore a problem more deeply through generating new questions based on observations, analysis, hypothesis posing, design, and more testing. This iterative process requires the learning and application of new and existing knowledge and skills.

As they work on their long-term projects, students create a range of artifacts that teachers can use in the formative process. Teachers know the knowledge, skills, and strategies to be learned to reach the G × G grade goals and ultimately the Anchor Standards by high school graduation, but the order of teaching standards within grades varies based on student needs as they explore the problems. Teachers use rubrics constructed from studying the Common Core goals and use them as the basis for their evaluations of student evidence. Learning is truly cross-disciplinary, and students understand the relevancy and authenticity of the work they are doing. Students push their own expectations, and succeed at high academic levels. It is worth viewing the Vimeo compilation of the 20-second commercials (*https://vimeo.com/96739623*) the students created to entice parents and others to come to their STEAM FAIR as well as their YouTube videos (e.g., *www.youtube.com/watch?v=mLMnwH1CMNE*). Both give a wonderful in-depth description of the project from the children's point of view. Amazing Grace and Renton Preparatory Schools offer inspiring examples for PreK–12 schools making the "big shifts" in instruction called for by the Standards.

Freestyle Academy of Communication Arts and Technology

The Freestyle Academy is a project-based program that has operated since 2006 in the Bay Area of Northern California. The program was created by the Mountain View–Los Altos Unified School District and is housed adjacent to Mountain View High School. This 2-year secondary education program is designed for up to 72 juniors and seniors attending either Mountain View High School, Los Altos High School, or Alta Vista High School—a district with a diverse student body. Students attend their home high school for half of the school day and go to the Freestyle campus for the other half. Students attending Freestyle take English, fine arts (design), and elective (either film or webaudio) classes totaling 60 credit hours in the 2 years, as part of their college preparatory coursework. The remainder of their coursework for graduation is taken at their home high school campus.

Hands-on, project-based learning that emphasizes a wide range of "new literacies" communication skills, with and without technology, forms the framework for Freestyle's coursework. Individualized student ideas for long-term projects are generated during their English class held at Freestyle and are based on their readings, discussions, critiques, brainstorming sessions, writings, and peer comments on written work. A goal for the Freestyle Academy is to help students "find or enhance an artistic/technological passion and develop their communicative skills" (*www.freestyle.mvla.net/about.php*) that can be used in the broader world. Challenging instruction in writing, digital film production, digital photography and graphic design, and Web production and audio engineering courses support students in developing multimedia projects that demonstrate their learning in creative and real-world ways. Their instruction allows for time to think, plan, test, revise and execute their ideas. Examples of student projects that attest to their achievement and motivation to learn can be viewed at *www.freestyle.mvla.net/featured_productions.php?v=featuredfilms*. These projects reflect the descriptors Freestyle uses about its program—relevant, unique, challenging, fun!

Although our readers may imagine that this program is earmarked for the students identified as gifted and talented, surprisingly it is not.

> Freestyle was created and envisioned to be another choice for those students who are "just doing school," not necessarily excelling in school or students with art or technical experience in hopes of getting these kinds of students once again excited about school. We are not looking for the "best" student or even a particular type of student. Our application process does not require any experience and does not require a portfolio to match the reason why Freestyle was created. This would hopefully entice students who are "just doing school" to apply. Our only requirements are a 2.0+ TGPA, a Junior or Senior within MVLAUHSD. We want a mix of all students and a lottery has resulted in a good mix of all levels of creative and passionate students with all levels of talents, skills and enthusiasm levels. (*www.freestyle.mvla.net/FAQs.php*)

Freestyle Academy's approach and the examples of student projects underscore the argument that project-based learning is indeed appropriate and motivating for a wide spectrum of students. This public school academy has demonstrated since 2006 that, when students are involved with authentic and complex projects and performances encompassing "big tasks," they exit the program as college- and career-ready. As proof of this claim, the Academy's website includes an impressive map (*www.google.com/maps/d/viewer?mid=zHsvD0BW145Y.kxj0A6NSGQyQ*) proudly displaying all of the institutions of higher education across the nation where Freestyle graduates have been or are currently enrolled. The academic achievements of many of these students, who when applying to the Freestyle Academy were "just doing school," gives testament to what can be done when schools venture away from traditional schooling to embrace a creative, student-centric project-based environment.

Response to Systems Intervention

Just as response-to-intervention (RTI) programs are designed to provide targeted instruction for students whose academic performance is below expectations for their grade level, schools and school districts experiencing difficulties in implementing and meeting the ELA Standards now have a response-to-systems intervention (RTSI) program available to them (Avelar La Salle, 2014). This unique program is provided by Principal's Exchange (*www.principals-exchange.org/index.php/about-us*), a Southern California-approved technical support provider, and was created to deliver significant support for the transition to the ELA Standards adoption at the systems level. This program's intended audience is districts designated as having low-performing schools. RTSI specialists work closely with teams of teachers at the elementary and secondary levels, school principals and assistant principals, guidance faculty in secondary schools, and central district data teams, superintendent's cabinets, and district educational services to study a variety of components that can make or break a successful embracing of the ELA Standards. RTSI addresses district-identified needs. Teams create a process to study a unit (districtwide to single schools) or to focus on a specific area of need, such as immigrant student achievement in the elementary schools.

The RTSI process begins with an "audit" of the unit designed to yield findings and recommendations that inform an action plan. The action plan incorporates six steps unique to the district involved, including:

1. Defining the desired end-of-the-year outcomes, based on the ELA Standards.
2. Determining a calendar of checkpoints during the year.
3. Designing formative assessments as progress-monitoring checks.
4. Facilitating structured data reflection sessions for teams to "tell their story."
5. Setting up collaboration sessions for teams to plan their responses (interventions) based on the data. Their responses are "agreements" they commit to implement prior to the next assessment. They measure the effects of those responses with the next assessment.
6. Establishing an administrative support/monitor plan (Avelar La Salle, 2014, p. 1).

Teams of teachers, either at each grade level or with a common course, create a Common Core Assessment Matrix that lays out a subset of standards they will address as units of instruction during that year. The units of instruction dictate the formative assessment calendar, indicating the cycle time during which students are assessed in common. Teachers are responsible for addressing all of the standards; the subset of targets forms the commonality that is measured during a particular timeframe. Teachers are encouraged to share lesson ideas, materials, and teaching and learning strategies for the units, and are encouraged to work collaboratively as much as possible across the year. Teachers are given blocks of time to design the five common units and their accompanying formative assessments with the support of the RTSI specialists. The maximum time for assessment across an academic year does not exceed 4 hours to allow more time for instruction. Typically, four Standards are assessed per unit to make time for including a short writing component. The assessment format mirrors the state assessments, so additional instruction time is not needed prior to state assessments for test prep. Following each common assessment, teachers meet for a Data Reflection session to determine students' gains and areas of need. The reflection is guided with RTSI protocols. The percentages of total students and subgroups of students (e.g., English learners, African Americans) demonstrating success in meeting the designated goals are added to a poster. This process helps teachers identify challenges for students and contributes to discussions of "next steps" and the selection of targets for the next unit of instruction by each team of teachers.

With the findings from the common formative assessments and the RTSI specialists' materials and support, the site leadership holds a structured open forum for reflecting on the school's achievement story and brainstorming next steps with the district staff. Through this process, leadership teams can more easily identify what the district "sweet spots" are and what happened to make them strengths in the districts. Conversely, the leadership teams can pinpoint the "hot spots" that need to be addressed to eliminate areas of weakness. The common assessments findings also aid guidance staff in the district's secondary schools to create an Early Warning Indicators Matrix for each grade. This matrix zeros in on what research and the district/school audit identifies as important metrics for college and career readiness. This information allows guidance staff to work closely with teachers and students in support of improved student achievement.

The RTSI model for districts and individual schools has demonstrated success in helping teachers provide instruction that addresses the ELA Standards in a coordinated fashion. Teachers and administrators at all levels are able to more knowledgeably interpret student achievement findings based on the common formative assessments, work collaboratively to address the identified student needs and strengths, and effectively communicate to all constituencies regarding student academic growth within the framework of the Common Core.

University Graduate Courses

During the summer of 2014, I (KMW) had the opportunity to test the innovative approach to learning and instruction advocated in this book. I taught two linked graduate courses at our university's Reading Center, one providing a practicum setting for the university students to put into action within 24 hours what they were learning during the lecture course. I decided to redesign the two courses from the format of previous years in order to pilot changes that incorporated the *New Shifts* introduced in Chapter 4: (1) integration of language and literacy with a linkage to the disciplines; (2) project-based learning that included original student productions or performances; (3) learning tasks that addressed multiple standards; (4) ongoing, embedded, authentic, formative assessment based on inquiry; and (5) technology integration. The primary goal of the courses was to support graduate students in establishing critical links between formative assessment, intervention, and student performance. Because the students enrolled in the courses were in the process of earning a K–12 Reading Specialist Endorsement, they would not only apply the Big Ideas to their work with students but also when working closely with teachers in their districts.

The layered design of the two courses included having each graduate student tutor a low-performing secondary reader, participate interactively in person and online in the lecture course, and provide individualized instructional coaching to a preservice undergraduate who was tutoring a struggling elementary grade reader in another course at the Reading Center. The classes met 4 days per week for lecture (4 hours/day), tutoring (1 hour/day), and coaching (1 hour/day) over a 5-week session—an intense experience for the graduate students. The practicum included close supervision, and the interactive lecture fostered collaboration among the graduate students. The layered design was ripe with opportunities for the formative process grounded in inquiry about student learning. The graduate students facilitated the children's project research in a self-selected topic and the creation of an authentic digital product to demonstrate their learning. The tutors wove their individualized literacy instruction into the reading and writing the children did with their projects.

The tutors based their literacy instruction on the formative evidence they continually gathered through observation and from the children's written work. The wide-ranging research topics chosen by the students included horror movie makeup, the process of securing a driver's license, roller-coasters around the world, bead-making from clay to the finished product, and lawnmowers. Definitely not typical teacher-chosen topics! The students' research process entailed such activities as reading a variety of hard copy and digital texts, locating and viewing videos on their tutor's iPads and laptops, completing graphic organizers to catalogue their findings and plan their presentations, writing scripts for videos and texts for books, learning new apps, and creating digital presentations with apps like *Glogster*, *Educreations*, *Tellagami*, *ebook Creator*, and the iPad video camera. Thus, the children's work regularly addressed multiple standards during each 1-hour tutoring session. The children proudly presented their learning to others with a combination of digitally generated and elaborated written texts, embedded photos/videos, and links to online websites. They knew that they had accomplished much with literacy in a short time. Even though they were assessed as performing one or more years below expectations in their literacy performance at the beginning of the summer session, they persevered in their project research with observable engagement. By the end of the 5-week session, the children showed remarkable growth across the summer session.

Guskey (2002) has posited that teachers are more likely to adopt new approaches to instruction after observing positive changes in student performance and when given support as they attempt implementation. The graduate students participating in this summer session demonstrated positive change in their pedagogical perspectives. They described how the summer graduate courses impacted their thinking as well as their plans for teaching in the coming academic year. One student, Jill (not her real name), described how the courses pushed her to thinking:

"At this point I was thinking a lot about my students and how this experience would change the way I talk to them about learning. Learning hurts. It strains you. It frustrates you. It makes you want to quit. But when it's got good purpose and when you can see the reward of it, like exercise, it makes you want to sacrifice for it. Or at least it makes you feel okay about sacrificing for it. It's a little heavy to think about how I will make learning purposeful and rewarding enough to ask them to endure that effort. . . .

"E. seemed to feel connected to the project; it was real to him because he likes mowing and spends a lot of time doing it. The reading, researching, writing, editing, and organizing he was doing was oftentimes self-directed. E. completed work at home that I hadn't asked him to do. At home he typed out paragraphs of what he wanted to say for when he'd be recording the ideas into the *Tellagami* app. He was timing how long it would take him to read certain sections and then breaking up the writing where necessary to fit into the app's 30-second time frames. E. would record himself and then determine where his mistakes were that he'd want to rework on a subsequent recording—all without my requests that he do so. In sum, he was owning the project. This project reminded me of the IRPA [Individual Research Project Activity] I used to do with my reading students. They got to choose a topic of interest, research it, and present what they learned in a PowerPoint (or similar) presentation to the class. Reading with a personal purpose and motivated by genuine interest appeared an effective way to practice reading and use strategies."

Leslie's experience with project-based learning, formative assessment, and learning to use new digital applications led her to share the following information:

"I feel that I now have an expansive toolbox for literacy instruction and dissecting the areas wherein students face challenges while reading. I also now look at classroom instruction differently by looking with a new perspective than I ever have before taking this class. For instance, I am really doubting the practice of having every student reading the same text in an English class. This now seems like such an archaic tradition. I definitely want to try incorporating student choice-centered literature circles into my American literature class this year. Unfortunately, I have a pretty limited supply of books, but, knowing what I know now about self-determination and motivation, I can make a good case for giving my students as much choice as possible. Additionally, after seeing J's incredibly high levels of engagement with this last project, I *know* that giving choice can change a student's entire attitude toward educational experiences.

"Additionally, my entire understanding of project-based learning has shifted. I used to think of incorporating projects by having students read a text and create something that represents some aspect of the text (think collage or diorama), and I always saw projects as fillers or less intense versions of tests. The ideas that I have accumulated throughout this course have really energized me for the upcoming year and for including projects into my curricula. Much like this course, I hope to have the project *be* the instruction. I intend on trying to incorporate a project where all of the reading and instruction will help guide the students to complete the independent work needed to complete a task or project. The platform I intend on incorporating first is the website *TouchCast* that Linda showed us. Overall, I think the project-based learning aspect to this course was great and really beneficial professionally."

Gabriella had the least amount of teaching experience—1 year. After the beginning of the new academic year, she wrote:

"The project-based learning gave me more incentive to focus on authentic assessment in the class. It has *drastically* cut down on the amount of daily homework tasks and asks them to work more creatively. For example, instead of asking students to read and answer a worksheet, I have gone over the geography information with them and then we use those theories we discovered through reading to create a world and cities. It will be a semester-long adventure and I am not sure how it is going to pan out, but instead of just having individual projects, they work individually, with partners and together to create a whole world as a class. It strives to give a balance to community–individual."

Linda is a doctoral student employed by a private education organization that works with high school and community college students primarily from high needs urban neighborhoods to prepare them to meet higher education requirements. In the fall she wrote about the impact of the summer experience on her work with teachers and students:

"The summer course and tutoring experience has impacted my planning and instructional implementation in several ways this year. First of all, in terms of feedback, I have been practicing the just-in-time coaching notes when I am in classrooms. The timely and specific feedback is much more meaningful and useful that way.

"The tutoring experience this summer pushed my thinking about how to implement project-based formative assessment and a project-based model for our high school students. Our mission is to ensure careers for students of hope and need through education and supportive relationships. What we have now developed are a series of student-centered projects that pave the way toward a career plan and an independent living plan. Because we've learned that transferrable job skills (communication, positive attitude, professionalism, responsibility, self-awareness) are areas of need, they form the basis of our formative assessment. We work with students on articulating what these skills look like, but student interest drives the projects. The five transferable skills provide the basis of our formative assessment structure. Students continually self-assess and receive feedback from staff in a consistent way, even though each student's short-term project and long-term plan look different.

"Finally, the academic individualization of assessment, planning, and tutoring for each student at the reading center is helping me advocate for a more individualized approach to developmental reading, writing, and math instruction at the community-college level. In this effort, the experience of *living it* this summer has been invaluable. Though we are not anywhere close yet to institutional change in this area, I am part of a leadership team that is in the early stages of proposing a new site and model for developmental education in [city's name]. This model includes an individualized approach as opposed to the one-size-fits-all sequence of courses. Also, the instructional model is project based with content driven by student interest and career relevance."

It is clear in each of the examples that when teachers are given support for beginning to implement the *New Shifts* advocated in this book, they not only quickly recognize the benefits for their students' learning and engagement, but also their need to adjust their conceptions of successful pedagogy. It is important to remember that the secondary students these teachers tutored were all struggling readers and writers with years of failure contributing to their self-conceptions as students. But, within an instructional context that applied the *New Shifts* their literacy achievement over the summer session was quite remarkable. They started as defeated readers and writers who composed little more than a sentence without much scaffolding, but left the summer sessions with products that they researched and wrote about in organized and detailed ways. We believe that what took place in the graduate school setting described above can be scaled up either through collaborations between K–12 school faculty and higher education or through collaborations between professional learning communities and specialists like literacy coaches, media specialists, and technology integration coaches. Teachers and coaches have several online resources that we will describe next to help them read about and view how others have successfully instituted the types of *New Shifts* changes that we call for.

RESOURCES

Teachers and schools who are intrigued by and see the sense of the ideas that we are recommending in this book have several excellent resources they can use when planning and implementing project-based learning to meet the full range of Common Core Standards for the English Language Arts and Literacy in History/Social Studies, Science and Technical Subjects. As we have shown above, project-based learning provides a context for authentic formative assessment to be used as the basis for ongoing inquiry into student learning. The following resources we suggest are a subset of possibilities that educators can access to read about and view teachers and students who are fully engaged in this alternative to traditional schooling. The Internet offers a wealth of websites to tap for useful information.

The Buck Institute

One source for information on how to implement and sustain project-based learning is the Buck Institute for Education (BIE). This nonprofit organization, based in Novato, California, is dedicated to fostering deeper learning for teachers and students through the implementation of project-based learning, their "highest priority so to help teachers prepare students for successful lives" (*http://bie.org/about*). The BIE espouses eight essential principles: (1) the projects that students conduct must have significant content; (2) students become proficient with 21st-century competencies through their project work; (3) the projects students embark on entail in-depth inquiry to enable them to answer the questions they pose; (4) students pose broad, driving questions that require multiple approaches to uncover answers; (5) the engaging processes and products of high-quality projects engender a "deep need to know" mentality in the students that supports their steadfastness in pursuing answers to their questions; (6) project-based learning is designed to give students choice in how to go about conducting their projects and develop their individual voices, based on their growing expertise in what they are learning; (7) students work in teams of critical friends from whom they receive feedback and suggestions upon which they can reflect and act on to revise their approach to the project at hand; and (8) public audiences for the projects' results are identified as the recipients of the fruits of the project, adding relevance to students' work and fostering students' consideration of how to frame their findings for particular audiences. Project-based learning, developed and researched by the BIE, addresses multiple ELA Common Core Standards and provides clear and long-standing alignment to the *New Shifts* discussed in this book.

Over the past 25 years, the BIE print materials, online resources, and professional development programs have spread internationally, attesting to its successful implementation in widely diverse settings. The BIE website offers visitors multiple project examples from elementary through high schools to demonstrate what classrooms and schools have accomplished through enacting the eight essential principles. Their well-designed website offers a wide range of resources for teachers and schools from videos, blogs, books, articles, research, planning guides, rubrics, curricula, archived webinars, interactive chats, conferences, and much more (*http://bie.org/resources*). For instance, a practical addition to the Buck Institute's book collection that schools will find helpful for establishing project-based learning in performance-based Common Core classrooms is *Setting the Standard for Project Based Learning: A Proven Approach to Rigorous Classroom Instruction* (Larmer, Mergendoller, & Boss, 2015). This website is well worth exploring to learn more about how to employ this instructional model to address the ELA Common Core Standards in very productive ways.

Edutopia

The George Lucas Educational Foundation created the comprehensive Edutopia website (*www.edutopia.org*) to be a resource and create an online community for educators, parents, and policymakers to access to increase "knowledge, sharing, and adoption of what works in K–12 education. We emphasize core strategies: project-based learning, comprehensive assessment, integrated studies, social and emotional learning, educational leadership and teacher development, and technology integration" (*www.edutopia.org/about*). For greater efficiency in searching for useful Web pages, teachers can choose to retrieve information focused on the primary grades, upper elementary, middle school, or high school. Other headings in drop-down menus include Core Strategies and Popular Topics, each with many choices available. Each linked subheading also indicates the number of resources presently available to readers. Project-based learning shows 1,112 entries, inquiry-based learning has 26 links, and the formative assessment subheading indicates 139 sources for information, just to name a few elements that fit the *New Shifts* for ELA Standards instruction.

For instance, educators can access *www.edutopia.org/blogs/tag/formative-assessment* to read and join in the discussions about ideas for incorporating formative assessment through the integration of technology into instruction in very creative ways. One article, "5 Fantastic, Fast, Formative Assessment Tools," featured was an entry by Vicki Davis (2015), a Georgia educator. It offers readers a narrative of her experiences with formative assessment through technology implementation accompanied by descriptions of useful apps teachers can try. Among the many choices found at the Edutopia website is a link to project-based learning Web pages where educators can read articles and blogs, view videos, read and take part in online discussions with teachers around the world, and access resources to promote deep learning through professional-based learning. Other Web pages are earmarked for the Common Core. Articles, blogs, videos, and other resources available at Edutopia provide an important and trustworthy venue for group and personal professional development for schools, reading specialists, and individual teachers.

The Teaching Channel

Teachers are invited to subscribe to broad topic areas on the free-access Teaching Channel. These include resources titled *Common Core, Deeper Learning,* and *Formative Assessment,* among many others. Viewers can watch short segments of teaching in action or groups of teachers discussing a variety of instructional and assessment applications. The videos and their accompanying commentary provide very accessible and clear modeling of the instruction, assessment, or professional development concepts featured within the main topic. Interested teachers are offered the option to join communities of other teachers matching their grade levels or areas of interest to have discussions on teaching, classroom management, assessment issues, and other issues that are either of concern to them or areas where they desire to deepen their pedagogical knowledge. Teachers can post questions for other Teaching Channel users to respond with suggestions. The website posts blogs from master teachers and blogs by the Teaching Channel teams.

I (KMW) have incorporated multiple Teaching Channel videos into my undergraduate and graduate teaching to great success. I have also had my graduate inservice teachers and undergraduate preservice teachers explore the website and choose pertinent videos that complement the "topic of discussion for the day" for which they are assigned. My students' enthusiasm for what they find and share in class is apparent in the lively discussions that naturally occur following the video viewings. Students have also stated that they independently end up watching more of the videos than they had planned to watch because placed below the video viewing window are links to additional videos on related topics. Extending the reach of the videos, the graduate students (class presenters for the day or the other class members) have shared them with fellow teachers at their schools. An advantage of the Teaching Channel videos is that they make abstract talk or readings real by enabling teachers to watch actual classroom applications. In most instances the teacher will point out why he or she believes the instructional approach works and highlight important aspects of his or her instructional choices that contribute to his or her students' high level of learning.

Expeditionary Learning

The final resource we want to highlight is Expeditionary Learning (*http://elschools.org*). The Expeditionary Learning organization partners with urban, suburban, and rural K–12 schools to provide professional development for teachers and administrators that enables schools to approach school improvement differently from what is commonly done. Since their establishment in 1992, they have developed a vibrant national network of Expeditionary Learning Schools that offer high-level learning for teachers and students. Their professional development is grounded in long-term learning projects of substance and relevance that fosters students in becoming self-motivated learners. Their model "challenges students to think critically and take active roles in their classrooms and communities. This results in higher achievement and greater engagement in school. Our schools give students the academic and character-building skills they need to reach their potential as learners and leaders" (*http://elschools.org/sites/default/files/Brochure_EL_2011.pdf*).

We found the detailed descriptions of student projects highlighted in their Center for Student Work (*http://elschools.org/csw*) to be particularly compelling examples of all students' potential to learn deeply and meet high expectations. Students show what they know in exciting ways. Like some of the other websites described previously, the Expeditionary Learning's website offers blogs for teachers, with entries written by experts such as Woodfin's "Would You Know Deeper Learning if You Saw It?" (2015), which also appeared as an *Education Week* blog, and Berger's article "What if Assessment Was Used to Elevate Learning Rather Than Rank Students" (Berger, 2015), which is also available on the Teaching Channel's TCHER'S VOICE.

One unique addition to the Experiential Learning website, not seen in other websites, is the Educator Resources link to Recommended Readings. This Web page offers visitors links to 23 categories of books to enrich teachers' and administrator's knowledge. Each book entry includes a link to the book's Amazon.com Web page for convenience, where readers can gain additional information about the book's content along with suggestions for other related books. Viewers may choose to order books of interest from Amazon, gather necessary information to purchase the book elsewhere, or seek access to it from university or public libraries. The categories range from 21st-century skills, to assessment to Inquiry, to project-based learning, to teaching and learning, just to name a few. All of these areas combine to provide guideposts for schools to make significant programmatic changes and provide teachers with the high-quality, multifaceted, and sustained professional development they are entitled to have in order to impact the learning of all students.

FINAL THOUGHTS

We believe the examples described above illustrate the changes from long-standing instructional traditions in U.S. schools that are necessary and possible for the vision described in the Introduction to the ELA Standards (NGA & CCSSO, pp. 3–8) to be realized. These *New Shifts* have already been adopted for ongoing instruction in public and private schools with diverse student bodies, and have been recognized broadly for their success. They are not pipedreams, but exciting realities that foster higher-order learning, excitement for attending school, motivation to learn, and engagement in worthwhile academic activities for *all* students from PreK through high school. These schools have decided to:

- Frame instruction around large, sustained project-based activities, PreK–12, that have been mapped backward by teachers from the *Research to Build and Present Knowledge* Anchor Standards of the Common Core to address the Standards, be developmentally appropriate, and communicate high, but achievable, expectations for their students.

- Create interactive classrooms, alive with the oral discourse that fosters creative thinking and learning that is enriched by the ideas of teachers and peers.
- Live in the Cloud, by integrating technology into schooling as an integral tool for teaching and learning and to be learned in its own right, thus preparing students for the flexibility in thinking needed as new technologies come on the scene and for full citizenship in the global society.
- Purposely plan and implement ongoing, embedded, and authentic formative assessments grounded in teacher inquiry about student academic progress toward achieving the goals of the Common Core.
- Help students make their thinking and learning visible by creating "information screens" all around for other students, teachers, parents, others, and themselves.

A PLAN OF ACTION

Clearly a large gap currently exists between the vision outlined here and present realities. And the stakes are very high indeed. If the nation's schools continue to be "factories" for the production of high test scores, tomorrow's graduates will be poorly prepared to meet tomorrow's challenges—even if they are designated as "college- and-career ready" based on year-end tests. The Assessment Consortia are explicit that the summative tests cover only a subset of the Standards, excluding those that require extensive time and resources, and that tap into the sustained projects called for by the *Research to Build and Present Knowledge* Anchor Standards cluster. They do not assess extended writing; they do not include the speaking/listening domains; selected-response multiple-choice items continue to be the primary activity. Those outcomes of the Standards that are most closely related to preparation for the future are not covered by the high-stakes summative tests. "What is tested (and what counts) is what will be taught"—this principle is likely to remain in full force.

What, if anything, can be done to change the present course of action? Here are several possibilities that build on local initiatives and widespread establishment of innovation.

- *For everyone:* Read the Standards! There is presently no common understanding of the Common Core State Standards. We hope that this book helps address this matter. We especially urge professional organizations, news organizations, and policymakers to do so—including the Introduction to the Standards. Readers may disagree with some or even many of the Standards, but closely reading all of the Standards may at least do something about the widespread double-talk that is so prevalent.

- *For schools, teachers, and professional organizations:* Initiate and defend the local teacher and school initiatives like the "bright spots" described earlier. Celebrate these accomplishments—but insist on transparency and generalizability.

- *For parents and concerned citizens:* Protest the tests. High-stakes accountability based on summative tests is a major barrier to the implementation of the Standards. Year-end tests can play a role in monitoring and comparing some educational outcomes, but are destructive when they become the goals of education, as is presently the case.

- *For leaders:* Beginning with the federal government and national "groups," take more responsibility for where you are leading the parade. The rapidly changing world our students will enter as adults will call for them to be innovative thinkers and creators with an entrepreneurial mind-set (Zhao, 2012). Support schools in their efforts to prepare students to be not only college and careerready, but also world ready to tackle future technological and social problems.

APPENDIX A

Common Core State Standards for English Language Arts and Literacy in History/Social Studies, Science, and Technical Subjects

Grades K–5

ENGLISH LANGUAGE ARTS STANDARDS FOR KINDERGARTEN

Reading: Literature » Kindergarten

Key Ideas and Details

- RL.K.1. With prompting and support, ask and answer questions about key details in a text.
- RL.K.2. With prompting and support, retell familiar stories, including key details.
- RL.K.3. With prompting and support, identify characters, settings, and major events in a story.

Craft and Structure

- RL.K.4. Ask and answer questions about unknown words in a text.
- RL.K.5. Recognize common types of texts (e.g., storybooks, poems).
- RL.K.6. With prompting and support, name the author and illustrator of a story and define the role of each in telling the story.

Integration of Knowledge and Ideas

- RL.K.7. With prompting and support, describe the relationship between illustrations and the story in which they appear (e.g., what moment in a story an illustration depicts).
- RL.K.8. (Not applicable to literature)
- RL.K.9. With prompting and support, compare and contrast the adventures and experiences of characters in familiar stories.

Range of Reading and Level of Text Complexity

- RL.K.10. Actively engage in group reading activities with purpose and understanding.

Reading: Informational Text » Kindergarten

Key Ideas and Details

- RI.K.1. With prompting and support, ask and answer questions about key details in a text.
- RI.K.2. With prompting and support, identify the main topic and retell key details of a text.
- RI.K.3. With prompting and support, describe the connection between two individuals, events, ideas, or pieces of information in a text.

Craft and Structure

- RI.K.4. With prompting and support, ask and answer questions about unknown words in a text.
- RI.K.5. Identify the front cover, back cover, and title page of a book.
- RI.K.6. Name the author and illustrator of a text and define the role of each in presenting the ideas or information in a text.

Integration of Knowledge and Ideas

- RI.K.7. With prompting and support, describe the relationship between illustrations and the text in which they appear (e.g., what person, place, thing, or idea in the text an illustration depicts).
- RI.K.8. With prompting and support, identify the reasons an author gives to support points in a text.
- RI.K.9. With prompting and support, identify basic similarities in and differences between two texts on the same topic (e.g., in illustrations, descriptions, or procedures).

Range of Reading and Level of Text Complexity

- RI.K.10. Actively engage in group reading activities with purpose and understanding.

Reading: Foundational Skills » Kindergarten

Print Concepts

- RF.K.1. Demonstrate understanding of the organization and basic features of print.
  - Follow words from left to right, top to bottom, and page by page.
  - Recognize that spoken words are represented in written language by specific sequences of letters.
  - Understand that words are separated by spaces in print.
  - Recognize and name all upper- and lowercase letters of the alphabet.

Phonological Awareness

- RF.K.2. Demonstrate understanding of spoken words, syllables, and sounds (phonemes).
  - Recognize and produce rhyming words.
  - Count, pronounce, blend, and segment syllables in spoken words.
  - Blend and segment onsets and rimes of single-syllable spoken words.
  - Isolate and pronounce the initial, medial vowel, and final sounds (phonemes) in three-phoneme (consonant–vowel–consonant, or CVC) words. (This does not include CVCs ending with /l/, /r/, or /x/.)
  - Add or substitute individual sounds (phonemes) in simple, one-syllable words to make new words.

Phonics and Word Recognition

- RF.K.3. Know and apply grade-level phonics and word analysis skills in decoding words.
  - Demonstrate basic knowledge of letter–sound correspondences by producing the primary or most frequent sound for each consonant.

- Associate the long and short sounds with the common spellings (graphemes) for the five major vowels.
- Read common high-frequency words by sight (e.g., *the, of, to, you, she, my, is, are, do, does*).
- Distinguish between similarly spelled words by identifying the sounds of the letters that differ.

Fluency

- RF.K.4. Read emergent-reader texts with purpose and understanding.

Writing » Kindergarten

Text Types and Purposes

- W.K.1. Use a combination of drawing, dictating, and writing to compose opinion pieces in which they tell a reader the topic or the name of the book they are writing about and state an opinion or preference about the topic or book (e.g., *My favorite book is . . .*).
- W.K.2. Use a combination of drawing, dictating, and writing to compose informative/explanatory texts in which they name what they are writing about and supply some information about the topic.
- W.K.3. Use a combination of drawing, dictating, and writing to narrate a single event or several loosely linked events, tell about the events in the order in which they occurred, and provide a reaction to what happened.

Production and Distribution of Writing

- W.K.4. (Begins in grade 3)
- W.K.5. With guidance and support from adults, respond to questions and suggestions from peers and add details to strengthen writing as needed.
- W.K.6. With guidance and support from adults, explore a variety of digital tools to produce and publish writing, including in collaboration with peers.

Research to Build and Present Knowledge

- W.K.7. Participate in shared research and writing projects (e.g., explore a number of books by a favorite author and express opinions about them).
- W.K.8. With guidance and support from adults, recall information from experiences or gather information from provided sources to answer a question.
- W.K.9. (Begins in grade 4)

Range of Writing

- W.K.10. (Begins in grade 3)

Speaking and Listening » Kindergarten

Comprehension and Collaboration

- SL.K.1. Participate in collaborative conversations with diverse partners about *kindergarten topics and texts* with peers and adults in small and larger groups.
  - Follow agreed-upon rules for discussions (e.g., listening to others and taking turns speaking about the topics and texts under discussion).
  - Continue a conversation through multiple exchanges.
- SL.K.2. Confirm understanding of a text read-aloud or information presented orally or through other media by asking and answering questions about key details and requesting clarification if something is not understood.
- SL.K.3. Ask and answer questions in order to seek help, get information, or clarify something that is not understood.

Presentation of Knowledge and Ideas

- SL.K.4. Describe familiar people, places, things, and events and, with prompting and support, provide additional detail.
- SL.K.5. Add drawings or other visual displays to descriptions as desired to provide additional detail.
- SL.K.6. Speak audibly and express thoughts, feelings, and ideas clearly.

Language » Kindergarten

Conventions of Standard English

- L.K.1. Demonstrate command of the conventions of standard English grammar and usage when writing or speaking.
  - Print many upper- and lowercase letters.
  - Use frequently occurring nouns and verbs.
  - Form regular plural nouns orally by adding /s/ or /es/ (e.g., *dog, dogs; wish, wishes*).
  - Understand and use question words (interrogatives) (e.g., *who, what, where, when, why, how*).
  - Use the most frequently occurring prepositions (e.g., *to, from, in, out, on, off, for, of, by, with*).
  - Produce and expand complete sentences in shared language activities.
- L.K.2. Demonstrate command of the conventions of standard English capitalization, punctuation, and spelling when writing.
  - Capitalize the first word in a sentence and the pronoun *I*.
  - Recognize and name end punctuation.
  - Write a letter or letters for most consonant and short-vowel sounds (phonemes).
  - Spell simple words phonetically, drawing on knowledge of sound–letter relationships.

Knowledge of Language

- L.K.3. (Begins in grade 2)

Vocabulary Acquisition and Use

- L.K.4. Determine or clarify the meaning of unknown and multiple-meaning words and phrases based on kindergarten reading and content.
  - Identify new meanings for familiar words and apply them accurately (e.g., knowing *duck* is a bird and learning the verb *to duck*).
  - Use the most frequently occurring inflections and affixes (e.g., *-ed, -s, re-, un-, pre-, -ful, -less*) as a clue to the meaning of an unknown word.
- L.K.5. With guidance and support from adults, explore word relationships and nuances in word meanings.
  - Sort common objects into categories (e.g., shapes, foods) to gain a sense of the concepts the categories represent.
  - Demonstrate understanding of frequently occurring verbs and adjectives by relating them to their opposites (antonyms).
  - Identify real-life connections between words and their use (e.g., note places at school that are colorful).
  - Distinguish shades of meaning among verbs describing the same general action (e.g., *walk, march, strut, prance*) by acting out the meanings.
- L.K.6. Use words and phrases acquired through conversations, reading and being read to, and responding to texts.

ENGLISH LANGUAGE ARTS STANDARDS FOR GRADE 1

Reading: Literature » Grade 1

Key Ideas and Details

- RL.1.1. Ask and answer questions about key details in a text.
- RL.1.2. Retell stories, including key details, and demonstrate understanding of their central message or lesson.
- RL.1.3. Describe characters, settings, and major events in a story, using key details.

Craft and Structure

- RL.1.4. Identify words and phrases in stories or poems that suggest feelings or appeal to the senses.
- RL.1.5. Explain major differences between books that tell stories and books that give information, drawing on a wide reading of a range of text types.
- RL.1.6. Identify who is telling the story at various points in a text.

Integration of Knowledge and Ideas

- RL.1.7. Use illustrations and details in a story to describe its characters, setting, or events.
- RL.1.8. (Not applicable to literature)
- RL.1.9. Compare and contrast the adventures and experiences of characters in stories.

Range of Reading and Level of Text Complexity

- RL.1.10. With prompting and support, read prose and poetry of appropriate complexity for grade 1.

Reading: Informational Text » Grade 1

Key Ideas and Details

- RI.1.1. Ask and answer questions about key details in a text.
- RI.1.2. Identify the main topic and retell key details of a text.
- RI.1.3. Describe the connection between two individuals, events, ideas, or pieces of information in a text.

Craft and Structure

- RI.1.4. Ask and answer questions to help determine or clarify the meaning of words and phrases in a text.
- RI.1.5. Know and use various text features (e.g., headings, tables of contents, glossaries, electronic menus, icons) to locate key facts or information in a text.
- RI.1.6. Distinguish between information provided by pictures or other illustrations and information provided by the words in a text.

Integration of Knowledge and Ideas

- RI.1.7. Use the illustrations and details in a text to describe its key ideas.
- RI.1.8. Identify the reasons an author gives to support points in a text.
- RI.1.9. Identify basic similarities in and differences between two texts on the same topic (e.g., in illustrations, descriptions, or procedures).

Range of Reading and Level of Text Complexity

- RI.1.10. With prompting and support, read informational texts appropriately complex for grade 1.

Reading: Foundational Skills » Grade 1

Print Concepts

- RF.1.1. Demonstrate understanding of the organization and basic features of print.
  - Recognize the distinguishing features of a sentence (e.g., first word, capitalization, ending punctuation).

Phonological Awareness

- RF.1.2. Demonstrate understanding of spoken words, syllables, and sounds (phonemes).
  - Distinguish long from short vowel sounds in spoken single-syllable words.
  - Orally produce single-syllable words by blending sounds (phonemes), including consonant blends.
  - Isolate and pronounce initial, medial vowel, and final sounds (phonemes) in spoken single-syllable words.
  - Segment spoken single-syllable words into their complete sequence of individual sounds (phonemes).

Phonics and Word Recognition

- RF.1.3. Know and apply grade-level phonics and word analysis skills in decoding words.
  - Know the spelling–sound correspondences for common consonant digraphs (two letters that represent one sound).
  - Decode regularly spelled one-syllable words.
  - Know final -e and common vowel team conventions for representing long vowel sounds.
  - Use knowledge that every syllable must have a vowel sound to determine the number of syllables in a printed word.
  - Decode two-syllable words following basic patterns by breaking the words into syllables.
  - Read words with inflectional endings.
  - Recognize and read grade-appropriate irregularly spelled words.

Fluency

- RF.1.4. Read with sufficient accuracy and fluency to support comprehension.
  - Read grade-level text with purpose and understanding.
  - Read grade-level text orally with accuracy, appropriate rate, and expression.
  - Use context to confirm or self-correct word recognition and understanding, rereading as necessary.

Writing » Grade 1

Text Types and Purposes

- W.1.1. Write opinion pieces in which they introduce the topic or name the book they are writing about, state an opinion, supply a reason for the opinion, and provide some sense of closure.
- W.1.2. Write informative/explanatory texts in which they name a topic, supply some facts about the topic, and provide some sense of closure.
- W.1.3. Write narratives in which they recount two or more appropriately sequenced events, include some details regarding what happened, use temporal words to signal event order, and provide some sense of closure.

Production and Distribution of Writing

- W.1.4. (Begins in grade 3)
- W.1.5. With guidance and support from adults, focus on a topic, respond to questions and suggestions from peers, and add details to strengthen writing as needed.

- W.1.6. With guidance and support from adults, use a variety of digital tools to produce and publish writing, including in collaboration with peers.

Research to Build and Present Knowledge

- W.1.7. Participate in shared research and writing projects (e.g., explore a number of "how-to" books on a given topic and use them to write a sequence of instructions).
- W.1.8. With guidance and support from adults, recall information from experiences or gather information from provided sources to answer a question.
- W.1.9. (Begins in grade 4)

Range of Writing

- W.1.10. (Begins in grade 3)

Speaking and Listening » Grade 1

Comprehension and Collaboration

- SL.1.1. Participate in collaborative conversations with diverse partners about *grade-1 topics and texts* with peers and adults in small and larger groups.
  - Follow agreed-upon rules for discussions (e.g., listening to others with care, speaking one at a time about the topics and texts under discussion).
  - Build on others' talk in conversations by responding to the comments of others through multiple exchanges.
  - Ask questions to clear up any confusion about the topics and texts under discussion.
- SL.1.2. Ask and answer questions about key details in a text read aloud or information presented orally or through other media.
- SL.1.3. Ask and answer questions about what a speaker says in order to gather additional information or clarify something that is not understood.

Presentation of Knowledge and Ideas

- SL.1.4. Describe people, places, things, and events with relevant details, expressing ideas and feelings clearly.
- SL.1.5. Add drawings or other visual displays to descriptions when appropriate to clarify ideas, thoughts, and feelings.
- SL.1.6. Produce complete sentences when appropriate to task and situation.

Language » Grade 1

Conventions of Standard English

- L.1.1. Demonstrate command of the conventions of standard English grammar and usage when writing or speaking.
  - Print all upper- and lowercase letters.
  - Use common, proper, and possessive nouns.
  - Use singular and plural nouns with matching verbs in basic sentences (e.g., *He hops; We hop*).
  - Use personal, possessive, and indefinite pronouns (e.g., *I, me, my; they, them, their, anyone, everything*).
  - Use verbs to convey a sense of past, present, and future (e.g., *Yesterday I walked home; Today I walk home; Tomorrow I will walk home*).
  - Use frequently occurring adjectives.
  - Use frequently occurring conjunctions (e.g., *and, but, or, so, because*).
  - Use determiners (e.g., articles, demonstratives).
  - Use frequently occurring prepositions (e.g., *during, beyond, toward*).
  - Produce and expand complete simple and compound declarative, interrogative, imperative, and exclamatory sentences in response to prompts.

- L.1.2. Demonstrate command of the conventions of standard English capitalization, punctuation, and spelling when writing.
  - Capitalize dates and names of people.
  - Use end punctuation for sentences.
  - Use commas in dates and to separate single words in a series.
  - Use conventional spelling for words with common spelling patterns and for frequently occurring irregular words.
  - Spell untaught words phonetically, drawing on phonemic awareness and spelling conventions.

Knowledge of Language
- L.1.3. (Begins in grade 2)

Vocabulary Acquisition and Use
- L.1.4. Determine or clarify the meaning of unknown and multiple-meaning words and phrases based on *grade-1 reading and content*, choosing flexibly from an array of strategies.
  - Use sentence-level context as a clue to the meaning of a word or phrase.
  - Use frequently occurring affixes as a clue to the meaning of a word.
  - Identify frequently occurring root words (e.g., *look*) and their inflectional forms (e.g., *looks, looked, looking*).
- L.1.5. With guidance and support from adults, demonstrate understanding of figurative language, word relationships, and nuances in word meanings.
  - Sort words into categories (e.g., colors, clothing) to gain a sense of the concepts the categories represent.
  - Define words by category and by one or more key attributes (e.g., a *duck* is a bird that swims; a *tiger* is a large cat with stripes).
  - Identify real-life connections between words and their use (e.g., note places at home that are *cozy*).
  - Distinguish shades of meaning among verbs differing in manner (e.g., *look, peek, glance, stare, glare, scowl*) and adjectives differing in intensity (e.g., *large, gigantic*) by defining or choosing them or by acting out the meanings.
- L.1.6. Use words and phrases acquired through conversations, reading and being read to, and responding to texts, including using frequently occurring conjunctions to signal simple relationships (e.g., *because*).

ENGLISH LANGUAGE ARTS STANDARDS FOR GRADE 2

Reading: Literature » Grade 2

Key Ideas and Details
- RL.2.1. Ask and answer such questions as *who, what, where, when, why,* and *how* to demonstrate understanding of key details in a text.
- RL.2.2. Recount stories, including fables and folktales from diverse cultures, and determine their central message, lesson, or moral.
- RL.2.3. Describe how characters in a story respond to major events and challenges.

Craft and Structure
- RL.2.4. Describe how words and phrases (e.g., regular beats, alliteration, rhymes, repeated lines) supply rhythm and meaning in a story, poem, or song.
- RL.2.5. Describe the overall structure of a story, including describing how the beginning introduces the story and the ending concludes the action.
- RL.2.6. Acknowledge differences in the points of view of characters, including by speaking in a different voice for each character when reading dialogue aloud.

Integration of Knowledge and Ideas
- RL.2.7. Use information gained from the illustrations and words in a print or digital text to demonstrate understanding of its characters, setting, or plot.
- RL.2.8. (Not applicable to literature)
- RL.2.9. Compare and contrast two or more versions of the same story (e.g., Cinderella stories) by different authors or from different cultures.

Range of Reading and Level of Text Complexity
- RL.2.10. By the end of the year, read and comprehend literature, including stories and poetry, in the grades 2–3 text complexity band proficiently, with scaffolding as needed at the high end of the range.

Reading: Informational Text » Grade 2
Key Ideas and Details
- RI.2.1. Ask and answer such questions as *who, what, where, when, why*, and *how* to demonstrate understanding of key details in a text.
- RI.2.2. Identify the main topic of a multiparagraph text as well as the focus of specific paragraphs within the text.
- RI.2.3. Describe the connection between a series of historical events, scientific ideas or concepts, or steps in technical procedures in a text.

Craft and Structure
- RI.2.4. Determine the meaning of words and phrases in a text relevant to a *grade-2 topic or subject area.*
- RI.2.5. Know and use various text features (e.g., captions, bold print, subheadings, glossaries, indexes, electronic menus, icons) to locate key facts or information in a text efficiently.
- RI.2.6. Identify the main purpose of a text, including what the author wants to answer, explain, or describe.

Integration of Knowledge and Ideas
- RI.2.7. Explain how specific images (e.g., a diagram showing how a machine works) contribute to and clarify a text.
- RI.2.8. Describe how reasons support specific points the author makes in a text.
- RI.2.9. Compare and contrast the most important points presented by two texts on the same topic.

Range of Reading and Level of Text Complexity
- RI.2.10. By the end of year, read and comprehend informational texts, including history/social studies, science, and technical texts, in the grades 2–3 text complexity band proficiently, with scaffolding as needed at the high end of the range.

Reading: Foundational Skills » Grade 2
Phonics and Word Recognition
- RF.2.3. Know and apply grade-level phonics and word analysis skills in decoding words.
  - Distinguish long and short vowels when reading regularly spelled one-syllable words.
  - Know spelling–sound correspondences for additional common vowel teams.
  - Decode regularly spelled two-syllable words with long vowels.
  - Decode words with common prefixes and suffixes.
  - Identify words with inconsistent but common spelling–sound correspondences.
  - Recognize and read grade-appropriate irregularly spelled words.

Fluency

- RF.2.4. Read with sufficient accuracy and fluency to support comprehension.
  - Read grade-level text with purpose and understanding.
  - Read grade-level text orally with accuracy, appropriate rate, and expression.
  - Use context to confirm or self-correct word recognition and understanding, reread-
    ing as necessary.

Writing » Grade 2

Text Types and Purposes

- W.2.1. Write opinion pieces in which they introduce the topic or book they are writing
  about, state an opinion, supply reasons that support the opinion, use linking words
  (e.g., *because, and, also*) to connect opinion and reasons, and provide a concluding
  statement or section.
- W.2.2. Write informative/explanatory texts in which they introduce a topic, use facts
  and definitions to develop points, and provide a concluding statement or section.
- W.2.3. Write narratives in which they recount a well-elaborated event or short
  sequence of events, include details to describe actions, thoughts, and feelings, use temporal words to signal event order, and provide a sense of closure.

Production and Distribution of Writing

- W.2.4. (Begins in grade 3)
- W.2.5. With guidance and support from adults and peers, focus on a topic and
  strengthen writing as needed by revising and editing.
- W.2.6. With guidance and support from adults, use a variety of digital tools to produce
  and publish writing, including in collaboration with peers.

Research to Build and Present Knowledge

- W.2.7. Participate in shared research and writing projects (e.g., read a number of books
  on a single topic to produce a report; record science observations).
- W.2.8. Recall information from experiences or gather information from provided
  sources to answer a question.
- W.2.9. (Begins in grade 4)

Range of Writing

- W.2.10. (Begins in grade 3)

Speaking and Listening » Grade 2

Comprehension and Collaboration

- SL.2.1. Participate in collaborative conversations with diverse partners about *grade-2
  topics and texts* with peers and adults in small and larger groups.
  - Follow agreed-upon rules for discussions (e.g., gaining the floor in respectful ways,
    listening to others with care, speaking one at a time about the topics and texts under
    discussion).
  - Build on others' talk in conversations by linking their comments to the remarks of
    others.
  - Ask for clarification and further explanation as needed about the topics and texts
    under discussion.
- SL.2.2. Recount or describe key ideas or details from a text read aloud or information
  presented orally or through other media.
- SL.2.3. Ask and answer questions about what a speaker says in order to clarify com-
  prehension, gather additional information, or deepen understanding of a topic or
  issue.

Presentation of Knowledge and Ideas
- SL.2.4. Tell a story or recount an experience with appropriate facts and relevant, descriptive details, speaking audibly in coherent sentences.
- SL.2.5. Create audio recordings of stories or poems; add drawings or other visual displays to stories or recounts of experiences when appropriate to clarify ideas, thoughts, and feelings.
- SL.2.6. Produce complete sentences when appropriate to task and situation in order to provide requested detail or clarification.

Language » Grade 2

Conventions of Standard English
- L.2.1. Demonstrate command of the conventions of standard English grammar and usage when writing or speaking.
  - Use collective nouns (e.g., *group*).
  - Form and use frequently occurring irregular plural nouns (e.g., *feet, children, teeth, mice, fish*).
  - Use reflexive pronouns (e.g., *myself, ourselves*).
  - Form and use the past tense of frequently occurring irregular verbs (e.g., *sat, hid, told*).
  - Use adjectives and adverbs, and choose between them depending on what is to be modified.
  - Produce, expand, and rearrange complete simple and compound sentences (e.g., *The boy watched the movie; The little boy watched the movie; The action movie was watched by the little boy*).
- L.2.2. Demonstrate command of the conventions of standard English capitalization, punctuation, and spelling when writing.
  - Capitalize holidays, product names, and geographic names.
  - Use commas in greetings and closings of letters.
  - Use an apostrophe to form contractions and frequently occurring possessives.
  - Generalize learned spelling patterns when writing words (e.g., *cage* → *badge*; *boy* → *boil*).
  - Consult reference materials, including beginning dictionaries, as needed to check and correct spellings.

Knowledge of Language
- L.2.3. Use knowledge of language and its conventions when writing, speaking, reading, or listening.
  - Compare formal and informal uses of English.

Vocabulary Acquisition and Use
- L.2.4. Determine or clarify the meaning of unknown and multiple-meaning words and phrases based on grade-2 reading and content, choosing flexibly from an array of strategies.
  - Use sentence-level context as a clue to the meaning of a word or phrase.
  - Determine the meaning of the new word formed when a known prefix is added to a known word (e.g., *happy/unhappy, tell/retell*).
  - Use a known root word as a clue to the meaning of an unknown word with the same root (e.g., *addition, additional*).
  - Use knowledge of the meaning of individual words to predict the meaning of compound words (e.g., *birdhouse, lighthouse, housefly; bookshelf, notebook, bookmark*).
  - Use glossaries and beginning dictionaries, both print and digital, to determine or clarify the meaning of words and phrases.

- L.2.5. Demonstrate understanding of figurative language, word relationships, and nuances in word meanings.
  - Identify real-life connections between words and their use (e.g., *describe foods that are spicy or juicy*).
  - Distinguish shades of meaning among closely related verbs (e.g., *toss, throw, hurl*) and closely related adjectives (e.g., *thin, slender, skinny, scrawny*).
- L.2.6. Use words and phrases acquired through conversations, reading and being read to, and responding to texts, including using adjectives and adverbs to describe (e.g., *When other kids are happy that makes me happy*).

ENGLISH LANGUAGE ARTS STANDARDS FOR GRADE 3

Reading: Literature » Grade 3

Key Ideas and Details

- RL.3.1. Ask and answer questions to demonstrate understanding of a text, referring explicitly to the text as the basis for the answers.
- RL.3.2. Recount stories, including fables, folktales, and myths from diverse cultures; determine the central message, lesson, or moral and explain how it is conveyed through key details in the text.
- RL.3.3. Describe characters in a story (e.g., their traits, motivations, or feelings) and explain how their actions contribute to the sequence of events.

Craft and Structure

- RL.3.4. Determine the meaning of words and phrases as they are used in a text, distinguishing literal from nonliteral language.
- RL.3.5. Refer to parts of stories, dramas, and poems when writing or speaking about a text, using terms such as chapter, scene, and stanza; describe how each successive part builds on earlier sections.
- RL.3.6. Distinguish their own point of view from that of the narrator or those of the characters.

Integration of Knowledge and Ideas

- RL.3.7. Explain how specific aspects of a text's illustrations contribute to what is conveyed by the words in a story (e.g., create mood, emphasize aspects of a character or setting).
- RL.3.8. (Not applicable to literature)
- RL.3.9. Compare and contrast the themes, settings, and plots of stories written by the same author about the same or similar characters (e.g., in books from a series).

Range of Reading and Complexity of Text

- RL.3.10. By the end of the year, read and comprehend literature, including stories, dramas, and poetry, at the high end of the grades 2–3 text complexity band independently and proficiently.

Reading: Informational Text » Grade 3

Key Ideas and Details

- RI.3.1. Ask and answer questions to demonstrate understanding of a text, referring explicitly to the text as the basis for the answers.
- RI.3.2. Determine the main idea of a text; recount the key details and explain how they support the main idea.
- RI.3.3. Describe the relationship between a series of historical events, scientific ideas or concepts, or steps in technical procedures in a text, using language that pertains to time, sequence, and cause/effect.

Craft and Structure
- RI.3.4. Determine the meaning of general academic and domain-specific words and phrases in a text relevant to a *grade-3 topic or subject area.*
- RI.3.5. Use text features and search tools (e.g., key words, sidebars, hyperlinks) to locate information relevant to a given topic efficiently.
- RI.3.6. Distinguish their own point of view from that of the author of a text.

Integration of Knowledge and Ideas
- RI.3.7. Use information gained from illustrations (e.g., maps, photographs) and the words in a text to demonstrate understanding of the text (e.g., where, when, why, and how key events occur).
- RI.3.8. Describe the logical connection between particular sentences and paragraphs in a text (e.g., comparison, cause/effect, first/second/third in a sequence).
- RI.3.9. Compare and contrast the most important points and key details presented in two texts on the same topic.

Range of Reading and Level of Text Complexity
- RI.3.10. By the end of the year, read and comprehend informational texts, including history/social studies, science, and technical texts, at the high end of the grades 2–3 text complexity band independently and proficiently.

Reading: Foundational Skills » Grade 3

Phonics and Word Recognition
- RF.3.3. Know and apply grade-level phonics and word analysis skills in decoding words.
  - Identify and know the meaning of the most common prefixes and derivational suffixes.
  - Decode words with common Latin suffixes.
  - Decode multisyllable words.
  - Read grade-appropriate irregularly spelled words.

Fluency
- RF.3.4. Read with sufficient accuracy and fluency to support comprehension.
  - Read grade-level text with purpose and understanding.
  - Read grade-level prose and poetry orally with accuracy, appropriate rate, and expression.
  - Use context to confirm or self-correct word recognition and understanding, rereading as necessary.

Writing » Grade 3

Text Types and Purposes
- W.3.1. Write opinion pieces on topics or texts, supporting a point of view with reasons.
  - Introduce the topic or text they are writing about, state an opinion, and create an organizational structure that lists reasons.
  - Provide reasons that support the opinion.
  - Use linking words and phrases (e.g., *because, therefore, since, for example*) to connect opinion and reasons.
  - Provide a concluding statement or section.
- W.3.2. Write informative/explanatory texts to examine a topic and convey ideas and information clearly.
  - Introduce a topic and group-related information together; include illustrations when useful to aiding comprehension.
  - Develop the topic with facts, definitions, and details.

- Use linking words and phrases (e.g., *also, another, and, more, but*) to connect ideas within categories of information.
- Provide a concluding statement or section.
- W.3.3. Write narratives to develop real or imagined experiences or events using effective technique, descriptive details, and clear event sequences.
  - Establish a situation and introduce a narrator and/or characters; organize an event sequence that unfolds naturally.
  - Use dialogue and descriptions of actions, thoughts, and feelings to develop experiences and events or show the response of characters to situations.
  - Use temporal words and phrases to signal event order.
  - Provide a sense of closure.

Production and Distribution of Writing

- W.3.4. With guidance and support from adults, produce writing in which the development and organization are appropriate to task and purpose. (Grade-specific expectations for writing types are defined in standards 1–3 above.)
- W.3.5. With guidance and support from peers and adults, develop and strengthen writing as needed by planning, revising, and editing.
- W.3.6. With guidance and support from adults, use technology to produce and publish writing (using keyboarding skills) as well as to interact and collaborate with others.

Research to Build and Present Knowledge

- W.3.7. Conduct short research projects that build knowledge about a topic.
- W.3.8. Recall information from experiences or gather information from print and digital sources; take brief notes on sources and sort evidence into provided categories.
- W.3.9. (Begins in grade 4)

Range of Writing

- W.3.10. Write routinely over extended time frames (time for research, reflection, and revision) and shorter time frames (a single sitting or a day or two) for a range of discipline-specific tasks, purposes, and audiences.

Speaking and Listening » Grade 3

Comprehension and Collaboration

- SL.3.1. Engage effectively in a range of collaborative discussions (one-on-one, in groups, and teacher-led) with diverse partners on *grade-3 topics and texts*, building on others' ideas and expressing their own clearly.
  - Come to discussions prepared, having read or studied required material; explicitly draw on that preparation and other information known about the topic to explore ideas under discussion.
  - Follow agreed-upon rules for discussions (e.g., gaining the floor in respectful ways, listening to others with care, speaking one at a time about the topics and texts under discussion).
  - Ask questions to check understanding of information presented, stay on topic, and link their comments to the remarks of others.
  - Explain their own ideas and understanding in light of the discussion.
- SL.3.2. Determine the main ideas and supporting details of a text read aloud or information presented in diverse media and formats, including visually, quantitatively, and orally.
- SL.3.3. Ask and answer questions about information from a speaker, offering appropriate elaboration and detail.

Presentation of Knowledge and Ideas

- SL.3.4. Report on a topic or text, tell a story, or recount an experience with appropriate facts and relevant, descriptive details, speaking clearly at an understandable pace.

- SL.3.5. Create engaging audio recordings of stories or poems that demonstrate fluid reading at an understandable pace; add visual displays when appropriate to emphasize or enhance certain facts or details.
- SL.3.6. Speak in complete sentences when appropriate to task and situation in order to provide requested detail or clarification.

Language » Grade 3

Conventions of Standard English

- L.3.1. Demonstrate command of the conventions of standard English grammar and usage when writing or speaking.
  - Explain the function of nouns, pronouns, verbs, adjectives, and adverbs in general and their functions in particular sentences.
  - Form and use regular and irregular plural nouns.
  - Use abstract nouns (e.g., *childhood*).
  - Form and use regular and irregular verbs.
  - Form and use the simple (e.g., *I walked*; *I walk*; *I will walk*) verb tenses.
  - Ensure subject–verb and pronoun–antecedent agreement.
  - Form and use comparative and superlative adjectives and adverbs, and choose between them depending on what is to be modified.
  - Use coordinating and subordinating conjunctions.
  - Produce simple, compound, and complex sentences.
- L.3.2. Demonstrate command of the conventions of standard English capitalization, punctuation, and spelling when writing.
  - Capitalize appropriate words in titles.
  - Use commas in addresses.
  - Use commas and quotation marks in dialogue.
  - Form and use possessives.
  - Use conventional spelling for high-frequency and other studied words and for adding suffixes to base words (e.g., *sitting, smiled, cries, happiness*).
  - Use spelling patterns and generalizations (e.g., *word families, position-based spellings, syllable patterns, ending rules, meaningful word parts*) in writing words.
  - Consult reference materials, including beginning dictionaries, as needed to check and correct spellings.

Knowledge of Language

- L.3.3. Use knowledge of language and its conventions when writing, speaking, reading, or listening.
  - Choose words and phrases for effect.
  - Recognize and observe differences between the conventions of spoken and written standard English.

Vocabulary Acquisition and Use

- L.3.4. Determine or clarify the meaning of unknown and multiple-meaning words and phrases based on *grade-3 reading and content*, choosing flexibly from a range of strategies.
  - Use sentence-level context as a clue to the meaning of a word or phrase.
  - Determine the meaning of the new word formed when a known affix is added to a known word (e.g., *agreeable/disagreeable, comfortable/uncomfortable, care/careless, heat/preheat*).
  - Use a known root word as a clue to the meaning of an unknown word with the same root (e.g., *company, companion*).
  - Use glossaries or beginning dictionaries, both print and digital, to determine or clarify the precise meaning of key words and phrases.
- L.3.5. Demonstrate understanding of figurative language, word relationships, and nuances in word meanings.

- Distinguish the literal and nonliteral meanings of words and phrases in context (e.g., *take steps*).
- Identify real-life connections between words and their use (e.g., describe people who are *friendly* or *helpful*).
- Distinguish shades of meaning among related words that describe states of mind or degrees of certainty (e.g., *knew, believed, suspected, heard, wondered*).
- L.3.6. Acquire and use accurately grade-appropriate conversational, general academic, and domain-specific words and phrases, including those that signal spatial and temporal relationships (e.g., *After dinner that night we went looking for them*).

ENGLISH LANGUAGE ARTS STANDARDS FOR GRADE 4

Reading: Literature » Grade 4

Key Ideas and Details

- RL.4.1. Refer to details and examples in a text when explaining what the text says explicitly and when drawing inferences from the text.
- RL.4.2. Determine a theme of a story, drama, or poem from details in the text; summarize the text.
- RL.4.3. Describe in depth a character, setting, or event in a story or drama, drawing on specific details in the text (e.g., a character's thoughts, words, or actions).

Craft and Structure

- RL.4.4. Determine the meaning of words and phrases as they are used in a text, including those that allude to significant characters found in mythology (e.g., *Herculean*).
- RL.4.5. Explain major differences between poems, drama, and prose, and refer to the structural elements of poems (e.g., verse, rhythm, meter) and drama (e.g., casts of characters, settings, descriptions, dialogue, stage directions) when writing or speaking about a text.
- RL.4.6. Compare and contrast the point of view from which different stories are narrated, including the difference between first- and third-person narrations.

Integration of Knowledge and Ideas

- RL.4.7. Make connections between the text of a story or drama and a visual or oral presentation of the text, identifying where each version reflects specific descriptions and directions in the text.
- RL.4.8. (Not applicable to literature)
- RL.4.9. Compare and contrast the treatment of similar themes and topics (e.g., opposition of good and evil) and patterns of events (e.g., the quest) in stories, myths, and traditional literature from different cultures.

Range of Reading and Complexity of Text

- RL.4.10. By the end of the year, read and comprehend literature, including stories, dramas, and poetry, in the grades 4–5 text complexity band proficiently, with scaffolding as needed at the high end of the range.

Reading: Informational Text » Grade 4

Key Ideas and Details

- RI.4.1. Refer to details and examples in a text when explaining what the text says explicitly and when drawing inferences from the text.
- RI.4.2. Determine the main idea of a text and explain how it is supported by key details; summarize the text.
- RI.4.3. Explain events, procedures, ideas, or concepts in a historical, scientific, or technical text, including what happened and why, based on specific information in the text.

Craft and Structure
- RI.4.4. Determine the meaning of general academic and domain-specific words or phrases in a text relevant to a *grade-4 topic or subject area.*
- RI.4.5. Describe the overall structure (e.g., chronology, comparison, cause/effect, problem/solution) of events, ideas, concepts, or information in a text or part of a text.
- RI.4.6. Compare and contrast a firsthand and secondhand account of the same event or topic; describe the differences in focus and the information provided.

Integration of Knowledge and Ideas
- RI.4.7. Interpret information presented visually, orally, or quantitatively (e.g., in charts, graphs, diagrams, timelines, animations, or interactive elements on Web pages) and explain how the information contributes to an understanding of the text in which it appears.
- RI.4.8. Explain how an author uses reasons and evidence to support particular points in a text.
- RI.4.9. Integrate information from two texts on the same topic in order to write or speak about the subject knowledgeably.

Range of Reading and Level of Text Complexity
- RI.4.10. By the end of year, read and comprehend informational texts, including history/social studies, science, and technical texts, in the grades 4–5 text complexity band proficiently, with scaffolding as needed at the high end of the range.

Reading: Foundational Skills » Grade 4
Phonics and Word Recognition
- RF.4.3. Know and apply grade-level phonics and word analysis skills in decoding words.
  - Use combined knowledge of all letter–sound correspondences, syllabication patterns, and morphology (e.g., roots and affixes) to read accurately unfamiliar multisyllabic words in context and out of context.

Fluency
- RF.4.4. Read with sufficient accuracy and fluency to support comprehension.
  - Read grade-level text with purpose and understanding.
  - Read grade-level prose and poetry orally with accuracy, appropriate rate, and expression.
  - Use context to confirm or self-correct word recognition and understanding, rereading as necessary.

Writing » Grade 4
Text Types and Purposes
- W.4.1. Write opinion pieces on topics or texts, supporting a point of view with reasons and information.
  - Introduce a topic or text clearly, state an opinion, and create an organizational structure in which related ideas are grouped to support the writer's purpose.
  - Provide reasons that are supported by facts and details.
  - Link opinion and reasons using words and phrases (e.g., *for instance, in order to, in addition*).
  - Provide a concluding statement or section related to the opinion presented.
- W.4.2. Write informative/explanatory texts to examine a topic and convey ideas and information clearly.
  - Introduce a topic clearly and group related information in paragraphs and sections; include formatting (e.g., headings), illustrations, and multimedia when useful to aiding comprehension.

- Develop the topic with facts, definitions, concrete details, quotations, or other information and examples related to the topic.
- Link ideas within categories of information using words and phrases (e.g., *another, for example, also, because*).
- Use precise language and domain-specific vocabulary to inform about or explain the topic.
- Provide a concluding statement or section related to the information or explanation presented.

- W.4.3. Write narratives to develop real or imagined experiences or events using effective technique, descriptive details, and clear event sequences.
  - Orient the reader by establishing a situation and introducing a narrator and/or characters; organize an event sequence that unfolds naturally.
  - Use dialogue and description to develop experiences and events or show the responses of characters to situations.
  - Use a variety of transitional words and phrases to manage the sequence of events.
  - Use concrete words and phrases and sensory details to convey experiences and events precisely.
  - Provide a conclusion that follows from the narrated experiences or events.

Production and Distribution of Writing

- W.4.4. Produce clear and coherent writing in which the development and organization are appropriate to task, purpose, and audience. (Grade-specific expectations for writing types are defined in standards 1–3 above.)
- W.4.5. With guidance and support from peers and adults, develop and strengthen writing as needed by planning, revising, and editing.
- W.4.6. With some guidance and support from adults, use technology, including the Internet, to produce and publish writing as well as to interact and collaborate with others; demonstrate sufficient command of keyboarding skills to type a minimum of one page in a single sitting.

Research to Build and Present Knowledge

- W.4.7. Conduct short research projects that build knowledge through investigation of different aspects of a topic.
- W.4.8. Recall relevant information from experiences or gather relevant information from print and digital sources; take notes and categorize information, and provide a list of sources.
- W.4.9. Draw evidence from literary or informational texts to support analysis, reflection, and research.
  - Apply *grade-4 Reading standards* to literature (e.g., "Describe in depth a character, setting, or event in a story or drama, drawing on specific details in the text [e.g., a character's thoughts, words, or actions]").
  - Apply *grade-4 Reading standards* to informational texts (e.g., "Explain how an author uses reasons and evidence to support particular points in a text").

Range of Writing

- W.4.10. Write routinely over extended time frames (time for research, reflection, and revision) and shorter time frames (a single sitting or a day or two) for a range of discipline-specific tasks, purposes, and audiences.

Speaking and Listening » Grade 4

Comprehension and Collaboration

- SL.4.1. Engage effectively in a range of collaborative discussions (one-on-one, in groups, and teacher-led) with diverse partners on *grade-4 topics and texts*, building on others' ideas and expressing their own clearly.
  - Come to discussions prepared, having read or studied required material; explicitly draw on that preparation and other information known about the topic to explore ideas under discussion.

- Follow agreed-upon rules for discussions and carry out assigned roles.
- Pose and respond to specific questions to clarify or follow up on information, and make comments that contribute to the discussion and link to the remarks of others.
- Review the key ideas expressed and explain their own ideas and understanding in light of the discussion.
- SL.4.2. Paraphrase portions of a text read aloud or information presented in diverse media and formats, including visually, quantitatively, and orally.
- SL.4.3. Identify the reasons and evidence a speaker provides to support particular points.

Presentation of Knowledge and Ideas

- SL.4.4. Report on a topic or text, tell a story, or recount an experience in an organized manner, using appropriate facts and relevant, descriptive details to support main ideas or themes; speak clearly at an understandable pace.
- SL.4.5. Add audio recordings and visual displays to presentations when appropriate to enhance the development of main ideas or themes.
- SL.4.6. Differentiate between contexts that call for formal English (e.g., presenting ideas) and situations where informal discourse is appropriate (e.g., small-group discussion); use formal English when appropriate to task and situation.

Language » Grade 4

Conventions of Standard English

- L.4.1. Demonstrate command of the conventions of standard English grammar and usage when writing or speaking.
  - Use relative pronouns (*who, whose, whom, which, that*) and relative adverbs (*where, when, why*).
  - Form and use the progressive (e.g., *I was walking; I am walking; I will be walking*) verb tenses.
  - Use modal auxiliaries (e.g., *can, may, must*) to convey various conditions.
  - Order adjectives within sentences according to conventional patterns (e.g., *a small red bag* rather than *a red small bag*).
  - Form and use prepositional phrases.
  - Produce complete sentences, recognizing and correcting inappropriate fragments and run-ons.
  - Correctly use frequently confused words (e.g., *to, too, two; there, their*).
- L.4.2. Demonstrate command of the conventions of standard English capitalization, punctuation, and spelling when writing.
  - Use correct capitalization.
  - Use commas and quotation marks to mark direct speech and quotations from a text.
  - Use a comma before a coordinating conjunction in a compound sentence.
  - Spell grade-appropriate words correctly, consulting references as needed.

Knowledge of Language

- L.4.3. Use knowledge of language and its conventions when writing, speaking, reading, or listening.
  - Choose words and phrases to convey ideas precisely.
  - Choose punctuation for effect.
  - Differentiate between contexts that call for formal English (e.g., presenting ideas) and situations where informal discourse is appropriate (e.g., small-group discussion).

Vocabulary Acquisition and Use

- L.4.4. Determine or clarify the meaning of unknown and multiple-meaning words and phrases based on grade-4 reading and content, choosing flexibly from a range of strategies.
  - Use context (e.g., definitions, examples, or restatements in text) as a clue to the meaning of a word or phrase.

- Use common, grade-appropriate Greek and Latin affixes and roots as clues to the meaning of a word (e.g., *telegraph, photograph, autograph*).
- Consult reference materials (e.g., dictionaries, glossaries, thesauruses), both print and digital, to find the pronunciation and determine or clarify the precise meaning of key words and phrases.

- L.4.5. Demonstrate understanding of figurative language, word relationships, and nuances in word meanings.
  - Explain the meaning of simple similes and metaphors (e.g., *as pretty as a picture*) in context.
  - Recognize and explain the meaning of common idioms, adages, and proverbs.
  - Demonstrate understanding of words by relating them to their opposites (antonyms) and to words with similar but not identical meanings (synonyms).

- L.4.6. Acquire and use accurately grade-appropriate general academic and domain-specific words and phrases, including those that signal precise actions, emotions, or states of being (e.g., *quizzed, whined, stammered*) and that are basic to a particular topic (e.g., *wildlife, conservation,* and *endangered* when discussing animal preservation).

ENGLISH LANGUAGE ARTS STANDARDS FOR GRADE 5

Reading: Literature » Grade 5

Key Ideas and Details

- RL.5.1. Quote accurately from a text when explaining what the text says explicitly and when drawing inferences from the text.
- RL.5.2. Determine a theme of a story, drama, or poem from details in the text, including how characters in a story or drama respond to challenges or how the speaker in a poem reflects upon a topic; summarize the text.
- RL.5.3. Compare and contrast two or more characters, settings, or events in a story or drama, drawing on specific details in the text (e.g., how characters interact).

Craft and Structure

- RL.5.4. Determine the meaning of words and phrases as they are used in a text, including figurative language such as metaphors and similes.
- RL.5.5. Explain how a series of chapters, scenes, or stanzas fits together to provide the overall structure of a particular story, drama, or poem.
- RL.5.6. Describe how a narrator's or speaker's point of view influences how events are described.

Integration of Knowledge and Ideas

- RL.5.7. Analyze how visual and multimedia elements contribute to the meaning, tone, or beauty of a text (e.g., graphic novel, multimedia presentation of fiction, folktale, myth, poem).
- RL.5.8. (Not applicable to literature)
- RL.5.9. Compare and contrast stories in the same genre (e.g., mysteries and adventure stories) on their approaches to similar themes and topics.

Range of Reading and Complexity of Text

- RL.5.10. By the end of the year, read and comprehend literature, including stories, dramas, and poetry, at the high end of the grades 4–5 text complexity band independently and proficiently.

Reading: Informational Text » Grade 5

Key Ideas and Details

- RI.5.1. Quote accurately from a text when explaining what the text says explicitly and when drawing inferences from the text.
- RI.5.2. Determine two or more main ideas of a text and explain how they are supported by key details; summarize the text.
- RI.5.3. Explain the relationships or interactions between two or more individuals, events, ideas, or concepts in a historical, scientific, or technical text based on specific information in the text.

Craft and Structure

- RI.5.4. Determine the meaning of general academic and domain-specific words and phrases in a text relevant to a *grade-5 topic or subject area.*
- RI.5.5. Compare and contrast the overall structure (e.g., chronology, comparison, cause/effect, problem/solution) of events, ideas, concepts, or information in two or more texts.
- RI.5.6. Analyze multiple accounts of the same event or topic, noting important similarities and differences in the point of view they represent.

Integration of Knowledge and Ideas

- RI.5.7. Draw on information from multiple print or digital sources, demonstrating the ability to locate an answer to a question quickly or to solve a problem efficiently.
- RI.5.8. Explain how an author uses reasons and evidence to support particular points in a text, identifying which reasons and evidence support which point(s).
- RI.5.9. Integrate information from several texts on the same topic in order to write or speak about the subject knowledgeably.

Range of Reading and Level of Text Complexity

- RI.5.10. By the end of the year, read and comprehend informational texts, including history/social studies, science, and technical texts, at the high end of the grades 4–5 text complexity band independently and proficiently.

Reading: Foundational Skills » Grade 5

Phonics and Word Recognition

- RF.5.3. Know and apply grade-level phonics and word analysis skills in decoding words.
  - Use combined knowledge of all letter–sound correspondences, syllabication patterns, and morphology (e.g., roots and affixes) to read accurately unfamiliar multi-syllabic words in context and out of context.

Fluency

- RF.5.4. Read with sufficient accuracy and fluency to support comprehension.
  - Read grade-level text with purpose and understanding.
  - Read grade-level prose and poetry orally with accuracy, appropriate rate, and expression.
  - Use context to confirm or self-correct word recognition and understanding, rereading as necessary.

Writing » Grade 5

Text Types and Purposes

- W.5.1. Write opinion pieces on topics or texts, supporting a point of view with reasons and information.

- Introduce a topic or text clearly, state an opinion, and create an organizational structure in which ideas are logically grouped to support the writer's purpose.
- Provide logically ordered reasons that are supported by facts and details.
- Link opinion and reasons using words, phrases, and clauses (e.g., *consequently*, *specifically*).
- Provide a concluding statement or section related to the opinion presented.
- W.5.2. Write informative/explanatory texts to examine a topic and convey ideas and information clearly.
  - Introduce a topic clearly, provide a general observation and focus, and group related information logically; include formatting (e.g., headings), illustrations, and multimedia when useful to aiding comprehension.
  - Develop the topic with facts, definitions, concrete details, quotations, or other information and examples related to the topic.
  - Link ideas within and across categories of information using words, phrases, and clauses (e.g., *in contrast*, *especially*).
  - Use precise language and domain-specific vocabulary to inform about or explain the topic.
  - Provide a concluding statement or section related to the information or explanation presented.
- W.5.3. Write narratives to develop real or imagined experiences or events using effective technique, descriptive details, and clear event sequences.
  - Orient the reader by establishing a situation and introducing a narrator and/or characters; organize an event sequence that unfolds naturally.
  - Use narrative techniques, such as dialogue, description, and pacing, to develop experiences and events or show the responses of characters to situations.
  - Use a variety of transitional words, phrases, and clauses to manage the sequence of events.
  - Use concrete words and phrases and sensory details to convey experiences and events precisely.
  - Provide a conclusion that follows from the narrated experiences or events.

Production and Distribution of Writing

- W.5.4. Produce clear and coherent writing in which the development and organization are appropriate to task, purpose, and audience. (Grade-specific expectations for writing types are defined in standards 1–3 above.)
- W.5.5. With guidance and support from peers and adults, develop and strengthen writing as needed by planning, revising, editing, rewriting, or trying a new approach.
- W.5.6. With some guidance and support from adults, use technology, including the Internet, to produce and publish writing as well as to interact and collaborate with others; demonstrate sufficient command of keyboarding skills to type a minimum of two pages in a single sitting.

Research to Build and Present Knowledge

- W.5.7. Conduct short research projects that use several sources to build knowledge through investigation of different aspects of a topic.
- W.5.8. Recall relevant information from experiences or gather relevant information from print and digital sources; summarize or paraphrase information in notes and finished work, and provide a list of sources.
- W.5.9. Draw evidence from literary or informational texts to support analysis, reflection, and research.
  - Apply *grade-5 Reading standards* to literature (e.g., "Compare and contrast two or more characters, settings, or events in a story or a drama, drawing on specific details in the text [e.g., how characters interact]").
  - Apply *grade-5 Reading standards* to informational texts (e.g., "Explain how an author uses reasons and evidence to support particular points in a text, identifying which reasons and evidence support which point[s]").

Range of Writing
- W.5.10. Write routinely over extended time frames (time for research, reflection, and revision) and shorter time frames (a single sitting or a day or two) for a range of discipline-specific tasks, purposes, and audiences.

Speaking and Listening » Grade 5
Comprehension and Collaboration
- SL.5.1. Engage effectively in a range of collaborative discussions (one-on-one, in groups, and teacher-led) with diverse partners on *grade-5 topics and texts*, building on others' ideas and expressing their own clearly.
  - Come to discussions prepared, having read or studied required material; explicitly draw on that preparation and other information known about the topic to explore ideas under discussion.
  - Follow agreed-upon rules for discussions and carry out assigned roles.
  - Pose and respond to specific questions by making comments that contribute to the discussion and elaborate on the remarks of others.
  - Review the key ideas expressed and draw conclusions in light of information and knowledge gained from the discussions.
- SL.5.2. Summarize a written text read aloud or information presented in diverse media and formats, including visually, quantitatively, and orally.
- SL.5.3. Summarize the points a speaker makes and explain how each claim is supported by reasons and evidence.

Presentation of Knowledge and Ideas
- SL.5.4. Report on a topic or text or present an opinion, sequencing ideas logically and using appropriate facts and relevant, descriptive details to support main ideas or themes; speak clearly at an understandable pace.
- SL.5.5. Include multimedia components (e.g., graphics, sound) and visual displays in presentations when appropriate to enhance the development of main ideas or themes.
- SL.5.6. Adapt speech to a variety of contexts and tasks, using formal English when appropriate to task and situation.

Language » Grade 5
Conventions of Standard English
- L.5.1. Demonstrate command of the conventions of standard English grammar and usage when writing or speaking.
  - Explain the function of conjunctions, prepositions, and interjections in general and their function in particular sentences.
  - Form and use the perfect (e.g., *I had walked*; *I have walked*; *I will have walked*) verb tenses.
  - Use verb tense to convey various times, sequences, states, and conditions.
  - Recognize and correct inappropriate shifts in verb tense.
  - Use correlative conjunctions (e.g., *either/or, neither/nor*).
- L.5.2. Demonstrate command of the conventions of standard English capitalization, punctuation, and spelling when writing.
  - Use punctuation to separate items in a series.
  - Use a comma to separate an introductory element from the rest of the sentence.
  - Use a comma to set off the words *yes* and *no* (e.g., *Yes, thank you*), to set off a tag question from the rest of the sentence (e.g., *It's true, isn't it?*), and to indicate direct address (e.g., *Is that you, Steve?*).
  - Use underlining, quotation marks, or italics to indicate titles of works.
  - Spell grade-appropriate words correctly, consulting references as needed.

Knowledge of Language

- L.5.3. Use knowledge of language and its conventions when writing, speaking, reading, or listening.
  - Expand, combine, and reduce sentences for meaning, reader/listener interest, and style.
  - Compare and contrast the varieties of English (e.g., *dialects, registers*) used in stories, dramas, or poems.

Vocabulary Acquisition and Use

- L.5.4. Determine or clarify the meaning of unknown and multiple-meaning words and phrases based on grade-5 reading and content, choosing flexibly from a range of strategies.
  - Use context (e.g., cause/effect relationships and comparisons in text) as a clue to the meaning of a word or phrase.
  - Use common, grade-appropriate Greek and Latin affixes and roots as clues to the meaning of a word (e.g., *photograph, photosynthesis*).
  - Consult reference materials (e.g., dictionaries, glossaries, thesauruses), both print and digital, to find the pronunciation and determine or clarify the precise meaning of key words and phrases.
- L.5.5. Demonstrate understanding of figurative language, word relationships, and nuances in word meanings.
  - Interpret figurative language, including similes and metaphors, in context.
  - Recognize and explain the meaning of common idioms, adages, and proverbs.
  - Use the relationship between particular words (e.g., synonyms, antonyms, homographs) to better understand each of the words.
- L.5.6. Acquire and use accurately grade-appropriate general academic and domain-specific words and phrases, including those that signal contrast, addition, and other logical relationships (e.g., *however, although, nevertheless, similarly, moreover, in addition*).

APPENDIX B

Common Core State Standards for English Language Arts and Literacy in History/Social Studies, Science, and Technical Subjects

Grades 6–12

ENGLISH LANGUAGE ARTS STANDARDS FOR GRADE 6

Reading: Literature » Grade 6

Key Ideas and Details

- RL.6.1. Cite textual evidence to support analysis of what the text says explicitly as well as inferences drawn from the text.
- RL.6.2. Determine a theme or central idea of a text and how it is conveyed through particular details; provide a summary of the text distinct from personal opinions or judgments.
- RL.6.3. Describe how a particular story's or drama's plot unfolds in a series of episodes as well as how the characters respond or change as the plot moves toward a resolution.

Craft and Structure

- RL.6.4. Determine the meaning of words and phrases as they are used in a text, including figurative and connotative meanings; analyze the impact of a specific word choice on meaning and tone
- RL.6.5. Analyze how a particular sentence, chapter, scene, or stanza fits into the overall structure of a text and contributes to the development of the theme, setting, or plot.
- RL.6.6. Explain how an author develops the point of view of the narrator or speaker in a text.

Integration of Knowledge and Ideas

- RL.6.7. Compare and contrast the experience of reading a story, drama, or poem to listening to or viewing an audio, video, or live version of the text, including contrasting what they "see" and "hear" when reading the text to what they perceive when they listen or watch.

- RL.6.8 (Not applicable to literature)
- RL.6.9. Compare and contrast texts in different forms or genres (e.g., stories and poems; historical novels and fantasy stories) in terms of their approaches to similar themes and topics.

Range of Reading and Level of Text Complexity

- RL.6.10. By the end of the year, read and comprehend literature, including stories, dramas, and poems, in the grades 6–8 text complexity band proficiently, with scaffolding as needed at the high end of the range.

Reading: Informational Text » Grade 6

Key Ideas and Details

- RI.6.1. Cite textual evidence to support analysis of what the text says explicitly as well as inferences drawn from the text.
- RI.6.2. Determine a central idea of a text and how it is conveyed through particular details; provide a summary of the text distinct from personal opinions or judgments.
- RI.6.3. Analyze in detail how a key individual, event, or idea is introduced, illustrated, and elaborated in a text (e.g., through examples or anecdotes).

Craft and Structure

- RI.6.4. Determine the meaning of words and phrases as they are used in a text, including figurative, connotative, and technical meanings.
- RI.6.5. Analyze how a particular sentence, paragraph, chapter, or section fits into the overall structure of a text and contributes to the development of the ideas.
- RI.6.6. Determine an author's point of view or purpose in a text and explain how it is conveyed in the text.

Integration of Knowledge and Ideas

- RI.6.7. Integrate information presented in different media or formats (e.g., visually, quantitatively) as well as in words to develop a coherent understanding of a topic or issue.
- RI.6.8. Trace and evaluate the argument and specific claims in a text, distinguishing claims that are supported by reasons and evidence from claims that are not.
- RI.6.9. Compare and contrast one author's presentation of events with that of another (e.g., a memoir written by and a biography on the same person).

Range of Reading and Level of Text Complexity

- RI.6.10. By the end of the year, read and comprehend literary nonfiction in the grades 6–8 text complexity band proficiently, with scaffolding as needed at the high end of the range.

Writing » Grade 6

Text Types and Purposes:

- W.6.1. Write arguments to support claims with clear reasons and relevant evidence.
  - W.6.1.A. Introduce claim(s) and organize the reasons and evidence clearly.
  - W.6.1.B. Support claim(s) with clear reasons and relevant evidence, using credible sources and demonstrating an understanding of the topic or text.
  - W.6.1.C. Use words, phrases, and clauses to clarify the relationships among claim(s) and reasons.
  - W.6.1.D. Establish and maintain a formal style.
  - W.6.1.E. Provide a concluding statement or section that follows from the argument presented.

- W.6.2. Write informative/explanatory texts to examine a topic and convey ideas, concepts, and information through the selection, organization, and analysis of relevant content.
  - W.6.2.A. Introduce a topic; organize ideas, concepts, and information, using strategies such as definition, classification, comparison/contrast, and cause/effect; include formatting (e.g., headings), graphics (e.g., charts, tables), and multimedia when useful to aiding comprehension.
  - W.6.2.B. Develop the topic with relevant facts, definitions, concrete details, quotations, or other information and examples.
  - W.6.2.C. Use appropriate transitions to clarify the relationships among ideas and concepts.
  - W.6.2.D. Use precise language and domain-specific vocabulary to inform about or explain the topic.
  - W.6.2.E. Establish and maintain a formal style.
  - W.6.2.F. Provide a concluding statement or section that follows from the information or explanation presented.
- W.6.3. Write narratives to develop real or imagined experiences or events using effective technique, relevant descriptive details, and well-structured event sequences.
  - W.6.3.A. Engage and orient the reader by establishing a context and introducing a narrator and/or characters; organize an event sequence that unfolds naturally and logically.
  - W.6.3.B. Use narrative techniques, such as dialogue, pacing, and description, to develop experiences, events, and/or characters.
  - W.6.3.C. Use a variety of transition words, phrases, and clauses to convey sequence and signal shifts from one time frame or setting to another.
  - W.6.3.D. Use precise words and phrases, relevant descriptive details, and sensory language to convey experiences and events.
  - W.6.3.E. Provide a conclusion that follows from the narrated experiences or events.

Production and Distribution of Writing

- W.6.4. Produce clear and coherent writing in which the development, organization, and style are appropriate to task, purpose, and audience. (Grade-specific expectations for writing types are defined in standards 1–3 above.)
- W.6.5. With some guidance and support from peers and adults, develop and strengthen writing as needed by planning, revising, editing, rewriting, or trying a new approach. (Editing for conventions should demonstrate command of Language standards 1–3 up to and including grade 6 here.)
- W.6.6. Use technology, including the Internet, to produce and publish writing as well as to interact and collaborate with others; demonstrate sufficient command of keyboarding skills to type a minimum of three pages in a single sitting.

Research to Build and Present Knowledge

- W.6.7. Conduct short research projects to answer a question, drawing on several sources and refocusing the inquiry when appropriate.
- W.6.8. Gather relevant information from multiple print and digital sources; assess the credibility of each source; and quote or paraphrase the data and conclusions of others while avoiding plagiarism and providing basic bibliographic information for sources.
- W.6.9. Draw evidence from literary or informational texts to support analysis, reflection, and research.
  - W.6.9.A. Apply grade-6 Reading standards to literature (e.g., "Compare and contrast texts in different forms or genres [e.g., stories and poems; historical novels and fantasy stories] in terms of their approaches to similar themes and topics").
  - W.6.9.B. Apply grade-6 Reading standards to literary nonfiction (e.g., "Trace and evaluate the argument and specific claims in a text, distinguishing claims that are supported by reasons and evidence from claims that are not").

Range of Writing

- W.6.10. Write routinely over extended time frames (time for research, reflection, and revision) and shorter time frames (a single sitting or a day or two) for a range of discipline-specific tasks, purposes, and audiences.

Speaking and Listening » Grade 6

Comprehension and Collaboration

- SL.6.1. Engage effectively in a range of collaborative discussions (one-on-one, in groups, and teacher-led) with diverse partners on *grade-6 topics, texts, and issues,* building on others' ideas and expressing their own clearly.
  - SL.6.1.A. Come to discussions prepared, having read or studied required material; explicitly draw on that preparation by referring to evidence on the topic, text, or issue to probe and reflect on ideas under discussion.
  - SL.6.1.B. Follow rules for collegial discussions, set specific goals and deadlines, and define individual roles as needed.
  - SL.6.1.C. Pose and respond to specific questions with elaboration and detail by making comments that contribute to the topic, text, or issue under discussion.
  - SL.6.1.D. Review the key ideas expressed and demonstrate understanding of multiple perspectives through reflection and paraphrasing.
- SL.6.2. Interpret information presented in diverse media and formats (e.g., visually, quantitatively, orally) and explain how it contributes to a topic, text, or issue under study.
- SL.6.3. Delineate a speaker's argument and specific claims, distinguishing claims that are supported by reasons and evidence from claims that are not.

Presentation of Knowledge and Ideas

- SL.6.4. Present claims and findings, sequencing ideas logically and using pertinent descriptions, facts, and details to accentuate main ideas or themes; use appropriate eye contact, adequate volume, and clear pronunciation.
- SL.6.5. Include multimedia components (e.g., graphics, images, music, sound) and visual displays in presentations to clarify information.
- SL.6.6. Adapt speech to a variety of contexts and tasks, demonstrating command of formal English when indicated or appropriate. (See grade-6 Language standards 1 and 3 for specific expectations.)

Language » Grade 6

Conventions of Standard English

- L.6.1. Demonstrate command of the conventions of standard English grammar and usage when writing or speaking.
  - L.6.1.A. Ensure that pronouns are in the proper case (subjective, objective, possessive).
  - L.6.1.B. Use intensive pronouns (e.g., *myself, ourselves*).
  - L.6.1.C. Recognize and correct inappropriate shifts in pronoun number and person.
  - L.6.1.D. Recognize and correct vague pronouns (i.e., ones with unclear or ambiguous antecedents).
  - L.6.1.E. Recognize variations from standard English in their own and others' writing and speaking, and identify and use strategies to improve expression in conventional language.
- L.6.2. Demonstrate command of the conventions of standard English capitalization, punctuation, and spelling when writing.
  - L.6.2.A. Use punctuation (commas, parentheses, dashes) to set off nonrestrictive/parenthetical elements.
  - L.6.2.B. Spell correctly.

Knowledge of Language

- L.6.3. Use knowledge of language and its conventions when writing, speaking, reading, or listening.
  - L.6.3.A. Vary sentence patterns for meaning, reader/listener interest, and style.
  - L.6.3.B. Maintain consistency in style and tone.

Vocabulary Acquisition and Use

- L.6.4. Determine or clarify the meaning of unknown and multiple-meaning words and phrases based on grade-6 reading and content, choosing flexibly from a range of strategies.
  - L.6.4.A. Use context (e.g., the overall meaning of a sentence or paragraph; a word's position or function in a sentence) as a clue to the meaning of a word or phrase.
  - L.6.4.B. Use common, grade-appropriate Greek or Latin affixes and roots as clues to the meaning of a word (e.g., *audience, auditory, audible*).
  - L.6.4.C. Consult reference materials (e.g., dictionaries, glossaries, thesauruses), both print and digital, to find the pronunciation of a word or determine or clarify its precise meaning or its part of speech.
  - L.6.4.D. Verify the preliminary determination of the meaning of a word or phrase (e.g., by checking the inferred meaning in context or in a dictionary).
- L.6.5. Demonstrate understanding of figurative language, word relationships, and nuances in word meanings.
  - L.6.5.A. Interpret figures of speech (e.g., personification) in context.
  - L.6.5.B. Use the relationship between particular words (e.g., *cause/effect, part/whole, item/category*) to better understand each of the words.
  - L.6.5.C. Distinguish among the connotations (associations) of words with similar denotations (definitions) (e.g., *stingy, scrimping, economical, unwasteful, thrifty*).
- L.6.6. Acquire and use accurately grade-appropriate general academic and domain-specific words and phrases; gather vocabulary knowledge when considering a word or phrase important to comprehension or expression.

ENGLISH LANGUAGE ARTS STANDARDS FOR GRADE 7

Reading: Literature » Grade 7

Key Ideas and Details

- RL.7.1. Cite several pieces of textual evidence to support analysis of what the text says explicitly as well as inferences drawn from the text.
- RL.7.2. Determine a theme or central idea of a text and analyze its development over the course of the text; provide an objective summary of the text.
- RL.7.3. Analyze how particular elements of a story or drama interact (e.g., how setting shapes the characters or plot).

Craft and Structure

- RL.7.4. Determine the meaning of words and phrases as they are used in a text, including figurative and connotative meanings; analyze the impact of rhymes and other repetitions of sounds (e.g., alliteration) on a specific verse or stanza of a poem or section of a story or drama.
- RL.7.5. Analyze how a drama's or poem's form or structure (e.g., soliloquy, sonnet) contributes to its meaning.
- RL.7.6. Analyze how an author develops and contrasts the points of view of different characters or narrators in a text.

Integration of Knowledge and Ideas

- RL.7.7. Compare and contrast a written story, drama, or poem to its audio, filmed, staged, or multimedia version, analyzing the effects of techniques unique to each medium (e.g., lighting, sound, color, or camera focus and angles in a film).

- RL.7.8 (Not applicable to literature)
- RL.7.9. Compare and contrast a fictional portrayal of a time, place, or character and a historical account of the same period as a means of understanding how authors of fiction use or alter history.

Range of Reading and Level of Text Complexity

- RL.7.10. By the end of the year, read and comprehend literature, including stories, dramas, and poems, in the grades 6–8 text complexity band proficiently, with scaffolding as needed at the high end of the range.

Reading: Informational Text » Grade 7

Key Ideas and Details

- RI.7.1. Cite several pieces of textual evidence to support analysis of what the text says explicitly as well as inferences drawn from the text.
- RI.7.2. Determine two or more central ideas in a text and analyze their development over the course of the text; provide an objective summary of the text.
- RI.7.3. Analyze the interactions between individuals, events, and ideas in a text (e.g., how ideas influence individuals or events, or how individuals influence ideas or events).

Craft and Structure

- RI.7.4. Determine the meaning of words and phrases as they are used in a text, including figurative, connotative, and technical meanings; analyze the impact of a specific word choice on meaning and tone.
- RI.7.5. Analyze the structure an author uses to organize a text, including how the major sections contribute to the whole and to the development of the ideas.
- RI.7.6. Determine an author's point of view or purpose in a text and analyze how the author distinguishes his or her position from that of others.

Integration of Knowledge and Ideas

- RI.7.7. Compare and contrast a text to an audio, video, or multimedia version of the text, analyzing each medium's portrayal of the subject (e.g., how the delivery of a speech affects the impact of the words).
- RI.7.8. Trace and evaluate the argument and specific claims in a text, assessing whether the reasoning is sound and the evidence is relevant and sufficient to support the claims.
- RI.7.9. Analyze how two or more authors writing about the same topic shape their presentations of key information by emphasizing different evidence or advancing different interpretations of facts.

Range of Reading and Level of Text Complexity

- RI.7.10. By the end of the year, read and comprehend literary nonfiction in the grades 6–8 text complexity band proficiently, with scaffolding as needed at the high end of the range.

Writing » Grade 7

Text Types and Purposes

- W.7.1. Write arguments to support claims with clear reasons and relevant evidence.
  - W.7.1.A. Introduce claim(s), acknowledge alternate or opposing claims, and organize the reasons and evidence logically.
  - W.7.1.B. Support claim(s) with logical reasoning and relevant evidence, using accurate, credible sources and demonstrating an understanding of the topic or text.
  - W.7.1.C. Use words, phrases, and clauses to create cohesion and clarify the relationships among claim(s), reasons, and evidence.

- W.7.1.D. Establish and maintain a formal style.
- W.7.1.E. Provide a concluding statement or section that follows from and supports the argument presented.

- W.7.2. Write informative/explanatory texts to examine a topic and convey ideas, concepts, and information through the selection, organization, and analysis of relevant content.
  - W.7.2.A. Introduce a topic clearly, previewing what is to follow; organize ideas, concepts, and information, using strategies such as definition, classification, comparison/contrast, and cause/effect; include formatting (e.g., headings), graphics (e.g., charts, tables), and multimedia when useful to aiding comprehension.
  - W.7.2.B. Develop the topic with relevant facts, definitions, concrete details, quotations, or other information and examples.
  - W.7.2.C. Use appropriate transitions to create cohesion and clarify the relationships among ideas and concepts.
  - W.7.2.D. Use precise language and domain-specific vocabulary to inform about or explain the topic.
  - W.7.2.E. Establish and maintain a formal style.
  - W.7.2.F. Provide a concluding statement or section that follows from and supports the information or explanation presented.

- W.7.3. Write narratives to develop real or imagined experiences or events using effective technique, relevant descriptive details, and well-structured event sequences.
  - W.7.3.A. Engage and orient the reader by establishing a context and point of view and introducing a narrator and/or characters; organize an event sequence that unfolds naturally and logically.
  - W.7.3.B. Use narrative techniques, such as dialogue, pacing, and description, to develop experiences, events, and/or characters.
  - W.7.3.C. Use a variety of transition words, phrases, and clauses to convey sequence and signal shifts from one time frame or setting to another.
  - W.7.3.D. Use precise words and phrases, relevant descriptive details, and sensory language to capture the action and convey experiences and events.
  - W.7.3.E. Provide a conclusion that follows from and reflects on the narrated experiences or events.

Production and Distribution of Writing

- W.7.4. Produce clear and coherent writing in which the development, organization, and style are appropriate to task, purpose, and audience. (Grade-specific expectations for writing types are defined in standards 1–3 above.)
- W.7.5. With some guidance and support from peers and adults, develop and strengthen writing as needed by planning, revising, editing, rewriting, or trying a new approach, focusing on how well purpose and audience have been addressed. (Editing for conventions should demonstrate command of Language standards 1–3 up to and including grade 7 here.)
- W.7.6. Use technology, including the Internet, to produce and publish writing and link to and cite sources as well as to interact and collaborate with others, including linking to and citing sources.

Research to Build and Present Knowledge

- W.7.7. Conduct short research projects to answer a question, drawing on several sources and generating additional related, focused questions for further research and investigation.
- W.7.8. Gather relevant information from multiple print and digital sources, using search terms effectively; assess the credibility and accuracy of each source; and quote or paraphrase the data and conclusions of others while avoiding plagiarism and following a standard format for citation.

- W.7.9. Draw evidence from literary or informational texts to support analysis, reflection, and research.
  - W.7.9.A. Apply grade-7 Reading standards to literature (e.g., "Compare and contrast a fictional portrayal of a time, place, or character and a historical account of the same period as a means of understanding how authors of fiction use or alter history").
  - W.7.9.B. Apply grade-7 Reading standards to literary nonfiction (e.g. "Trace and evaluate the argument and specific claims in a text, assessing whether the reasoning is sound and the evidence is relevant and sufficient to support the claims").

Range of Writing

- W.7.10. Write routinely over extended time frames (time for research, reflection, and revision) and shorter time frames (a single sitting or a day or two) for a range of discipline-specific tasks, purposes, and audiences.

Speaking and Listening » Grade 7

Comprehension and Collaboration

- SL.7.1. Engage effectively in a range of collaborative discussions (one-on-one, in groups, and teacher-led) with diverse partners on *grade-7 topics, texts, and issues,* building on others' ideas and expressing their own clearly.
  - SL.7.1.A. Come to discussions prepared, having read or researched material under study; explicitly draw on that preparation by referring to evidence on the topic, text, or issue to probe and reflect on ideas under discussion.
  - SL.7.1.B. Follow rules for collegial discussions, track progress toward specific goals and deadlines, and define individual roles as needed.
  - SL.7.1.C. Pose questions that elicit elaboration and respond to others' questions and comments with relevant observations and ideas that bring the discussion back on topic as needed.
  - SL.7.1.D. Acknowledge new information expressed by others and, when warranted, modify their own views.
- SL.7.2. Analyze the main ideas and supporting details presented in diverse media and formats (e.g., visually, quantitatively, orally) and explain how the ideas clarify a topic, text, or issue under study.
- SL.7.3. Delineate a speaker's argument and specific claims, evaluating the soundness of the reasoning and the relevance and sufficiency of the evidence.

Presentation of Knowledge and Ideas

- SL.7.4. Present claims and findings, emphasizing salient points in a focused, coherent manner with pertinent descriptions, facts, details, and examples; use appropriate eye contact, adequate volume, and clear pronunciation.
- SL.7.5. Include multimedia components and visual displays in presentations to clarify claims and findings and emphasize salient points.
- SL.7.6. Adapt speech to a variety of contexts and tasks, demonstrating command of formal English when indicated or appropriate. (See grade-7 Language standards 1 and 3 for specific expectations.)

Language » Grade 7

Conventions of Standard English

- L.7.1. Demonstrate command of the conventions of standard English grammar and usage when writing or speaking.
  - L.7.1.A. Explain the function of phrases and clauses in general and their function in specific sentences.
  - L.7.1.B. Choose among simple, compound, complex, and compound-complex sentences to signal differing relationships among ideas.

- L.7.1.C. Place phrases and clauses within a sentence, recognizing and correcting misplaced and dangling modifiers.
- L.7.2. Demonstrate command of the conventions of standard English capitalization, punctuation, and spelling when writing.
    - L.7.2.A. Use a comma to separate coordinate adjectives (e.g., *It was a fascinating, enjoyable movie* but not *He wore an old[,] green shirt*).
    - L.7.2.B. Spell correctly.

Knowledge of Language

- L.7.3. Use knowledge of language and its conventions when writing, speaking, reading, or listening.
    - L.7.3.A. Choose language that expresses ideas precisely and concisely, recognizing and eliminating wordiness and redundancy.

Vocabulary Acquisition and Use

- L.7.4. Determine or clarify the meaning of unknown and multiple-meaning words and phrases based on grade-7 reading and content, choosing flexibly from a range of strategies.
    - L.7.4.A. Use context (e.g., the overall meaning of a sentence or paragraph; a word's position or function in a sentence) as a clue to the meaning of a word or phrase.
    - L.7.4.B. Use common, grade-appropriate Greek or Latin affixes and roots as clues to the meaning of a word (e.g., *belligerent, bellicose, rebel*).
    - L.7.4.C. Consult general and specialized reference materials (e.g., dictionaries, glossaries, thesauruses), both print and digital, to find the pronunciation of a word or determine or clarify its precise meaning or its part of speech.
    - L.7.4.D. Verify the preliminary determination of the meaning of a word or phrase (e.g., by checking the inferred meaning in context or in a dictionary).
- L.7.5. Demonstrate understanding of figurative language, word relationships, and nuances in word meanings.
    - L.7.5.A. Interpret figures of speech (e.g., literary, biblical, and mythological allusions) in context.
    - L.7.5.B. Use the relationship between particular words (e.g., *synonym/antonym, analogy*) to better understand each of the words.
    - L.7.5.C. Distinguish among the connotations (associations) of words with similar denotations (definitions) (e.g., *refined, respectful, polite, diplomatic, condescending*).
- L.7.6. Acquire and use accurately grade-appropriate general academic and domain-specific words and phrases; gather vocabulary knowledge when considering a word or phrase important to comprehension or expression.

ENGLISH LANGUAGE ARTS STANDARDS FOR GRADE 8

Reading: Literature » Grade 8

Key Ideas and Details

- RL.8.1. Cite the textual evidence that most strongly supports an analysis of what the text says explicitly as well as inferences drawn from the text.
- RL.8.2. Determine a theme or central idea of a text and analyze its development over the course of the text, including its relationship to the characters, setting, and plot; provide an objective summary of the text.
- RL.8.3. Analyze how particular lines of dialogue or incidents in a story or drama propel the action, reveal aspects of a character, or provoke a decision.

Craft and Structure

- RL.8.4. Determine the meaning of words and phrases as they are used in a text, including figurative and connotative meanings; analyze the impact of specific word choices on meaning and tone, including analogies or allusions to other texts.
- RL.8.5. Compare and contrast the structure of two or more texts and analyze how the differing structure of each text contributes to its meaning and style.
- RL.8.6. Analyze how differences in the points of view of the characters and the audience or reader (e.g., created through the use of dramatic irony) create such effects as suspense or humor.

Integration of Knowledge and Ideas

- RL.8.7. Analyze the extent to which a filmed or live production of a story or drama stays faithful to or departs from the text or script, evaluating the choices made by the director or actors.
- RL.8.8 (not applicable to literature)
- RL.8.9. Analyze how a modern work of fiction draws on themes, patterns of events, or character types from myths, traditional stories, or religious works such as the Bible, including describing how the material is rendered new.

Range of Reading and Level of Text Complexity

- RL.8.10. By the end of the year, read and comprehend literature, including stories, dramas, and poems, at the high end of grades 6–8 text complexity band independently and proficiently.

Reading: Informational Text » Grade 8

Key Ideas and Details

- RI.8.1. Cite the textual evidence that most strongly supports an analysis of what the text says explicitly as well as inferences drawn from the text.
- RI.8.2. Determine a central idea of a text and analyze its development over the course of the text, including its relationship to supporting ideas; provide an objective summary of the text.
- RI.8.3. Analyze how a text makes connections among and distinctions between individuals, ideas, or events (e.g., through comparisons, analogies, or categories).

Craft and Structure

- RI.8.4. Determine the meaning of words and phrases as they are used in a text, including figurative, connotative, and technical meanings; analyze the impact of specific word choices on meaning and tone, including analogies or allusions to other texts.
- RI.8.5. Analyze in detail the structure of a specific paragraph in a text, including the role of particular sentences in developing and refining a key concept.
- RI.8.6. Determine an author's point of view or purpose in a text and analyze how the author acknowledges and responds to conflicting evidence or viewpoints.

Integration of Knowledge and Ideas

- RI.8.7. Evaluate the advantages and disadvantages of using different mediums (e.g., print or digital text, video, multimedia) to present a particular topic or idea.
- RI.8.8. Delineate and evaluate the argument and specific claims in a text, assessing whether the reasoning is sound and the evidence is relevant and sufficient; recognize when irrelevant evidence is introduced.
- RI.8.9. Analyze a case in which two or more texts provide conflicting information on the same topic and identify where the texts disagree on matters of fact or interpretation.

Range of Reading and Level of Text Complexity

- RI.8.10. By the end of the year, read and comprehend literary nonfiction at the high end of the grades 6–8 text complexity band independently and proficiently.

Writing » Grade 8

Text Types and Purposes

- W.8.1. Write arguments to support claims with clear reasons and relevant evidence.
  - W.8.1.A. Introduce claim(s), acknowledge and distinguish the claim(s) from alternate or opposing claims, and organize the reasons and evidence logically.
  - W.8.1.B. Support claim(s) with logical reasoning and relevant evidence, using accurate, credible sources and demonstrating an understanding of the topic or text.
  - W.8.1.C. Use words, phrases, and clauses to create cohesion and clarify the relationships among claim(s), counterclaims, reasons, and evidence.
  - W.8.1.D. Establish and maintain a formal style.
  - W.8.1.E. Provide a concluding statement or section that follows from and supports the argument presented.
- W.8.2. Write informative/explanatory texts to examine a topic and convey ideas, concepts, and information through the selection, organization, and analysis of relevant content.
  - W.8.2.A. Introduce a topic clearly, previewing what is to follow; organize ideas, concepts, and information into broader categories; include formatting (e.g., headings), graphics (e.g., charts, tables), and multimedia when useful to aiding comprehension.
  - W.8.2.B. Develop the topic with relevant, well-chosen facts, definitions, concrete details, quotations, or other information and examples.
  - W.8.2.C. Use appropriate and varied transitions to create cohesion and clarify the relationships among ideas and concepts.
  - W.8.2.D. Use precise language and domain-specific vocabulary to inform about or explain the topic.
  - W.8.2.E. Establish and maintain a formal style.
  - W.8.2.F. Provide a concluding statement or section that follows from and supports the information or explanation presented.
- W.8.3. Write narratives to develop real or imagined experiences or events using effective technique, relevant descriptive details, and well-structured event sequences.
  - W.8.3.A. Engage and orient the reader by establishing a context and point of view and introducing a narrator and/or characters; organize an event sequence that unfolds naturally and logically.
  - W.8.3.B. Use narrative techniques, such as dialogue, pacing, description, and reflection, to develop experiences, events, and/or characters.
  - W.8.3.C. Use a variety of transition words, phrases, and clauses to convey sequence, signal shifts from one time frame or setting to another, and show the relationships among experiences and events.
  - W.8.3.D. Use precise words and phrases, relevant descriptive details, and sensory language to capture the action and convey experiences and events.
  - W.8.3.E. Provide a conclusion that follows from and reflects on the narrated experiences or events.

Production and Distribution of Writing

- W.8.4. Produce clear and coherent writing in which the development, organization, and style are appropriate to task, purpose, and audience. (Grade-specific expectations for writing types are defined in standards 1–3 above.)
- W.8.5. With some guidance and support from peers and adults, develop and strengthen writing as needed by planning, revising, editing, rewriting, or trying a new approach, focusing on how well purpose and audience have been addressed. (Editing for conventions should demonstrate command of Language standards 1–3 up to and including grade 8 here.)
- W.8.6. Use technology, including the Internet, to produce and publish writing and present the relationships between information and ideas efficiently as well as to interact and collaborate with others.

Research to Build and Present Knowledge
- W.8.7. Conduct short research projects to answer a question (including a self-generated question), drawing on several sources and generating additional related, focused questions that allow for multiple avenues of exploration.
- W.8.8. Gather relevant information from multiple print and digital sources, using search terms effectively; assess the credibility and accuracy of each source; and quote or paraphrase the data and conclusions of others while avoiding plagiarism and following a standard format for citation.
- W.8.9. Draw evidence from literary or informational texts to support analysis, reflection, and research.
  - W.8.9.A. Apply grade-8 Reading standards to literature (e.g., "Analyze how a modern work of fiction draws on themes, patterns of events, or character types from myths, traditional stories, or religious works such as the Bible, including describing how the material is rendered new").
  - W.8.9.B. Apply grade-8 Reading standards to literary nonfiction (e.g., "Delineate and evaluate the argument and specific claims in a text, assessing whether the reasoning is sound and the evidence is relevant and sufficient; recognize when irrelevant evidence is introduced").

Range of Writing
- W.8.10. Write routinely over extended time frames (time for research, reflection, and revision) and shorter time frames (a single sitting or a day or two) for a range of discipline-specific tasks, purposes, and audiences.

Speaking and Listening » Grade 8
Comprehension and Collaboration
- SL.8.1. Engage effectively in a range of collaborative discussions (one-on-one, in groups, and teacher-led) with diverse partners on *grade-8 topics, texts, and issues*, building on others' ideas and expressing their own clearly.
  - SL.8.1.A. Come to discussions prepared, having read or researched material under study; explicitly draw on that preparation by referring to evidence on the topic, text, or issue to probe and reflect on ideas under discussion.
  - SL.8.1.B. Follow rules for collegial discussions and decision-making, track progress toward specific goals and deadlines, and define individual roles as needed.
  - SL.8.1.C. Pose questions that connect the ideas of several speakers and respond to others' questions and comments with relevant evidence, observations, and ideas.
  - SL.8.1.D. Acknowledge new information expressed by others, and, when warranted, qualify or justify their own views in light of the evidence presented.
- SL.8.2. Analyze the purpose of information presented in diverse media and formats (e.g., visually, quantitatively, orally) and evaluate the motives (e.g., social, commercial, political) behind its presentation.
- SL.8.3. Delineate a speaker's argument and specific claims, evaluating the soundness of the reasoning and relevance and sufficiency of the evidence and identifying when irrelevant evidence is introduced.

Presentation of Knowledge and Ideas
- SL.8.4. Present claims and findings, emphasizing salient points in a focused, coherent manner with relevant evidence, sound valid reasoning, and well-chosen details; use appropriate eye contact, adequate volume, and clear pronunciation.
- SL.8.5. Integrate multimedia and visual displays into presentations to clarify information, strengthen claims and evidence, and add interest.
- SL.8.6. Adapt speech to a variety of contexts and tasks, demonstrating command of formal English when indicated or appropriate. (See grade-8 Language standards 1 and 3 here for specific expectations.)

Language » Grade 8

Conventions of Standard English

- L.8.1. Demonstrate command of the conventions of standard English grammar and usage when writing or speaking.
  - L.8.1.A. Explain the function of verbals (gerunds, participles, infinitives) in general and their function in particular sentences.
  - L.8.1.B. Form and use verbs in the active and passive voice.
  - L.8.1.C. Form and use verbs in the indicative, imperative, interrogative, conditional, and subjunctive mood.
  - L.8.1.D. Recognize and correct inappropriate shifts in verb voice and mood.
- L.8.2. Demonstrate command of the conventions of standard English capitalization, punctuation, and spelling when writing.
  - L.8.2.A. Use punctuation (comma, ellipsis, dash) to indicate a pause or break.
  - L.8.2.B. Use an ellipsis to indicate an omission.
  - L.8.2.C. Spell correctly.

Knowledge of Language

- L.8.3. Use knowledge of language and its conventions when writing, speaking, reading, or listening.
  - L.8.3.A. Use verbs in the active and passive voice and in the conditional and subjunctive mood to achieve particular effects (e.g., emphasizing the actor or the action; expressing uncertainty or describing a state contrary to fact).

Vocabulary Acquisition and Use

- L.8.4. Determine or clarify the meaning of unknown and multiple-meaning words or phrases based on *grade-8 reading and content*, choosing flexibly from a range of strategies.
  - L.8.4.A. Use context (e.g., the overall meaning of a sentence or paragraph; a word's position or function in a sentence) as a clue to the meaning of a word or phrase.
  - L.8.4.B. Use common, grade-appropriate Greek or Latin affixes and roots as clues to the meaning of a word (e.g., *precede, recede, secede*).
  - L.8.4.C. Consult general and specialized reference materials (e.g., dictionaries, glossaries, thesauruses), both print and digital, to find the pronunciation of a word or determine or clarify its precise meaning or its part of speech.
  - L.8.4.D. Verify the preliminary determination of the meaning of a word or phrase (e.g., by checking the inferred meaning in context or in a dictionary).
- L.8.5. Demonstrate understanding of figurative language, word relationships, and nuances in word meanings.
  - L.8.5.A. Interpret figures of speech (e.g. verbal irony, puns) in context.
  - L.8.5.B. Use the relationship between particular words to better understand each of the words.
  - L.8.5.C. Distinguish among the connotations (associations) of words with similar denotations (definitions) (e.g., *bullheaded, willful, firm, persistent, resolute*).
- L.8.6. Acquire and use accurately grade-appropriate general academic and domain-specific words and phrases; gather vocabulary knowledge when considering a word or phrase important to comprehension or expression.

ENGLISH LANGUAGE ARTS STANDARDS FOR GRADES 9–10

Reading: Literature » Grades 9–10

Key Ideas and Details

- RL.9–10.1. Cite strong and thorough textual evidence to support analysis of what the text says explicitly as well as inferences drawn from the text.

- RL.9–10.2. Determine a theme or central idea of a text and analyze in detail its development over the course of the text, including how it emerges and is shaped and refined by specific details; provide an objective summary of the text.
- RL.9–10.3. Analyze how complex characters (e.g., those with multiple or conflicting motivations) develop over the course of a text, interact with other characters, and advance the plot or develop the theme.

Craft and Structure

- RL.9–10.4. Determine the meaning of words and phrases as they are used in the text, including figurative and connotative meanings; analyze the cumulative impact of specific word choices on meaning and tone (e.g., how the language evokes a sense of time and place; how it sets a formal or informal tone).
- RL.9–10.5. Analyze how an author's choices concerning how to structure a text, order events within it (e.g., parallel plots), and manipulate time (e.g., pacing, flashbacks) create such effects as mystery, tension, or surprise.
- RL.9–10.6. Analyze a particular point of view or cultural experience reflected in a work of literature from outside the United States, drawing on a wide reading of world literature.

Integration of Knowledge and Ideas

- RL.9–10.7. Analyze the representation of a subject or a key scene in two different artistic mediums, including what is emphasized or absent in each treatment (e.g., Auden's "Musée des Beaux Arts" and Breughel's *Landscape with the Fall of Icarus*).
- RL.9–10.8 (not applicable to literature)
- RL.9–10.9. Analyze how an author draws on and transforms source material in a specific work (e.g., how Shakespeare treats a theme or topic from Ovid or the Bible or how a later author draws on a play by Shakespeare).

Range of Reading and Level of Text Complexity

- RL.9–10.10. By the end of grade 9, read and comprehend literature, including stories, dramas, and poems, in the grades 9–10 text complexity band proficiently, with scaffolding as needed at the high end of the range.
  By the end of grade 10, read and comprehend literature, including stories, dramas, and poems, at the high end of the grades 9–10 text complexity band independently and proficiently.

Reading: Informational Text » Grades 9–10

Key Ideas and Details

- RI.9–10.1. Cite strong and thorough textual evidence to support analysis of what the text says explicitly as well as inferences drawn from the text.
- RI.9–10.2. Determine a central idea of a text and analyze its development over the course of the text, including how it emerges and is shaped and refined by specific details; provide an objective summary of the text.
- RI.9–10.3. Analyze how the author unfolds an analysis or series of ideas or events, including the order in which the points are made, how they are introduced and developed, and the connections that are drawn between them.

Craft and Structure

- RI.9–10.4. Determine the meaning of words and phrases as they are used in a text, including figurative, connotative, and technical meanings; analyze the cumulative impact of specific word choices on meaning and tone (e.g., how the language of a court opinion differs from that of a newspaper).
- RI.9–10.5. Analyze in detail how an author's ideas or claims are developed and refined by particular sentences, paragraphs, or larger portions of a text (e.g., a section or chapter).

- RI.9–10.6. Determine an author's point of view or purpose in a text and analyze how an author uses rhetoric to advance that point of view or purpose.

Integration of Knowledge and Ideas

- RI.9–10.7. Analyze various accounts of a subject told in different mediums (e.g., a person's life story in both print and multimedia), determining which details are emphasized in each account.
- RI.9–10.8. Delineate and evaluate the argument and specific claims in a text, assessing whether the reasoning is valid and the evidence is relevant and sufficient; identify false statements and fallacious reasoning.
- RI.9–10.9. Analyze seminal U.S. documents of historical and literary significance (e.g., Washington's Farewell Address, the Gettysburg Address, Roosevelt's Four Freedoms speech, King's "Letter from Birmingham Jail"), including how they address related themes and concepts.

Range of Reading and Level of Text Complexity

- RI.9–10.10. By the end of grade 9, read and comprehend literacy nonfiction in the grades 9–10 text complexity band proficiently, with scaffolding as needed at the high end of the range.
  By the end of grade 10, read and comprehend literary nonfiction at the high end of the grades 9–10 text complexity band independently and proficiently.

Writing » Grades 9–10

Text Types and Purposes

- W.9–10.1. Write arguments to support claims in an analysis of substantive topics or texts, using valid reasoning and relevant and sufficient evidence.
  - W.9–10.1.A. Introduce precise claim(s), distinguish the claim(s) from alternate or opposing claims, and create an organization that establishes clear relationships among claim(s), counterclaims, reasons, and evidence.
  - W.9–10.1.B. Develop claim(s) and counterclaims fairly, supplying evidence for each while pointing out the strengths and limitations of both in a manner that anticipates the audience's knowledge level and concerns.
  - W.9–10.1.C. Use words, phrases, and clauses to link the major sections of the text, create cohesion, and clarify the relationships between claim(s) and reasons, between reasons and evidence, and between claim(s) and counterclaims.
  - W.9–10.1.D. Establish and maintain a formal style and objective tone while attending to the norms and conventions of the discipline in which they are writing.
  - W.9–10.1.E. Provide a concluding statement or section that follows from and supports the argument presented.
- W.9–10.2. Write informative/explanatory texts to examine and convey complex ideas, concepts, and information clearly and accurately through the effective selection, organization, and analysis of content.
  - W.9–10.2.A. Introduce a topic; organize complex ideas, concepts, and information to make important connections and distinctions; include formatting (e.g., headings), graphics (e.g., figures, tables), and multimedia when useful to aiding comprehension.
  - W.9–10.2.B. Develop the topic with well-chosen, relevant, and sufficient facts, extended definitions, concrete details, quotations, or other information and examples appropriate to the audience's knowledge of the topic.
  - W.9–10.2.C. Use appropriate and varied transitions to link the major sections of the text, create cohesion, and clarify the relationships among complex ideas and concepts.
  - W.9–10.2.D. Use precise language and domain-specific vocabulary to manage the complexity of the topic.

- W.9–10.2.E. Establish and maintain a formal style and objective tone while attending to the norms and conventions of the discipline in which they are writing.
- W.9–10.2.F. Provide a concluding statement or section that follows from and supports the information or explanation presented (e.g., articulating implications or the significance of the topic).

- W.9–10.3. Write narratives to develop real or imagined experiences or events using effective technique, well-chosen details, and well-structured event sequences.
  - W.9–10.3.A. Engage and orient the reader by setting out a problem, situation, or observation, establishing one or multiple point(s) of view, and introducing a narrator and/or characters; create a smooth progression of experiences or events.
  - W.9–10.3.B. Use narrative techniques, such as dialogue, pacing, description, reflection, and multiple plot lines, to develop experiences, events, and/or characters.
  - W.9–10.3.C. Use a variety of techniques to sequence events so that they build on one another to create a coherent whole.
  - W.9–10.3.D. Use precise words and phrases, telling details, and sensory language to convey a vivid picture of the experiences, events, setting, and/or characters.
  - W.9–10.3.E. Provide a conclusion that follows from and reflects on what is experienced, observed, or resolved over the course of the narrative.

Production and Distribution of Writing

- W.9–10.4. Produce clear and coherent writing in which the development, organization, and style are appropriate to task, purpose, and audience. (Grade-specific expectations for writing types are defined in standards 1–3 above.)
- W.9–10.5. Develop and strengthen writing as needed by planning, revising, editing, rewriting, or trying a new approach, focusing on addressing what is most significant for a specific purpose and audience. (Editing for conventions should demonstrate command of Language standards 1–3 up to and including grades 9–10 here.)
- W.9–10.6. Use technology, including the Internet, to produce, publish, and update individual or shared writing products, taking advantage of technology's capacity to link to other information and to display information flexibly and dynamically.

Research to Build and Present Knowledge

- W.9–10.7. Conduct short as well as more sustained research projects to answer a question (including a self-generated question) or solve a problem; narrow or broaden the inquiry when appropriate; synthesize multiple sources on the subject, demonstrating understanding of the subject under investigation.
- W.9–10.8. Gather relevant information from multiple authoritative print and digital sources, using advanced searches effectively; assess the usefulness of each source in answering the research question; integrate information into the text selectively to maintain the flow of ideas, avoiding plagiarism and following a standard format for citation.
- W.9–10.9. Draw evidence from literary or informational texts to support analysis, reflection, and research.
  - W.9–10.9.A. Apply grades 9–10 Reading standards to literature (e.g., "Analyze how an author draws on and transforms source material in a specific work [e.g., how Shakespeare treats a theme or topic from Ovid or the Bible or how a later author draws on a play by Shakespeare]").
  - W.9–10.9.B. Apply grades 9–10 Reading standards to literary nonfiction (e.g., "Delineate and evaluate the argument and specific claims in a text, assessing whether the reasoning is valid and the evidence is relevant and sufficient; identify false statements and fallacious reasoning").

Range of Writing

- W.9–10.10. Write routinely over extended time frames (time for research, reflection, and revision) and shorter time frames (a single sitting or a day or two) for a range of tasks, purposes, and audiences.

Speaking and Listening » Grades 9–10

Comprehension and Collaboration

- SL.9–10.1. Initiate and participate effectively in a range of collaborative discussions (one-on-one, in groups, and teacher-led) with diverse partners on *grades 9–10 topics, texts, and issues*, building on others' ideas and expressing their own clearly and persuasively.
  - SL.9–10.1.A. Come to discussions prepared, having read and researched material under study; explicitly draw on that preparation by referring to evidence from texts and other research on the topic or issue to stimulate a thoughtful, well-reasoned exchange of ideas.
  - SL.9–10.1.B. Work with peers to set rules for collegial discussions and decision making (e.g., informal consensus, taking votes on key issues, presentation of alternate views), clear goals and deadlines, and individual roles as needed.
  - SL.9–10.1.C. Propel conversations by posing and responding to questions that relate the current discussion to broader themes or larger ideas; actively incorporate others into the discussion; and clarify, verify, or challenge ideas and conclusions.
  - SL.9–10.1.D. Respond thoughtfully to diverse perspectives, summarize points of agreement and disagreement, and, when warranted, qualify or justify their own views and understanding and make new connections in light of the evidence and reasoning presented.
- SL.9–10.2. Integrate multiple sources of information presented in diverse media or formats (e.g., visually, quantitatively, orally) evaluating the credibility and accuracy of each source.
- SL.9–10.3. Evaluate a speaker's point of view, reasoning, and use of evidence and rhetoric, identifying any fallacious reasoning or exaggerated or distorted evidence.

Presentation of Knowledge and Ideas

- SL.9–10.4. Present information, findings, and supporting evidence clearly, concisely, and logically such that listeners can follow the line of reasoning and the organization, development, substance, and style are appropriate to purpose, audience, and task.
- SL.9–10.5. Make strategic use of digital media (e.g., textual, graphical, audio, visual, and interactive elements) in presentations to enhance understanding of findings, reasoning, and evidence and to add interest.
- SL.9–10.6. Adapt speech to a variety of contexts and tasks, demonstrating command of formal English when indicated or appropriate. (See grades 9–10 Language standards 1 and 3 here for specific expectations.)

Language » Grades 9–10

Conventions of Standard English

- L.9–10.1. Demonstrate command of the conventions of standard English grammar and usage when writing or speaking.
  - L.9–10.1.A. Use parallel structure.
  - L.9–10.1.B. Use various types of phrases (noun, verb, adjectival, adverbial, participial, prepositional, absolute) and clauses (independent, dependent; noun, relative, adverbial) to convey specific meanings and add variety and interest to writing or presentations.
- L.9–10.2. Demonstrate command of the conventions of standard English capitalization, punctuation, and spelling when writing.
  - L.9–10.2.A. Use a semicolon (and perhaps a conjunctive adverb) to link two or more closely related independent clauses.
  - L.9–10.2.B. Use a colon to introduce a list or quotation.
  - L.9–10.2.C. Spell correctly.

Knowledge of Language

- L.9–10.3. Apply knowledge of language to understand how language functions in different contexts, to make effective choices for meaning or style, and to comprehend more fully when reading or listening.
    - L.9–10.3.A. Write and edit work so that it conforms to the guidelines in a style manual (e.g., *MLA Handbook*, Turabian's *Manual for Writers*) appropriate for the discipline and writing type.

Vocabulary Acquisition and Use

- L.9–10.4. Determine or clarify the meaning of unknown and multiple-meaning words and phrases based on *grades 9–10 reading and content*, choosing flexibly from a range of strategies.
    - L.9–10.4.A. Use context (e.g., the overall meaning of a sentence, paragraph, or text; a word's position or function in a sentence) as a clue to the meaning of a word or phrase.
    - L.9–10.4.B. Identify and correctly use patterns of word changes that indicate different meanings or parts of speech (e.g., *analyze, analysis, analytical; advocate, advocacy*).
    - L.9–10.4.C. Consult general and specialized reference materials (e.g., dictionaries, glossaries, thesauruses), both print and digital, to find the pronunciation of a word or determine or clarify its precise meaning, its part of speech, or its etymology.
    - L.9–10.4.D. Verify the preliminary determination of the meaning of a word or phrase (e.g., by checking the inferred meaning in context or in a dictionary).
- L.9–10.5. Demonstrate understanding of figurative language, word relationships, and nuances in word meanings.
    - L.9–10.5.A. Interpret figures of speech (e.g., euphemism, oxymoron) in context and analyze their role in the text.
    - L.9–10.5.B. Analyze nuances in the meaning of words with similar denotations.
- L.9–10.6. Acquire and use accurately general academic and domain-specific words and phrases, sufficient for reading, writing, speaking, and listening at the college and career readiness level; demonstrate independence in gathering vocabulary knowledge when considering a word or phrase important to comprehension or expression.

ENGLISH LANGUAGE ARTS STANDARDS FOR GRADES 11–12

Reading: Literature » Grades 11–12

Key Ideas and Details

- RL.11–12.1. Cite strong and thorough textual evidence to support analysis of what the text says explicitly as well as inferences drawn from the text, including determining where the text leaves matters uncertain.
- RL.11–12.2. Determine two or more themes or central ideas of a text and analyze their development over the course of the text, including how they interact and build on one another to produce a complex account; provide an objective summary of the text.
- RL.11–12.3. Analyze the impact of the author's choices regarding how to develop and relate elements of a story or drama (e.g., where a story is set, how the action is ordered, how the characters are introduced and developed).

Craft and Structure

- RL.11–12.4. Determine the meaning of words and phrases as they are used in the text, including figurative and connotative meanings; analyze the impact of specific word choices on meaning and tone, including words with multiple meanings or language that is particularly fresh, engaging, or beautiful. (Include Shakespeare as well as other authors.)

- RL.11–12.5. Analyze how an author's choices concerning how to structure specific parts of a text (e.g., the choice of where to begin or end a story, the choice to provide a comedic or tragic resolution) contribute to its overall structure and meaning as well as its aesthetic impact.
- RL.11–12.6. Analyze a case in which grasping a point of view requires distinguishing what is directly stated in a text from what is really meant (e.g., satire, sarcasm, irony, or understatement).

Integration of Knowledge and Ideas

- RL.11–12.7. Analyze multiple interpretations of a story, drama, or poem (e.g., recorded or live production of a play or recorded novel or poetry), evaluating how each version interprets the source text. (Include at least one play by Shakespeare and one play by an American dramatist.)
- RL.11–12.8 (Not applicable to literature)
- RL.11–12.9. Demonstrate knowledge of eighteenth-, nineteenth- and early-twentieth-century foundational works of American literature, including how two or more texts from the same period treat similar themes or topics.

Range of Reading and Level of Text Complexity

- RL.11–12.10. By the end of grade 11, read and comprehend literature, including stories, dramas, and poems, in the grades 11–CCR text complexity band proficiently, with scaffolding as needed at the high end of the range.

    By the end of grade 12, read and comprehend literature, including stories, dramas, and poems, at the high end of the grades 11–CCR text complexity band independently and proficiently.

Reading: Informational Text » Grades 11–12

Key Ideas and Details

- RI.11–12.1. Cite strong and thorough textual evidence to support analysis of what the text says explicitly as well as inferences drawn from the text, including determining where the text leaves matters uncertain.
- RI.11–12.2. Determine two or more central ideas of a text and analyze their development over the course of the text, including how they interact and build on one another to provide a complex analysis; provide an objective summary of the text.
- RI.11–12.3. Analyze a complex set of ideas or sequence of events and explain how specific individuals, ideas, or events interact and develop over the course of the text.

Craft and Structure

- RI.11–12.4. Determine the meaning of words and phrases as they are used in a text, including figurative, connotative, and technical meanings; analyze how an author uses and refines the meaning of a key term or terms over the course of a text (e.g., how Madison defines *faction* in *Federalist* No. 10).
- RI.11–12.5. Analyze and evaluate the effectiveness of the structure an author uses in his or her exposition or argument, including whether the structure makes points clear, convincing, and engaging.
- RI.11–12.6. Determine an author's point of view or purpose in a text in which the rhetoric is particularly effective, analyzing how style and content contribute to the power, persuasiveness, or beauty of the text.

Integration of Knowledge and Ideas

- RI.11–12.7. Integrate and evaluate multiple sources of information presented in different media or formats (e.g., visually, quantitatively) as well as in words in order to address a question or solve a problem.
- RI.11–12.8. Delineate and evaluate the reasoning in seminal U.S. texts, including the application of constitutional principles and use of legal reasoning (e.g., in U.S. Supreme

Court majority opinions and dissents) and the premises, purposes, and arguments in works of public advocacy (e.g., *The Federalist*, presidential addresses).

- RI.11–12.9. Analyze seventeenth-, eighteenth-, and nineteenth-century foundational U.S. documents of historical and literary significance (including The Declaration of Independence, the Preamble to the Constitution, the Bill of Rights, and Lincoln's Second Inaugural Address) for their themes, purposes, and rhetorical features.

Range of Reading and Level of Text Complexity

- RI.11–12.10. By the end of grade 11, read and comprehend literary nonfiction in the grades 11–CCR text complexity band proficiently, with scaffolding as needed at the high end of the range.

    By the end of grade 12, read and comprehend literary nonfiction at the high end of the grades 11–CCR text complexity band independently and proficiently.

Writing » Grades 11–12

Text Types and Purposes

- W.11–12.1. Write arguments to support claims in an analysis of substantive topics or texts, using valid reasoning and relevant and sufficient evidence.
    - W.11–12.1.A. Introduce precise, knowledgeable claim(s), establish the significance of the claim(s), distinguish the claim(s) from alternate or opposing claims, and create an organization that logically sequences claim(s), counterclaims, reasons, and evidence.
    - W.11–12.1.B. Develop claim(s) and counterclaims fairly and thoroughly, supplying the most relevant evidence for each while pointing out the strengths and limitations of both in a manner that anticipates the audience's knowledge level, concerns, values, and possible biases.
    - W.11–12.1.C. Use words, phrases, and clauses as well as varied syntax to link the major sections of the text, create cohesion, and clarify the relationships between claim(s) and reasons, between reasons and evidence, and between claim(s) and counterclaims.
    - W.11–12.1.D. Establish and maintain a formal style and objective tone while attending to the norms and conventions of the discipline in which they are writing.
    - W.11–12.1.E. Provide a concluding statement or section that follows from and supports the argument presented.
- W.11–12.2. Write informative/explanatory texts to examine and convey complex ideas, concepts, and information clearly and accurately through the effective selection, organization, and analysis of content.
    - W.11–12.2.A. Introduce a topic; organize complex ideas, concepts, and information so that each new element builds on that which precedes it to create a unified whole; include formatting (e.g., headings), graphics (e.g., figures, tables), and multimedia when useful to aiding comprehension.
    - W.11–12.2.B. Develop the topic thoroughly by selecting the most significant and relevant facts, extended definitions, concrete details, quotations, or other information and examples appropriate to the audience's knowledge of the topic.
    - W.11–12.2.C. Use appropriate and varied transitions and syntax to link the major sections of the text, create cohesion, and clarify the relationships among complex ideas and concepts.
    - W.11–12.2.D. Use precise language, domain-specific vocabulary, and techniques such as metaphor, simile, and analogy to manage the complexity of the topic.
    - W.11–12.2.E. Establish and maintain a formal style and objective tone while attending to the norms and conventions of the discipline in which they are writing.
    - W.11–12.2.F. Provide a concluding statement or section that follows from and supports the information or explanation presented (e.g., articulating implications or the significance of the topic).

- W.11–12.3. Write narratives to develop real or imagined experiences or events using effective technique, well-chosen details, and well-structured event sequences.
  - W.11–12.3.A. Engage and orient the reader by setting out a problem, situation, or observation and its significance, establishing one or multiple point(s) of view, and introducing a narrator and/or characters; create a smooth progression of experiences or events.
  - W.11–12.3.B. Use narrative techniques, such as dialogue, pacing, description, reflection, and multiple plot lines, to develop experiences, events, and/or characters.
  - W.11–12.3.C. Use a variety of techniques to sequence events so that they build on one another to create a coherent whole and build toward a particular tone and outcome (e.g., a sense of mystery, suspense, growth, or resolution).
  - W.11–12.3.D. Use precise words and phrases, telling details, and sensory language to convey a vivid picture of the experiences, events, setting, and/or characters.
  - W.11–12.3.E. Provide a conclusion that follows from and reflects on what is experienced, observed, or resolved over the course of the narrative.

Production and Distribution of Writing

- W.11–12.4. Produce clear and coherent writing in which the development, organization, and style are appropriate to task, purpose, and audience. (Grade-specific expectations for writing types are defined in standards 1–3 above.)
- W.11–12.5. Develop and strengthen writing as needed by planning, revising, editing, rewriting, or trying a new approach, focusing on addressing what is most significant for a specific purpose and audience. (Editing for conventions should demonstrate command of Language standards 1–3 up to and including grades 11–12 here.)
- W.11–12.6. Use technology, including the Internet, to produce, publish, and update individual or shared writing products in response to ongoing feedback, including new arguments or information.

Research to Build and Present Knowledge

- W.11–12.7. Conduct short as well as more sustained research projects to answer a question (including a self-generated question) or solve a problem; narrow or broaden the inquiry when appropriate; synthesize multiple sources on the subject, demonstrating understanding of the subject under investigation.
- W.11–12.8. Gather relevant information from multiple authoritative print and digital sources, using advanced searches effectively; assess the strengths and limitations of each source in terms of the task, purpose, and audience; integrate information into the text selectively to maintain the flow of ideas, avoiding plagiarism and overreliance on any one source and following a standard format for citation.
- W.11–12.9. Draw evidence from literary or informational texts to support analysis, reflection, and research.
  - W.11–12.9.A. Apply grades 11–12 Reading standards to literature (e.g., "Demonstrate knowledge of eighteenth-, nineteenth- and early-twentieth-century foundational works of American literature, including how two or more texts from the same period treat similar themes or topics").
  - W.11–12.9.B. Apply grades 11–12 Reading standards to literary nonfiction (e.g., "Delineate and evaluate the reasoning in seminal U.S. texts, including the application of constitutional principles and use of legal reasoning [e.g., in U.S. Supreme Court Case majority opinions and dissents] and the premises, purposes, and arguments in works of public advocacy [e.g., *The Federalist*, presidential addresses]").

Range of Writing

- W.11–12.10. Write routinely over extended time frames (time for research, reflection, and revision) and shorter time frames (a single sitting or a day or two) for a range of tasks, purposes, and audiences.

Speaking and Listening » Grades 11–12

Comprehension and Collaboration

- SL.11–12.1. Initiate and participate effectively in a range of collaborative discussions (one-on-one, in groups, and teacher-led) with diverse partners on *grades 11–12 topics, texts, and issues*, building on others' ideas and expressing their own clearly and persuasively.
  - SL.11–12.1.A. Come to discussions prepared, having read and researched material under study; explicitly draw on that preparation by referring to evidence from texts and other research on the topic or issue to stimulate a thoughtful, well-reasoned exchange of ideas.
  - SL.11–12.1.B. Work with peers to promote civil, democratic discussions and decision making, set clear goals and deadlines, and establish individual roles as needed.
  - SL.11–12.1.C. Propel conversations by posing and responding to questions that probe reasoning and evidence; ensure a hearing for a full range of positions on a topic or issue; clarify, verify, or challenge ideas and conclusions; and promote divergent and creative perspectives.
  - SL.11–12.1.D. Respond thoughtfully to diverse perspectives; synthesize comments, claims, and evidence made on all sides of an issue; resolve contradictions when possible; and determine what additional information or research is required to deepen the investigation or complete the task.
- SL.11–12.2. Integrate multiple sources of information presented in diverse formats and media (e.g., visually, quantitatively, orally) in order to make informed decisions and solve problems, evaluating the credibility and accuracy of each source and noting any discrepancies among the data.
- SL.11–12.3. Evaluate a speaker's point of view, reasoning, and use of evidence and rhetoric, assessing the stance, premises, links among ideas, word choice, points of emphasis, and tone used.

Presentation of Knowledge and Ideas

- SL.11–12.4. Present information, findings, and supporting evidence, conveying a clear and distinct perspective, such that listeners can follow the line of reasoning, alternative or opposing perspectives are addressed, and the organization, development, substance, and style are appropriate to purpose, audience, and a range of formal and informal tasks.
- SL.11–12.5. Make strategic use of digital media (e.g., textual, graphical, audio, visual, and interactive elements) in presentations to enhance understanding of findings, reasoning, and evidence and to add interest.
- SL.11–12.6. Adapt speech to a variety of contexts and tasks, demonstrating a command of formal English when indicated or appropriate. (See grades 11–12 Language standards 1 and 3 here for specific expectations.)

Language » Grades 11–12

Conventions of Standard English

- L.11–12.1. Demonstrate command of the conventions of standard English grammar and usage when writing or speaking.
  - L.11–12.1.A. Apply the understanding that usage is a matter of convention, can change over time, and is sometimes contested.
  - L.11–12.1.B. Resolve issues of complex or contested usage, consulting references (e.g., *Merriam-Webster's Dictionary of English Usage, Garner's Modern American Usage*) as needed.
- L.11–12.2. Demonstrate command of the conventions of standard English capitalization, punctuation, and spelling when writing.
  - L.11–12.2.A. Observe hyphenation conventions.
  - L.11–12.2.B. Spell correctly.

Knowledge of Language

- L.11–12.3. Apply knowledge of language to understand how language functions in different contexts, to make effective choices for meaning or style, and to comprehend more fully when reading or listening.
    - L.11–12.3.A. Vary syntax for effect, consulting references (e.g., Tufte's *Artful Sentences*) for guidance as needed; apply an understanding of syntax to the study of complex texts when reading.

Vocabulary Acquisition and Use

- L.11–12.4. Determine or clarify the meaning of unknown and multiple-meaning words and phrases based on *grades 11–12 reading and content*, choosing flexibly from a range of strategies.
    - L.11–12.4.A. Use context (e.g., the overall meaning of a sentence, paragraph, or text; a word's position or function in a sentence) as a clue to the meaning of a word or phrase.
    - L.11–12.4.B. Identify and correctly use patterns of word changes that indicate different meanings or parts of speech (e.g., *conceive, conception, conceivable*).
    - L.11–12.4.C. Consult general and specialized reference materials (e.g., dictionaries, glossaries, thesauruses), both print and digital, to find the pronunciation of a word or determine or clarify its precise meaning, its part of speech, its etymology, or its standard usage.
    - L.11–12.4.D. Verify the preliminary determination of the meaning of a word or phrase (e.g., by checking the inferred meaning in context or in a dictionary).
- L.11–12.5. Demonstrate understanding of figurative language, word relationships, and nuances in word meanings.
    - L.11–12.5.A. Interpret figures of speech (e.g., hyperbole, paradox) in context and analyze their role in the text.
    - L.11–12.5.B. Analyze nuances in the meaning of words with similar denotations.
- L.11–12.6. Acquire and use accurately general academic and domain-specific words and phrases, sufficient for reading, writing, speaking, and listening at the college and career readiness level; demonstrate independence in gathering vocabulary knowledge when considering a word or phrase important to comprehension or expression.

LITERACY STANDARDS IN HISTORY/SOCIAL STUDIES, SCIENCE, AND TECHNICAL SUBJECTS FOR GRADES 6–12

History/Social Studies » Grades 6–8

Key Ideas and Details

- RH.6–8.1. Cite specific textual evidence to support analysis of primary and secondary sources.
- RH.6–8.2. Determine the central ideas or information of a primary or secondary source; provide an accurate summary of the source distinct from prior knowledge or opinions.
- RH.6–8.3. Identify key steps in a text's description of a process related to history/social studies (e.g., how a bill becomes law, how interest rates are raised or lowered).

Craft and Structure

- RH.6–8.4. Determine the meaning of words and phrases as they are used in a text, including vocabulary specific to domains related to history/social studies.
- RH.6–8.5. Describe how a text presents information (e.g., sequentially, comparatively, causally).
- RH.6–8.6. Identify aspects of a text that reveal an author's point of view or purpose (e.g., loaded language, inclusion or avoidance of particular facts).

Integration of Knowledge and Ideas

- RH.6–8.7. Integrate visual information (e.g., in charts, graphs, photographs, videos, or maps) with other information in print and digital texts.
- RH.6–8.8. Distinguish among fact, opinion, and reasoned judgment in a text.
- RH.6–8.9. Analyze the relationship between a primary and secondary source on the same topic.

Range of Reading and Level of Text Complexity

- RH.6–8.10. By the end of grade 8, read and comprehend history/social studies texts in the grades 6–8 text complexity band independently and proficiently.

History/Social Studies » Grades 9–10

Key Ideas and Details

- RH.9–10.1. Cite specific textual evidence to support analysis of primary and secondary sources, attending to such features as the date and origin of the information.
- RH.9–10.2. Determine the central ideas or information of a primary or secondary source; provide an accurate summary of how key events or ideas develop over the course of the text.
- RH.9–10.3. Analyze in detail a series of events described in a text; determine whether earlier events caused later ones or simply preceded them.

Craft and Structure

- RH.9–10.4. Determine the meaning of words and phrases as they are used in a text, including vocabulary describing political, social, or economic aspects of history/social science.
- RH.9–10.5. Analyze how a text uses structure to emphasize key points or advance an explanation or analysis.
- RH.9–10.6. Compare the point of view of two or more authors for how they treat the same or similar topics, including which details they include and emphasize in their respective accounts.

Integration of Knowledge and Ideas

- RH.9–10.7. Integrate quantitative or technical analysis (e.g., charts, research data) with qualitative analysis in print or digital text.
- RH.9–10.8. Assess the extent to which the reasoning and evidence in a text support the author's claims.
- RH.9–10.9. Compare and contrast treatments of the same topic in several primary and secondary sources.

Range of Reading and Level of Text Complexity

- RH.9–10.10. By the end of grade 10, read and comprehend history/social studies texts in the grades 9–10 text complexity band independently and proficiently.

History/Social Studies » Grades 11–12

Key Ideas and Details

- RH.11–12.1. Cite specific textual evidence to support analysis of primary and secondary sources, connecting insights gained from specific details to an understanding of the text as a whole.
- RH.11–12.2. Determine the central ideas or information of a primary or secondary source; provide an accurate summary that makes clear the relationships among the key details and ideas.
- RH.11–12.3. Evaluate various explanations for actions or events and determine which explanation best accords with textual evidence, acknowledging where the text leaves matters uncertain.

Craft and Structure

- RH.11–12.4. Determine the meaning of words and phrases as they are used in a text, including analyzing how an author uses and refines the meaning of a key term over the course of a text (e.g., how Madison defines *faction* in *Federalist* No. 10).
- RH.11–12.5. Analyze in detail how a complex primary source is structured, including how key sentences, paragraphs, and larger portions of the text contribute to the whole.
- RH.11–12.6. Evaluate authors' differing points of view on the same historical event or issue by assessing the authors' claims, reasoning, and evidence.

Integration of Knowledge and Ideas

- RH.11–12.7. Integrate and evaluate multiple sources of information presented in diverse formats and media (e.g., visually, quantitatively, as well as in words) in order to address a question or solve a problem.
- RH.11–12.8. Evaluate an author's premises, claims, and evidence by corroborating or challenging them with other information.
- RH.11–12.9. Integrate information from diverse sources, both primary and secondary, into a coherent understanding of an idea or event, noting discrepancies among sources.

Range of Reading and Level of Text Complexity

- RH.11–12.10. By the end of grade 12, read and comprehend history/social studies texts in the grades 11–CCR text complexity band independently and proficiently.

Science and Technical Subjects » Grades 6–8

Key Ideas and Details

- RST.6–8.1. Cite specific textual evidence to support analysis of science and technical texts.
- RST.6–8.2. Determine the central ideas or conclusions of a text; provide an accurate summary of the text distinct from prior knowledge or opinions.
- RST.6–8.3. Follow precisely a multistep procedure when carrying out experiments, taking measurements, or performing technical tasks.

Craft and Structure

- RST.6–8.4. Determine the meaning of symbols, key terms, and other domain-specific words and phrases as they are used in a specific scientific or technical context relevant to grades 6–8 texts and topics.
- RST.6–8.5. Analyze the structure an author uses to organize a text, including how the major sections contribute to the whole and to an understanding of the topic.
- RST.6–8.6. Analyze the author's purpose in providing an explanation, describing a procedure, or discussing an experiment in a text.

Integration of Knowledge and Ideas

- RST.6–8.7. Integrate quantitative or technical information expressed in words in a text with a version of that information expressed visually (e.g., in a flowchart, diagram, model, graph, or table).
- RST.6–8.8. Distinguish among facts, reasoned judgment based on research findings, and speculation in a text.
- RST.6–8.9. Compare and contrast the information gained from experiments, simulations, video, or multimedia sources with that gained from reading a text on the same topic.

Range of Reading and Level of Text Complexity

- RST.6–8.10. By the end of grade 8, read and comprehend science/technical texts in the grades 6–8 text complexity band independently and proficiently.

Science and Technical Subjects » Grades 9–10

Key Ideas and Details

- RST.9–10.1. Cite specific textual evidence to support analysis of science and technical texts, attending to the precise details of explanations or descriptions.
- RST.9–10.2. Determine the central ideas or conclusions of a text; trace the text's explanation or depiction of a complex process, phenomenon, or concept; provide an accurate summary of the text.
- RST.9–10.3. Follow precisely a complex multistep procedure when carrying out experiments, taking measurements, or performing technical tasks, attending to special cases or exceptions defined in the text.

Craft and Structure

- RST.9–10.4. Determine the meaning of symbols, key terms, and other domain-specific words and phrases as they are used in a specific scientific or technical context relevant to grades 9–10 texts and topics.
- RST.9–10.5. Analyze the structure of the relationships among concepts in a text, including relationships among key terms (e.g., *force, friction, reaction force, energy*).
- RST.9–10.6. Analyze the author's purpose in providing an explanation, describing a procedure, or discussing an experiment in a text, defining the question the author seeks to address.

Integration of Knowledge and Ideas

- RST.9–10.7. Translate quantitative or technical information expressed in words in a text into visual form (e.g., a table or chart) and translate information expressed visually or mathematically (e.g., in an equation) into words.
- RST.9–10.8. Assess the extent to which the reasoning and evidence in a text support the author's claim or a recommendation for solving a scientific or technical problem.
- RST.9–10.9. Compare and contrast findings presented in a text to those from other sources (including their own experiments), noting when the findings support or contradict previous explanations or accounts.

Range of Reading and Level of Text Complexity

- RST.9–10.10. By the end of grade 10, read and comprehend science/technical texts in the grades 9–10 text complexity band independently and proficiently.

Science and Technical Subjects » Grades 11–12

Key Ideas and Details

- RST.11–12.1. Cite specific textual evidence to support analysis of science and technical texts, attending to important distinctions the author makes and to any gaps or inconsistencies in the account.
- RST.11–12.2. Determine the central ideas or conclusions of a text; summarize complex concepts, processes, or information presented in a text by paraphrasing them in simpler but still accurate terms.
- RST.11–12.3. Follow precisely a complex multistep procedure when carrying out experiments, taking measurements, or performing technical tasks; analyze the specific results based on explanations in the text.

Craft and Structure

- RST.11–12.4. Determine the meaning of symbols, key terms, and other domain-specific words and phrases as they are used in a specific scientific or technical context relevant to grades 11–12 texts and topics.
- RST.11–12.5. Analyze how the text structures information or ideas into categories or hierarchies, demonstrating understanding of the information or ideas.
- RST.11–12.6. Analyze the author's purpose in providing an explanation, describing a procedure, or discussing an experiment in a text, identifying important issues that remain unresolved.

Integration of Knowledge and Ideas

- RST.11–12.7. Integrate and evaluate multiple sources of information presented in diverse formats and media (e.g., quantitative data, video, multimedia) in order to address a question or solve a problem.
- RST.11–12.8. Evaluate the hypotheses, data, analysis, and conclusions in a science or technical text, verifying the data when possible and corroborating or challenging conclusions with other sources of information.
- RST.11–12.9. Synthesize information from a range of sources (e.g., texts, experiments, simulations) into a coherent understanding of a process, phenomenon, or concept, resolving conflicting information when possible.

Range of Reading and Level of Text Complexity

- RST.11–12.10. By the end of grade 12, read and comprehend science/technical texts in the grades 11–CCR text complexity band independently and proficiently.

References

Achieve: New Room. (2014). news@achieve.org. Retrieved October 20, 2014, from *http://achieve.org/dont-let-politics-block-common-core*.

Achieve the Core. (2014). Publishers' criteria: K–2, 3–12. Available at *http://achievethecore.org*.

Adler, M. J., & Van Doren, C. (1972). *How to read a book*. New York: Touchstone.

Avelar La Salle, R. (2014). Principal's Exchange. Retrieved August 5, 2015, from *www.principals-exchange.org/index.php*.

Amendum, S., & Fitzgerald, J. (2013). Does structure of content delivery or degree of professional development support matter for student reading growth in high poverty settings? *Journal of Literacy Research, 45,* 465–502.

American Federation of Teachers. (2014). Debunking myths of the Common Core. Retrieved January 14, 2015, from *www.aft.org/position/common-core-state-standards/debunking-myths-common-core*.

Bear, D. R., Templeton, S., Invernizzi, M. A., & Johnston, F. A. (2011). *Words their way: Word study for phonics, vocabulary, and spelling instruction* (5th ed.). Harlow, UK: Pearson.

Berger, R. (2015, January 8). What if assessment was used to elevate learning rather than rank students? Retrieved March 16, 2015, from *www.teachingchannel.org/blog/2015/01/08/assessing-to-elevate-students*.

Black, P., Harrison, C., Lee, C., & Marshall, B. (2003). *Assessment for learning: Putting it into practice*. New York: McGraw-Hill.

Black, P., & Wiliam, D. (1998a). Assessment and classroom learning. *Assessment in Education: Principles, Policy, and Practice, 5*(1), 7–74.

Black, P., & Wiliam, D. (1998b). Inside the black box: Raising standards through classroom assessment. *Phi Delta Kappan, 80,* 139–148.

Brown, S., & Kappes, L. (2012, October). *Implementing the Common Core State Standards: A primer on "close reading of text."* Washington, DC: Aspen Institute.

Bruning, R., & Schweiger, B. M. (1997). Integrating science and literacy experiences to motivate student learning. In J. T. Guthrie & A. Wigfield (Eds.), *Reading engagement: Motivating readers through integrated instruction* (pp. 149–167). Newark, DE: International Reading Association.

Calfee, R. C. (2013, November). *Defining and Fulfilling the Vision of the Common Core Standards.* Presentation to the annual meeting of the Association of Literacy Educators and Researchers, Dallas, TX.

Calfee, R. C., & Patrick, C. L. (1995). *Teach our children well.* Stanford, CA: Stanford University Alumni Association.

Calfee, R. C., & Wilson, K. M. (2013). *LP+FA: Learning progression framework for constructing a formative assessment system for K–5 Literacy Standards.* Unpublished manuscript.

Calfee, R. C., Wilson, K. M., Flannery, B., & Kapinus, B. (2014). Formative assessments for the Common Core Literacy Standards. *Teachers College Record, 116*(11), 1–32.

Carroll, J. B., & Chall, J. S. (1975). *Toward a literate society: The report of the Committee on Reading of the National Academy of Education with a series of papers commissioned by the committee.* New York: McGraw-Hill.

Center on Education Policy. (2011, December). AYP results for 2010–11. Retrieved June 8, 2015, from *www.cep.-dc.org.*

Chambliss, M. J., & Calfee, R. C. (1998). *Textbooks for learning: Nurturing children's minds.* Malden, MA: Blackwell.

Christenson, S. L., Rounds, T., & Gorney, D. (1992). Family factors and student achievement: An avenue to increase students' success. *School Psychology Quarterly, 7*(3), 178–206.

Coleman, D., & Pimentel, S. (2011a). Publishers' Criteria for the Common Core State Standards in English Language Arts and Literacy, Grades K–2. Retrieved August 4, 2015, from *www.corestandards.org/assets/Publishers_Criteria_for_K-2_old.pdf.*

Coleman, D., & Pimentel, S. (2011b). Publishers criteria for the Common Core State Standards in English Language Arts and Literacy, Grades 3–12. Retrieved August 4, 2015, from *www.edweek.org/media/3-12-criteria-blog.pdf.*

Coleman, D., & Pimentel, S. (2012). Revised Publishers' Criteria for the Common Core State Standards in English Language Arts and Literacy, Grades K–2. Retrieved August 4, 2015, from *www.corestandards.org/assets/Publishers_Criteria_for_K-2.pdf.*

Coleman, J. S., Campbell, E. Q., Hobson, C. J., McPartland, J., Mood, A. M., Weinfeld, F. D., et al. (1966). *The Coleman Report. Equality of educational opportunity.* Washington, DC: U.S. Government Printing Office.

Council of the Greater City Schools. (2013). Implementing the Common Core State Standards: Year two progress report from the Greater City Schools. Retrieved October 21, 2014, from *www.cgcs.org/cms/lib/ DC00001581/Centricity/Domain/87/CC%20Survey%20Report%20 FINAL.pdf.*

Danielson, C. (2011). *Enhancing professional practice: A framework for teaching.* Alexandria, VA: ASCD.

Darling-Hammond, L. (2010). *Performance counts: Assessment systems that support high-quality learning.* Washington, DC: Council of Chief State School Officers.

Darling-Hammond, L. (2014, November 17). Transforming assessment to improve teaching and learning. Retrieved February 22, 2015, from *http:// blogs.edweek.org/edweek/learning_deeply/2014/11/transforming_ assessment_to_improve_teaching_and_learning.html?qs=Transforming +Assessment+Darling-Hammond.*

Davis, V. (2015, January 15). 5 fantastic, fast, formative assessment tools. Retrieved March 16, 2015, from *www.edutopia.org/blog/5-fast-formative-assessment-tools-vicki-davis.*

Deci, E. L., & Ryan, R. M. (1985). The General Causality Orientations Scale: Self-determination in personality. *Journal of Research in Personality,* 19(2), 109–134.

Editorial Projects in Education. (2014). *From adoption to practice: Findings from a national survey of teachers.* Bethesda, MD: Education Week Research Center. Retrieved October 20, 2014, from *www.edweek.org/ media/ewrc_teacherscommoncore_2014.pdf.*

Editorial Projects in Education Research Center. (2013). *Findings from a national survey of teacher perspectives on the Common Core.* Bethesda, MD: Author. Retrieved September 4, 2013, from *www.edweek.org/ media/epe_survey_teacher_perspctives_common_core_2013.pdf.*

Education Week. (2014). Resistance to the Common Core mounts. Retrieved October 20, 2014, from *www.edweek.org/ew/articles/2014/04/23/29cc-backlash.h33.html.*

Education Week Report Roundup. (2014, November 11). Common-Core testing: "Smarter balanced 'tests of the tests' successful." *Education Week,* 34(12), 5.

Educational Testing Service. (2011, July). *Coming together to raise achievement: New assessments for the Common Core State Standards.* Austin, TX: Author.

Educational Testing Service. (2013, June). *Coming together to raise achievement: New assessments for the Common Core State Standards* (4th ed.). Austin, TX: Author.

Elawar, M. C., & Corno, L. (1985). A factorial experiment in teacher's written feedback on students' homework. *Journal of Educational Psychology,* 77(2), 162–173.

engageNY. (n.d.). Pedagogical shifts demanded by the Common Core State

Standards. Retrieved January 31, 2015, from *www.engageny.org/sites/default/files/resource/attachments/common-core-shifts.pdf.*

Frangos, E. M. (2011). The Common Core State Standards for English Language Arts and literacy in history/social studies, science and technical subjects. In *Coming together to raise achievement: New assessments for the Common Core State Standards* (pp. 5–6). Center for K–12 Assessment and Performance Management at ETS. Retrieved August 3, 2015, from *www.k12center.org/rsc/pdf/coming_together_february_2011.pdf*

Gambrell, L. B., & Morrow, L. M. (Eds.). (2014). *Best practices in literacy instruction* (5th ed.). New York: Guilford Press.

Gamse, B. C., Bloom, H. S., Kemple, J. J., & Jacob, R. T. (2008a). *Reading First Impact Study: Interim Report. Executive Summary* (NCEE 2008-4019). National Center for Education Evaluation and Regional Assistance. Washington, DC: National Center for Education Evaluation and Regional Assistance, Institute of Education Sciences, U.S. Department of Education.

Gamse, B. C., Bloom, H. S., Kemple, J. J., & Jacob, R. T. (2008b). *Reading First Impact Study: Interim Report* (NCEE 2008-4016). Washington, DC: National Center for Education Evaluation and Regional Assistance, Institute of Education Sciences, U.S. Department of Education

Gardner, D. P., Larsen, Y. W., Baker, W., & Campbell, A. (1983). *A nation at risk: The imperative for educational reform.* Washington, DC: U.S. Government Printing Office.

Gewertz, C. (2013a, May 22). District bets big on Standards. *Education Week, 32*(32), 1, 10, 12–14.

Gewertz, C. (2013b, June 5). One class takes on the Standards. *Education Week, 32*(33), 1, 18–21.

Gewertz, C. (2013c, June 12). Year-end exams add urgency to teaching. *Education Week, 32*(34), 1, 26–28.

Gewertz, C. (2013d, September 9). D.C. teachers tally results of year's work. *Education Week, 33*(3), 1, 18–20.

Gewertz, C. (2014a, April 21). Common Core at four: Sizing up the enterprise: Common Core penetrates K–12 system, but big challenges remain. *Education Week, 33*(29), 4–6.

Gewertz, C. (2014b, May 5). Early reports suggest few field-testing snags. *Education Week, 33*(30), 1, 20–21.

Gewertz, C. (2014c, September 3). Big year looms for Common-Core testing. *Education Week, 34*(3), 1, 16–17.

Gewertz, C. (2015, February 23). As Common-Core test season begins, teachers feel pressure. *Education Week, 34*(22), 6.

Gibbons, G. (2008). *The vegetables we eat.* New York: Holiday House.

Good, R. H. III, & Kaminski, R. A. (1996). Assessment for instructional decisions: Toward a proactive/prevention model of decision-making for early literacy skills. *School Psychology Quarterly, 11*(4), 326–336.

Goodman, K. S., Calfee, R. C., & Goodman, Y. M. (Eds.). (2013). *Whose knowledge counts in government literacy policies?: Why expertise matters.* New York: Routledge.

Goodman, Y. M. (1978). Kid watching: An alternative to testing. *National Elementary Principal, 57*(4), 41–45.

Gough, P. B., & Tunmer, W. E. (1986). Decoding, reading, and reading disability. *Remedial and Special Education, 7*(1), 6–10.

Gray, W. S., Baruch, D., & Montgomery, E. R. (1940a). *Sally, Dick, and Jane.* Glenview, IL: Scott Foresman.

Gray, W. S., Baruch, D., & Montgomery, E. [R.] (1940b). *We look and see.* Glenview, IL: Scott Foresman.

Guskey, T. R. (2002). Professional development and teacher change. *Teachers and Teaching: Theory and Practice, 8*(3–4), 381–391.

Guthrie, J. T., Hoa, A. L. W., Wigfield, A., Tonks, S. M., Humenick, N. M., & Littles, E. (2007). Reading motivation and reading comprehension growth in the later elementary years. *Contemporary Educational Psychology, 32*(3), 282–313.

Guthrie, J. T., Van Meter, P., McCann, A. D., Wigfield, A., Bennett, L., Poundstone, C. C., et al. (1996). Growth of literacy engagement: Changes in motivations and strategies during concept-oriented reading instruction. *Reading Research Quarterly, 31*(3), 306–332.

Hawking, S. (1998). *A brief history of time.* New York: Bantam Books.

Heincke, P. (2013). *To assess, to teach, to learn: A vision for the future of Assessment Executive Summary.* Princeton, NJ: Gordon Commission on the Future of Assessment in Education.

Heritage, M. (2010). *Formative assessment: Making it happen in the classroom.* Thousand Oaks, CA: Corwin Press.

Heritage, M. (2013). *Formative assessment in practice: A process of inquiry and action.* Cambridge, MA: Harvard Education Press.

Homeroom. (2013, June 18). *New flexibility for states implementing fast-moving reforms: Laying out our thinking.* Washington, DC: U.S. Department of Education. Retrieved February 1, 2015, from *www.ed.gov/blog/2013/06/new-flexibility-for-states-implementing-fast-moving-reforms-laying-out-our-thinking.*

Hosseini, K. (2003). *The kite runner.* New York: Riverhead Books.

Jordan, H. J. (1960). *How a seed grows.* New York: HarperCollins.

K–12 Center at ETS. (2013). *Coming together to raise achievement: New Assessments for the Common Core State Standards.* Princeton, NJ: Educational Testing Service.

Kilpatrick, W. H. (1933). *Others: The educational frontier.* New York: Appleton-Century.

Krauss, R. (1945). *The carrot seed.* New York: Harper & Row

Larmer, J., Mergendoller, J. J., & Boss, S. (2015). *Setting the standard for project based learning: A proven approach to rigorous classroom instruction.* Alexandria, VA: ASCD.

Lin, G. (1999). *The ugly vegetables.* Watertown, MA: Charlesbridge.

Linn, R. L., Baker, E. L., & Betebenner, D. W. (2002). Accountability systems: Implications of requirements of the No Child Left Behind act of 2001. *Educational Researcher*, 31(6), 3–16.

Lionni, L. (1963). *Swimmy*. New York: Random House Children's Books.

Martin, B., Jr. (1967). *Brown bear, brown bear, what do you see?* New York: Holt, Rinehart, & Winston.

McGraw-Hill. (2014). *Reading Wonders*. New York: McGraw-Hill Education Global Holdings. Retrieved from *www.mheonline.com/program/view/1/1/2729/READWONDER*.

McGuinn, P. J. (2006). *No Child Left Behind and the transformation of federal education policy, 1965–2005*. Lawrence: University Press of Kansas.

Mioduser, D., Nachmias, R., & Forkosh-Baruch, A. (2008). New literacies for the knowledge society. In *International handbook of information technology in primary and secondary education* (pp. 23–42). New York: Springer.

Nafizi, A. (2003). *Reading Lolita in Tehran*. New York: Random House.

National Governors Association. (2014). Trends in state implementation of the Common Core State Standards: Making the shift to better tests. Retrieved November 20, 2014, from *www.nga.org/cms/home/nga-center-for-best-practices/center-divisions/center-issues/page-edu-issues/col2-content/main-content-list/common-core-state-standards.html*.

National Governors Association Center for Best Practices & Council of Chief State School Officers. (2010). *The Common Core Standards for English Language Arts and literacy in history/social studies, science, and technical subjects*. Washington, DC: Authors.

National Reading Panel. (2000). *Report of the National Reading Panel: Teaching children to read: An evidence-based assessment of the scientific research literature on reading and its implications for reading instruction: Reports of the subgroups*. Washington, DC: National Institute of Child Health and Human Development, National Institutes of Health.

National school standards, at last. (2010, March 13). *New York Times*. Retrieved August 1, 2015, from *http://nyti.ms/1KKtUlp*.

Neuman, S. B. (2013). Foreword. In L. M. Morrow, K. K. Wixson, & T. Shanahan (Eds.), *Teaching with the Common Core State Standards for English language arts: Grades 3–5* (pp. ix–x). New York: Guilford Press.

Norris, S. P., & Phillips, L. M. (2003). How literacy in its fundamental sense is central to scientific literacy. *Science Education*, 87(2), 224–240.

Partnership for Readiness for College and Careers (PARCC). (2015). Contents of the grade- and subject-specific performance level descriptors: ELA/Literacy. Retrieved February 1, 2015. from *www.parcconline.org/ela-plds*.

Pearson, P. D. (2013). Research foundations of the Common Core State Standards in English Language Arts. In S. Neuman & L. Gambrell (Eds.), *Quality reading instruction in the age of Common Core State Standards* (pp. 237–262). Newark, DE: International Reading Association.

Pondiscio, R. (2009). Voluntary national standards dead on arrival. Retrieved July 22, 2009, from *http://blog.coreknowledge.org/2009/07*.

Popham, W. J. (2008). *Transformative assessment*. Alexandria, VA: ASCD.

Ravitch, D. (2011). *The death and life of the great American school system: How testing and choice are undermining education*. New York: Basic Books.

Rebora, A. (2013, March 13). Interview: Charlotte Danielson on teaching and the Common Core. *Education Week* (Web only). Retrieved March 1, 2015, from *www.edweek.org/tm/articles/2013/03/13/ccio_danielson_teaching.html?tkn=LXYDdgll%2Fx5Ld0kKNHSOGAa9RYiCkMmVq zyE&intc=es*.

Rich, M. (2013, August 15). School standards' debut is rocky, and critics pounce. *New York Times*. Retrieved January 22, 2015, from *www.nytimes.com/2013/08/16/education/new-education-standards-face-growing-opposition.html?pagewanted=all&_r=0*.

The right to read: Report of Forum 7, White House Conference on Children 1970. (1972). *Journal of Reading, 15*(6), 472–516.

Rose, M. (1981). Sophisticated, ineffective books: The dismantling of process in composition texts. *College Composition and Communication, 1*, 65–74.

Rothman, R. (2011a). Five myths about the Common Core Standards. *Harvard Education Newsletter, 25*(5), 1–3.

Rothman, R. (2011b). *Something in common: The Common Core Standards and the next chapter in American education*. Cambridge, MA: Harvard Education Press.

Rothman, R. (2013). *Fewer, cleaner, higher: How the Common Core State Standards can change classroom practice*. Cambridge, MA: Harvard Education Press.

Ryan, R. M., & Deci, E. L. (2000). Self-determination theory and the facilitation of intrinsic motivation, social development, and well-being. *American Psychologist, 55*(1), 68–78.

Samuels, C. A. (2012, July 17). Districts push of texts aligned with Common Core. *Education Week, 31*(36), 10–11.

Saracho, O. N., & Spodek, B. (2002). Contemporary views of research and practice in early childhood literacy programs. In O. N. Saracho & B. Spodek (Eds.), *Contemporary perspectives in literacy in early childhood education* (pp. 171–183). Greenwich, CT: Information Age.

Sawchuk, S. (2012, November 13). Retooled textbooks aim to capture Common Core. *Education Week, 32*(12), s21–s22.

Schmoker, M. (2012). Refocus professional development. *Phi Delta Kappan, 93*(6), 68–69.

Shanahan, T. (2013). Letting the text take center stage: How the Common Core State Standards will transform English Language Arts instruction. *American Educator, 37*(3), 4–11, 43.

Shepard, L., Hammerness, K., Darling-Hammond, L., Rust, F., Gordon, E., Gutierrez, C., et al. (2005). Assessment. In L. Darling-Hammond & J. Bransford (Eds.), *Preparing teachers for a changing world: What teachers should learn and be able to do* (pp. 275–326). San Francisco: Jossey-Bass.

Smarter Balanced. (n. d.). Smarter balanced assessments. Retrieved February 1, 2015, from *www.smarterbalanced.org/smarter-balanced-assessments.*

Stiggins, R. J. (2002). Assessment crisis: The absence of assessment for learning. *Phi Delta Kappan, 83*(10), 758–765.

Strauss, V. (2012, March 3). Teacher: One (maddening) day working with the Common Core. *Washington Post.* Retrieved February 1, 2015, from *www. washingtonpost.com/blogs/answer-sheet/post/teacher-one-maddening-day-working-with-the-common-core/2012/03/15/gIQA8J4WUS_blog. html.*

Ujifusa, A. (2014, March 31). Common-Core backlash: Track state efforts. *Education Week.* Retrieved February 27, 2015, from *www.edweek.org/ ew/section/multimedia/2014-anti-cc-tracker.html.*

Ujifusa, A. (2015, January 8). Surveying the Common-Core chatter: How will the Standards fare in 2015? *Education Week State Ed Watch.* Retrieved February 27, 2015, from *http://blogs.edweek.org/edweek/state_ edwatch/2015/01/surveying_the_commoncore_chatter_how_will_the_ standards_fare_in_2015.html?qs=Common+Core+controversy.*

Vinovskis, M. (2009). *From A Nation at Risk to No Child Left Behind: National education goals and the creation of federal education policy.* New York: Teachers College Press.

Vygotsky, L. (1978). Interaction between learning and development. In M. Gauvain & M. Cole (Eds.), *Readings on the development of children* (5th ed., pp. 22–29). New York: Worth.

Wagner, T. (2008). *The global achievement gap: Why even our best schools don't teach the new survival skills our children need—and what we can do about it.* New York: Basic Books.

Wigfield, A., Guthrie, J. T., Tonks, S., & Perencevich, K. C. (2004). Children's motivation for reading: Domain specificity and instructional influences. *Journal of Educational Research, 97*(6), 299–310.

Wiggins, G. P., & McTighe, J. (1998, 2005). *Understanding by design.* Alexandria, VA: ASCD.

Wilder, L. I. (1932). *Little house in the big woods.* New York: HarperTrophy.

Wildsmith, B. (1962). *Brian Wildsmith's ABC.* New York: Oxford University Press.

Wiliam, D. (2011). *Embedded formative assessment.* Bloomington, IN: Solution Tree Press.

Wiliam, D., & Thompson, M. (2006). Integrating assessment with instruction: What will it take to make it work? In C. A. Dwyer (Ed.), *The future of assessment: Shaping teaching and learning* (pp. 53–82). Mahwah, NJ: Erlbaum.

Wilson, K. M., & Calfee, R. C. (2007). Classroom assessment. In M. F. Graves, C. Juel, & B. B. Graves (Eds.), *Teaching reading in the 21st century* (4th ed., pp. 426–473). Boston: Allyn & Bacon.

Woodfin, L. (2015, February 2). Would you know deeper learning if you saw it? Retrieved March 16, 2015, from *http://elschools.org/best-practices/would-you-know-deeper-learning-if-you-saw-it*.

Zhao, Y. (2012). *World class learners: Educating creative and entrepreneurial students*. Thousand Oaks, CA: Corwin Press.

Zwiers, J., & Crawford, M. (2011). *Academic conversations: Classroom talk that fosters critical thinking and content understandings*. Portland, ME: Stenhouse.

Index

Page numbers followed by *f* indicate figure, *t* indicate table

F

Feedback, 95–96
Fifth grade. *See* Grade 5
50/50 recommendation, 62–63
First grade. *See* Grade 1
Formative assessments
  Common Core State Standards (CCSS) and,
    46
  examples of, 80–84, 94, 105
  grain-size and cycle-time dimensions of, 88,
    89*f*, 91–99, 93*f*
  implementation of CCSS and, 71–73, 78–80,
    84–86, 103
  resources for, 119–120
  response-to-systems intervention (RTSI)
    program and, 112
  teacher inquiry model and, 86–91, 87*f*, 89*f*
  transition to Standards implementation and,
    73–77
  See also Assessment
Foundational Skills standards. *See* Reading:
    Foundational Skills Standards K–5
Fourth grade. *See* Grade 4
Freestyle Academy of Communication Arts and
    Technology, 109–110
Funding, 19, 23–24
Future possibilities
  comparing to present practices, 16–17
  example of, 1–3
  grade 3 example of, 6–9
  grade 7 example of, 9–10
  grade 9 example of, 10–13
  grade 11 example of, 13–15
  implementation of CCSS and, 77–78
  kindergarten example of, 3–6

G

Gewertz's reports, 47–55
Grade 1, ELA standards for, 129–132
Grade 2, ELA standards for, 132–136
Grade 3
  ELA standards for, 136–140
  example of future possibilities in, 6–9
Grade 4, ELA standards for, 140–144
Grade 5, ELA standards for, 144–148
Grade 6
  ELA standards for, 149–153
  history/social studies literacy standards for,
    171–172
  science and technical studies literacy
    standards for, 173
Grade 7
  ELA standards for, 153–157
  example of future possibilities in, 9–10
  history/social studies literacy standards for,
    171–172
  science and technical studies literacy
    standards for, 173

Grade 8
  ELA standards for, 157–161
  history/social studies literacy standards for,
    171–172
  science and technical studies literacy
    standards for, 173
Grade 9
  ELA standards for, 161–166
  example of future possibilities in, 10–13
  history/social studies literacy standards for,
    172
  science and technical studies literacy
    standards for, 174
Grade 10
  ELA standards for, 161–166
  history/social studies literacy standards for,
    172
  science and technical studies literacy
    standards for, 174
Grade 11
  ELA standards for, 166–171
  example of future possibilities in, 13–15
  history/social studies literacy standards for,
    172–173
  science and technical studies literacy
    standards for, 174–175
Grade 12
  ELA standards for, 166–171
  history/social studies literacy standards for,
    172–173
  science and technical studies literacy
    standards for, 174–175
Grade-by-grade (G × G) entries, 36–38
Grades 6–12 content-area standards, 32–38,
    171–175. *See also* Content-area
    standards; English Language Arts (ELA)
    Standards
Grades 6–12 ELA standards, 32–38, 149–175.
    See also English Language Arts (ELA)
    Standards; Language Standards 6–12;
    Writing Standards 6–12
Grades K–5 ELA standards, 32–38, 125–148.
    See also English Language Arts (ELA)
    Standards; Language Standards K–5;
    Reading Standards K–5; Speaking
    and Listening Standards K–5; Writing
    Standards K–5
Graduate schools of education, 103, 112–117
Grain-size dimensions of formative assessment,
    88, 89*f*, 93*f*, 96–99. *See also* Formative
    assessments

H

"Highly qualified teacher" (HQT) requirement,
    22–23
High-stakes testing, 102–103. *See also*
    Assessment; Standardized testing
History, 171–173